D0622397

MAKING INDIA GREAT

Praise for *From Chanakya to Modi*

'Dr Aparna Pande's *From Chanakya to Modi: The Evolution of India's Foreign Policy* is that rare book. It is written by someone outside government, unencumbered by policy fatigue or being too close to the powers that be.'

– Neena Gopal in the *Deccan Chronicle*

'Pande's book is not a simple narrative, but a deep analysis which looks at foreign policy through the prism of India's heritage, as well as the ideas and individuals who shaped it, the principles and interests that they pursued and the institutions and strategic culture they have created.'

– Manoj Joshi in the *Outlook*

'*From Chanakya to Modi: The Evolution of India's Foreign Policy* not only explains the continuity and the constancy of certain concepts but also their growth, evolution and adaptation to an ever-changing world.'

– Seema Sirohi in The Wire

'Pande's book is an excellent primer on how India has engaged with the world and will continue to do so – through realism with imperial hues, tempered by its civilizational responsibilities and grace. As such, it will be widely read by those who want to understand the neural roots of contemporary India's strategic intent.'

– Abhijnan Rej in *Swarajya* magazine

'Aparna Pande's sleek offer in less than 200 pages, *From Chanakya to Modi: The Evolution of India's Foreign Policy*, is an overview of an Indian view of the world over two millennia, in which the emphasis is on continuity. Not that she is unmindful or dismissive of the changes that are taking place in India's strategic posture under Modi, but her focus is on the underlying principles that guide them all—from Chanakya to Modi, as the ambitious title suggests.'

– Varghese K. George in *The Hindu*

'*From Chanakya to Modi* is a magnificently readable survey of Indian foreign policy ... This book is a wonderful primer that will help a broad readership make sense of the persistent tensions in Indian foreign policy.'

– Ashley J. Tellis, Tata Chair for Strategic Affairs, Carnegie Endowment for International Peace

MAKING INDIA GREAT

THE PROMISE OF A RELUCTANT GLOBAL POWER

APARNA PANDE

HarperCollins *Publishers* India

First published in hardback in India in 2020 by
HarperCollins *Publishers* India
A-75, Sector 57, Noida, Uttar Pradesh 201301, India
www.harpercollins.co.in

2 4 6 8 10 9 7 5 3 1

Copyright © Aparna Pande 2020

P-ISBN: 978-93-5357-801-5
E-ISBN: 978-93-5357-802-2

The views and opinions expressed in this book are the author's
own and the facts are as reported by her, and the publishers are
not in any way liable for the same.

Aparna Pande asserts the moral right
to be identified as the author of this work.

All rights reserved. No part of this publication may be reproduced,
stored in a retrieval system, or transmitted, in any form or by any means,
electronic, mechanical, photocopying, recording or otherwise,
without the prior permission of the publishers.

Typeset in 11/14 Sabon MT
Manipal Technology Ltd, Manipal

Printed and bound at
Thomson Press (India) Ltd

To my teacher and mentor, Ambassador Husain Haqqani, who, after my father, has been my greatest source of support and inspiration. His faith and guidance have been invaluable.

Contents

Introduction
Potential and Promise

*Let us remember first that India is not a little island, nor a
continent sparsely inhabited by savages, but a vast territory
containing 320,000,000 souls – three times as many as in
the United States, more than in North and South America
combined, more than in all Europe, west of Russia combined;
all in all, one-fifth of the world's population.*[1]

HISTORIAN WILL DURANT makes this argument in his book, *The
Case for India*, written after his visit to the subcontinent in 1930.
Since then, two new countries have been carved out of what was
then India, with a combined population of 1,800,000,000. The
country that carries the historic name and traditions of ancient
India has a population of 1.4 billion and is still as vast a country
as it was in Durant's time. Every sixth person in the world today
is Indian.

The promise of India, therefore, is old: it lies in the centuries-old
culture, the possibilities of the large and youthful population, the
size and potential of the economy, and the capability and capacity of
its military. The Indian national movement, which initiated the end
of the colonial era worldwide, was built on India's great prospects.
The sense of Indian exceptionalism that the country's founding
fathers spoke about and that the average Indian believes in, comes
from the seeming inevitability of its rise to great power status. For
Indians, India's greatness is a given. The only question is when and
how it will manifest itself on the world stage.

As one of the only two countries in the world with a population of over 1 billion, half of it under the age of twenty-five, India has a huge labour force, a massive recruitment pool for soldiers and a formidable consumer market.[2] Its ability to build and consistently maintain a democratic political system has made it a natural partner for Western democracies.

India will be the most populous country by 2024 and the world's third largest economy by 2028. It already has the fourth largest military and one of the largest English-speaking populations in the world. India ranks fourth in the global rankings of countries that produce the most doctoral students, with over 24,000 PhDs annually.[3] Over 90,000 books are published annually in India placing it sixth in the ranking of countries publishing the largest number of books. In two decades, between 1994 and 2014, India halved the number of people living under poverty.[4]

It is, therefore, natural that the prospect of India's rise attracts global attention. China has quadrupled its GDP in the last two decades.[5] If India can manage to do the same, it is the natural competitor for China in what is dubbed as the Asian century that lies ahead. But India's march towards great power status is not likely to be as smooth as it sounds. Much as Indians want their country to be a global leader, there is also hesitance in building and exercising hard power. It is almost as if India wants to be a great power because it is its right to be one. Methodical development of the wherewithal of global power has thus far not proved to be its strong suit.

⁓

As early as February 1947, the United States saw a united India as 'making its rightful and honourable contribution to the maintenance of international peace and prosperity'.[6] Even after Partition, the consensus in Washington was that India was 'the natural political and economic centre of South Asia'.[7]

When the former Connecticut governor, Chester Bowles, asked President Harry Truman in 1951 to appoint him US ambassador to India, the president was surprised why a political figure of his stature would want to serve in that poor country. Bowles argued that the future of the world would rest on the 'competition between democratic India on the one hand and communist China on the other.'[8]

In 1957, Senator John F. Kennedy – who, as president, sent Bowles back to India for a second stint as ambassador in 1961 – asserted that India represented 'the free world's strongest bulwark to the seductive appeal of Peking and Moscow'.[9] India's appeal remained alive despite losing a border war with China in 1962 and the slow growth of its economy during the 1960s and 1970s.

At the end of the Cold War, India's economic liberalization, its sustained democracy, its embrace of technology – especially information technology – and its open, plural and diverse society, once again led to the resurrection of the promise of India. Strobe Talbott, who as deputy secretary of state under President Clinton invested heavily in building the US–India relationship, declared, 'India – with its resilient democracy, its vibrant high-tech sector, its liberal reforms that had begun to revitalize a statist and sclerotic economy, and its huge consumer market – as a natural beneficiary of globalization and therefore potentially a much more important partner for the United States.'[10]

Indians have also believed in the promise of India. Five thousand years of continuous civilization has bred a sense of Indian exceptionalism. Others might judge the modern state by its economic indicators, its low ranking on the human development index, or its apparent political and social chaos. For Indians, however, the subcontinent represents one civilization and one indivisible historical entity, whose past achievements are a source of immense pride, justification for a sense of superiority and the expectation of an equally great future.

India is seen by some as suffering from political, social and cultural lethargy, bred by the baggage of its long history. In the words of Nobel laureate, Sir Vidiadhar Surajprasad (V.S.) Naipaul (a Trinidadian of Indian descent), the country is plagued with the crisis of what he refers to as a 'wounded old civilization'; while Indians are 'aware of its inadequacies', their culture seems to lack 'the intellectual means to move ahead'.[11]

Unlike much of the Muslim Middle East that has been reluctant to embrace modernity, India has embraced modernity, but only partially. Even as the promise of a rising India keeps resurfacing, it is held back by inadequate modernization. Thus, India's history and its modern parts breed optimism about its future. But the same history and the parts that are not modern hold the country back.

India's promise cannot be realized without acknowledging its failings. As one of the two oldest continuous civilizations in the world, India could certainly be a global power. But to get there, it would have to deal with its handicaps. Indians living abroad, in particular, tend to gloss over widespread superstition, caste and ethnic prejudice, as well as religious antagonisms that impede India's progress. They speak often of the India they want, not the India that is.

One of its foremost encumbrances is its relationship with the past. India is an ancient land, unified by geography and tradition. Many Indian languages use the same word for yesterday and tomorrow, reflecting a belief in life as an eternal cycle. There are those, like Booker Prize–winner Salman Rushdie, who argue, 'No people whose word for "yesterday" is the same as their word for "tomorrow" can be said to have a firm grip on time.'[12]

In the view of such critics, Indians spend far greater time dwelling on their past than they do on planning for their future. They might not be wrong. Every now and then, Indian cities shut down amidst protests over the perceived wrong portrayal of a historical figure in a book or film. Instead of conducting such arguments in classrooms or the media, Indians seem prepared to waste an entire day's, or a few days' productivity, resulting in loss of earnings. The argument over honour of a deity or hero, who may or may not have existed centuries ago, matters more than the substantive matters relating to the here and now. More often than not, this is used to assert a new identity and drive a new political argument.

It is claimed by some that India's rich heritage keeps it going even if it is not up to par with the world's developed nations. Politician and author Shashi Tharoor insists that 'India is not, as people keep calling it, an underdeveloped country, but rather, in the context of its history and cultural heritage, a highly developed one in an advanced state of decay.'[13]

The Indians' unique relationship with time, where past greatness somehow compensates for current decay, means that in the country, different eras must coexist instead of one era replacing the last. In most countries, horse-driven carriages disappeared within a few years of the arrival of motor cars. A century after the first motor car appeared on the streets of India, bullock carts, a host of animals – cows, buffaloes, and stray dogs – and humans all share Indian streets with motor vehicles.

In 2015, a Delhi-based motor accidents' tribunal adjudicated that animal-driven slow-moving vehicles (mainly bullock carts) often caused serious accidents. But the court still did not bar these vehicles from the road, asking for their regulation instead.[14] This attitude is not limited to forcing the motor car to share space with the bullock cart. There are dozens of issues that embroil India in culture wars with grave consequences for economic development.

Another example is the issue of language. India has one of the largest English-speaking populations in the world. This is a significant economic advantage. India has benefited from having English as one of the twenty-three recognized national languages and one of the languages for official correspondence, as well as the language of business.[15] But ultra-nationalists insist on scrapping the teaching of English notwithstanding its economic cost.

English did not replace any of India's own languages – it has only augmented them. But that does not keep some politicians from demanding that English must be completely replaced with Sanskrit or Hindi in schools, and the language of official correspondence should mandatorily be Hindi.[16] Such moves might stoke the national ego, but it would unnecessarily take away one of India's comparative advantages in the process of globalization.

India could keep its religions, cultures and history, and still avoid adverse economic or political consequences. But the current environment in India does not seem conducive to such sensible decision-making. The recent escalation in the desire to protect the cow, a sacred symbol for some Hindus, offers a major example of turning gains into losses. Until recently, India was the second largest exporter of beef in the world (after Brazil), accounting for 20 per cent of global beef exports in 2016, earning US $4 billion annually.[17] India has also been one of the world's top five producers of leather, with skins primarily from cows or buffalos, and earning US $16 billion in annual sales.[18]

All that has been put at risk with religious vigilantism claiming to protect the cow. Public attacks on Muslims, Christians and lower caste Hindus over eating beef, the ban on slaughter of cattle, sale and consumption of beef and the shutting down of abattoirs has had enormous economic and social consequences. The livelihood of over a million people involved in the cattle and leather industries has been threatened.[19]

Ironically, the government of Prime Minister Narendra Modi has not effectively tackled the religion-based cow protection vigilantism even as it is hoping to double leather revenues to US $27 billion by 2020. The government expects the leather sector to expand job creation without realizing the incompatibility of its ambition with the ban on the slaughter and sale of cows and buffalos encouraged by the ruling party in most Indian states.[20]

At a time when India and Indians need to debate issues of national and global importance, from economic reforms to the country's role in Asia, the discussion in Indian mainstream and social media focuses preponderantly on divisive cultural and religious issues. India has yet to find the balance between philosophical debates and conversation on practical matters. Getting carried away by emotions about other people's beliefs or views on history often comes in the way of determining a course of action in the present moment.

For example, in the same week that the Indian prime minister met his American, Australian and Japanese counterparts in the Philippines to discuss their strategic collaboration under the Quad – a strategic grouping of the United States, India, Australia, and Japan – India's tech capital, Bengaluru, was shut down because of protests against a Bollywood film, *Padmaavat*. The protestors threatened violence simply because they disagreed with the movie's portrayal of a sixteenth century fictional account of a figure from the fourteenth century AD.[21]

The recent focus on religious and cultural disputes could end up reversing India's success in nation-building since Independence. It was one of the few postcolonial countries that, despite years of colonial rule, appeared to be forging national unity among its diverse populace without violence or use of force. It attempted to educate its people and lay down the foundations of a prosperous economy. It remained a democracy when others resorted to military coups. Its society was pluralist, open and tolerant, where all its minorities – linguistic, ethnic or religious – had equal opportunities.

In the foreign policy realm, India did not join any military alliances, tried to stay out of the Cold War and adopted a policy of non-alignment to build relations with both the Western countries and other developing nations. Its leaders sought to advance the country's interest by securing technology and modern know-how from capitalist countries as well as communist ones.

Unlike many of its peers, including neighbour Pakistan, India did not insist on creating a falsified national narrative through history textbooks. Its school curriculum reflected 5000 years of Indian history, including phases of Hindu, Muslim and Western ascendance. This resulted in the creation of a reasonably literate generation that was taught about India's diverse multicultural, multi religious history.

Indian textbooks are now being rewritten to erase parts of India's historical heritage. Mention of rulers or empires that are seen as detrimental to Hindutva ('Hinduness') is being deliberately omitted to portray India as exclusively Hindu.[22] Given that India is home to at least 220 million non-Hindus, efforts to create a purely Hindu – as opposed to a pluralist – India could prove divisive.

Attempts to coerce students at universities to shout slogans about the Hindu motherland or stand up for the national anthem, and the placement of out-of-service Indian army tanks on university campuses are all meant to elicit patriotism.[23] But such measures are leading to debates about what patriotism truly entails, distracting students and professors from their real task of imparting and receiving education. This threatens the quality of India's university education.

According to The Times Higher Education (THE) World University Rankings of 2018, Indian institutes of higher learning performed poorly and fell in their global rankings from previous years. The highest-ranking Indian university, the Indian Institute of Science (IISc) Bangalore, fell from 200–250 ranking in 2017 to 251–300 in 2018. Indian Institute of Technology (IIT) Bombay remained in the 351–400 slot, but IIT Delhi and IIT Kanpur fell from 401–500 ranking to 501–600.[24]

At a time when China is moving ahead by focusing on building its economic and military capacity, and the US, Japan, Southeast Asia and Australia are looking to India as a potential partner and competitor to China, India should not appear to be more concerned about rewriting history or being mired in culture wars.

⤴

India has a potential demographic dividend that could be of immense benefit with correct planning and execution. With approximately half of its 1.4 billion population under the age of twenty-five,[25] India is forecast to be one of the youngest countries in the world by 2020, with a median age of 29.[26] Almost 20 per cent of the world's working age population will live in India by 2025.[27] But the large, young population could become a serious problem if it cannot be educated and employed productively.

India needs to expand its investment in human capital to take advantage of its demographic profile. As of 2015, the global average for government expenditure on education as a percentage of GDP was 4.8 per cent, but according to the World Bank, India has only invested between 3 and 4 per cent of GDP in education annually.[28]

India's literacy rate currently stands at 74 per cent, but it ranks second after Malawi in a list of twelve countries 'wherein a grade two student could not read a single word of a short text'. India is also at the top of a list of seven countries 'in which a grade two student could not perform two-digit subtraction'.[29]

According to a 2017 study, which surveyed 36,000 engineering students, in over 500 colleges across India, 95 per cent of Indian engineers 'are not fit to take up software development jobs'. In addition to lacking technical skills, more than 67 per cent of the engineering graduates are not fluent in the English language and more than three-fourths of these students 'lack spoken English skills required for any job in the knowledge economy'.[30]

India would have to increase resource allocation to expand both the access and value of its education. In addition to ensuring that students leave primary and secondary school with basic reading and arithmetic skills, the quality of tertiary education needs serious improvement. Indian universities would have to become centres of excellence, research and development rather than diploma mills.

Economies seeking high growth rates tend to invest in research and development (R&D). The global expenditure on R&D as a percentage of GDP stands at 2.29 per cent with the United States investing 2.74 per cent, China 2.11 per cent, Japan 3.14 per cent, and India less than 0.63 per cent.[31] India's unemployment rate has risen from 2.2 per cent in 2011–12 to 6.7 per cent in 2018, and it is particularly high in the key age group between fifteen and twenty-nine years: 27.2 per cent for urban men and women, and 17.4 per cent and 13.6 per cent for rural men and women.[32]

Less than 5 per cent of India's 487 million workers have received any formal skill training, and this hurts their future potential. This is in sharp contrast to industrialized countries where the figure is closer to 60 per cent.[33] Similarly, global female labour force participation stands at 39 per cent, with China at 43.6 per cent but India only at 22.1 per cent.

There is considerable room for improvement in India's skills training as well as in raising female labour force participation.[34] India cannot expect to be a global economic powerhouse without expanding its women's participation in productive economic activity.

∽

India's strategy to realize its promise would require more than just planning for economic growth. It requires a shift in attitudes, which in turn needs a leadership that can think beyond getting elected by consolidating vote banks on the basis of religion, caste, or ethnicity. Indian leaders need to bear in mind that attempts to build a homogenous society amidst actual heterogeneity do not succeed.

For example, China is ethnically more homogenous than India, but it has reached the outer limit of the advantage of homogeneity. As the Han Chinese state moves towards the non-Han periphery, it is facing problems of integrating groups that it has so far treated as outsiders. The Sinification of Tibet and Xinjiang is becoming increasingly more problematic for China and is beginning to expose its fissures.

India, on the other hand, has a tradition of recognizing and embracing its diversity. India has always been diverse: ethnically, linguistically and culturally. There are many differences between India's regions, states, and even within its states. India has twenty-eight states, nine Union Territories, twenty-three national languages, and over 1000 spoken languages. Instead of seeking to homogenize a vast nation, India could continue to build on its pluralist tradition. Attempts to homogenize a diverse populace aggravates and hardens the differences.

India is urbanizing fast with almost 30 per cent of its population living in the over 8000 cities and towns. Yet, there is also wide divergence between rural and urban areas. Today, India has five megacities, each of which have more 10 million people – Delhi (around 30 million), Mumbai (21.4 million), Kolkata (15 million), Bengaluru (11.4 million) and Chennai (10.4 million). By 2030, India would have two more megacities: Hyderabad and Ahmedabad.[35]

Cities are known the world over as engines of growth – they encourage creation of wealth, generate employment and help drive human progress.[36] Cities are also always more diverse than rural areas. This is true of India as well: whether it is Delhi or Mumbai, Bengaluru or Chennai, India's cities are more diverse, and their diversity is their strength.

Actions such as the shutting down of Bengaluru by protestors enraged over a film, or attacks in the name of the cow and other attempts to marginalize minorities hurt the country's economic potential. Politicians often find it easy to use identity politics to win elections and ensure their voter base along religious, caste, or ethnic lines, but this risks losing the city's advantage as an engine of growth.

Cities also need investment and nurturing. India needs to spend over US $1.5 trillion over the next decade to modernize its railways, build highways and roads, and provide energy and water to its cities and villages.[37]

More than 300 million Indians have zero access to electricity and a vast majority are still experiencing electricity shortages on a daily basis.[38] Not a single Indian city can provide clean water that can be consumed from the tap on a 24/7 basis.[39] According to estimates, India's electricity woes cost the economy from 1 to 3 per cent of GDP. The government has only recently launched an ambitious project to supply 24-hour power to its towns and villages by 2022.[40]

In addition to clean water and energy, Indians also need clean air. According to a report published by The Lancet Commission on Pollution and Health, a staggering 2.5 million Indians died in 2015 due to non-communicable diseases, including strokes and lung cancer, caused by pollution.[41] In 2019, the pollution levels in Delhi hit a high even earlier than usual. In addition to industrial smog, vehicle exhaust and dust, one of the major sources of pollution every year in north India is that farmers in these states burn the stubble of the previous crop before they plant anew. For poorer farmers, that is the cheapest way of getting rid of agricultural waste without hiring additional labour or incurring costs.

If agricultural reforms had been undertaken farmers would have been provided with more eco-friendly alternatives. The Central and state governments know what to do and yet are reluctant to do so, both because of complacency as well as a reluctance to apply pressure on farm owners, who deliver critical votes.

While NITI Aayog, a policy advisory group, estimated that the government would need around US $600 million to ensure farmers receive alternatives to burning farm waste, the Union Cabinet only plans to spend US $230 million over two years to prevent crop residue burning.[42] Such decision by the Indian government will do little to circumvent the air pollution that envelops the capital region. The air pollution around cities like Delhi would not significantly subside and the higher costs of shutdowns, delays, and healthcare due to smog would not diminish.

India also needs to think through the social and cultural consequences. Advances made in birth control changed social mores and male–female relationships. As India adopts new technologies, it must adapt to the social changes that accompany them.

Moreover, the Internet, smartphones and wireless connectivity can help India resolve issues ranging from providing online education to remote areas, digital payments and avoiding bureaucratic red tape and regulations. But that would require changes in the mindset of rigid bureaucracies seeking old-fashioned control and religious leaders seeking to enforce social conservatism. That is, by no means, an easy task.

Across the United States and Europe, the political marriage between social conservatives and classical economic liberals calling themselves economic conservatives is gradually coming apart. Small government and low tax advocates worked with those opposed to social change – from women's emancipation to LGBT rights – because it helped create a working coalition against the liberal left. For the most part, the centre inspired by ideas of free enterprise wielded power with the votes of those with more right-wing or even religious ideas. Now, however, the ever-expanding demands of social conservatism are dividing centre-right political parties in most Western countries.

In India, the centre-left has dominated politics for most of its seventy-year history as an independent modern state. Centre-right economic ideas have found resonance among urban Indians, but many have often been content to express them through a socially conservative, even religiously founded political party.

During the 1950s and 60s, India had a real economic conservative party – the Swatantra (Independent) Party – that did not embrace religious conservativism while advocating a market economy. But it failed to build a mass base. Today there is no Swatantra Party, and the only expression of the centre-right can be found in the politics of Hindutva.

India's middle class rallied to the Bharatiya Janata Party (BJP) in pursuit of economic reform and the dismantling of the socialist state. The first BJP prime minister, Atal Bihari Vajpayee, moderated the demands of his party's Hindutva ideologues from 1999 to 2004, showing that good leadership can direct an essentially social movement into being an inclusive pro-growth political party.

Since then, the Hindutva organizations have reverted to religious and social issues – cow protection,[43] rebuilding of temples allegedly destroyed by Muslim invaders centuries ago,[44] forbidding young men and women from dating in public parks,[45] shutting down movies or banning books that do not depict Hinduism or Hindus as they ought to be portrayed from the point of view of Hindutva leaders.[46]

Content analysis of India's electronic and print media shows that economic issues receive scant attention amid the clutter and noise about recasting India in a mould free of influences of the last several centuries. To achieve its promise, the country's economy needs an annual GDP growth rate of between 8 and 10 per cent. That is within the grasp of India if only it speeds up its process of economic reform and its leaders refrain from lighting fires of social and cultural conflicts.

India jumped thirty ranks on the World Bank Ease of Business Rankings from 130 in 2016 to 100 in 2017. Its rank on that score in 2018 was 77,[47] and went up fourteen places to land at 63 in 2019.[48] In 2017, the international credit rating company Moody's Investors Service upgraded India's sovereign rating from the lowest investment grade of Baa3 to Baa2 and changed the outlook from stable to positive. It was the first upgrade of India's rating in fourteen years and was based on 'Moody's expectation that continued progress on economic and institutional reforms will, over time, enhance India's high growth potential'.[49] Two years later, in November 2019, Moody's downgraded India from 'stable' to 'negative' based on concerns of a 'more entrenched slowdown'.[50]

But India's economy slowed down from over 8 per cent in 2015 and 7.1 per cent in 2016 to 6.7 per cent in 2017. In 2018, it went up to 7.2 per cent,[51] and in 2019 it fell down to 4.5 per cent[52] – less than half of India's goal. The double shock of demonetization of high-value currency notes and the implementation of a nationwide Goods and Services Tax hit large sectors of the economy leading companies to scale back investments, lay off workers and adopt a wait and watch approach.

It is said that most Indian politicians consider their electorate insufficiently mature and engage in identity politics because economic reforms do not win elections. Ironically, that belief persists without the alternative ever being tried out. The average

Indian will probably reward a government that performs well in the economic sphere. Some leader someday has to shift the political discourse towards substantive issues.

⁓

In addition to domestic political constraints, India's leaders also tend to seek a greater role on the global stage without committing requisite resources for such an expanded role. To be big, you need to think and act big. If India seeks to become a great power, it needs to spend more money on its military and defence, and expand its diplomatic corps.

India is still stuck with the British Indian army legacy of a 'spit and polish' army. It has a small officer base, a large number of soldiers who can serve as cannon fodder, and does not spend much money on protective gear, equipment or training. That has to change for India to be considered a global power by its enemies and rivals.

India's army has fared well against Pakistan, which also inherited a similar military. But Pakistan is not India's only competitor and a purely conventional war in the plains of Punjab and Sindh is not all that India has to think about. China confronts India along a high-altitude mountainous frontier. To exercise influence across the Indo-Pacific, India also needs a twenty-first century navy and air force, which, in turn, require significant allocation of resources.

During the early decades of independence, Indian leaders believed that India, as a status quo power that stayed out of the Cold War blocs, did not need to really build a large military as it lacked enemies. Civilian supremacy and keeping the services out of security and defence policy meant that India never built the structural wherewithal, which would ensure periodic modernization and overhaul of the armed forces.

During the 1980s, India spent over 3 per cent of its GDP on its military. By the 1990s, defence spending was over 2 per cent, but less than 3 per cent and since then it has been between 2 per cent and 3 per cent of GDP.[53] For some years now, there was talk of India spending approximately US $100 billion over ten years on defence modernization. The 2020-21 budget allocation for defence is only Rs 4.71 trillion (US $65.9 billion), of which Rs 1.3 trillion are for pensions.[54] This means that only 1.5 per cent of India's GDP has been set aside for defence, which continues the steady reduction in expenditure on defence spending at a time when the reverse is required. This will not be enough to play catch up, especially with China.

Available estimates indicate that India has a US $400-billion military equipment deficit. To get over this, India would need to spend at least 6 per cent of its GDP on military modernization for a few years. That might not be easy and is likely to run into political headwinds.

India started its military modernization before China announced its modernization plans. China's military expansion and modernization is under way and will be complete by 2020, as scheduled. India, on the other hand, has spoken of military modernization since 2002, but nothing much happened till 2014.

India's purchase of heavy military equipment – fighter jets, tanks, heavy artillery, submarines and naval surface craft – has been piecemeal since the purchase of Bofors guns for the Indian army in the 1980s. The scandal of alleged kickbacks in that purchase has paralysed major Indian defence equipment acquisitions. Fear of corruption and scandal have made the purchase process onerous. Several contracts have been cancelled after being signed.

India also remains reluctant to buy military equipment from other countries without significant technology transfer. The desire for technological self-sufficiency is not bad, but the negotiations over technology transfer, especially with the United States, drag on forever. Similarly, the US–India joint development of the next generation aircraft carrier has not even advanced to the serious designing stage. The project is still more talked about than being implemented.

As of now, India's military modernization plan simply focuses on purchasing equipment to reduce the equipment deficit for each of the military services. What is missing is strategic intent: if India seeks to become a competitor to China, it needs to grow faster economically, build a large technological and industrial base, and expand its domestic defence production base.

The desire for military self-sufficiency led to decades of support for public sector enterprises that have not built the same capability or capacity and are not as efficient as China. A large amount of India's military hardware needs replacement and the country continues to debate endlessly on how much it should purchase from abroad and how much should it manufacture domestically.

India's armed forces, and its ambition to be a global power, need an earlier resolution to that argument than seems feasible within India's political and bureaucratic system so far. The Ministry of Defence has to be something greater than a glorified acquisitions and budgets office for India to successfully modernize its armed forces.

In most countries strategic planning is undertaken by the Department of Defence and the uniformed services. In India's case, the legacy of colonial rule and the fears of modern India's founding fathers about erosion of civilian supremacy put control of strategic planning in the hands of civil servants. Bringing the uniformed services into strategic and defence planning remains one of the challenges India must address in the near future.

⁓

India and China see each other as long-term rivals, but neither wants to provoke the other. India may be able to balance its relations with China for now because of China's caution, as well as the prospect of India's large consumer market being open to Chinese goods. But given the underlying tensions, incidents like the June 2017 Doklam crisis will continue to occur.

China, however, will continue to try and encircle India through relationships with its many neighbours. To be able to counter China's ambitions in South Asia, India needs to do a better job within its own neighbourhood. In 2015, India's then foreign secretary (and now foreign minister) S. Jaishankar stated that to become a great power you need the neighbourhood rooting for you.[55]

It has taken decades for New Delhi to learn that managing a sphere of influence is not only a function of telling others what to do but being able to expend resources that deny space to competitors. India gives US $1.6 billion annually in aid with the majority going to South Asia, followed by countries in Africa.[56] For decades India's performance with respect to building infrastructure – whether dams or roads – was abysmal, inside India and in the neighbourhood. The country often promised and failed to deliver on its promises.

Its recent experience in Afghanistan, where Indian assistance has been instrumental in building the country's parliament and key infrastructure, demonstrates that it can perform when it sets its mind to it. India would have to replicate its success in winning hearts and minds in Afghanistan to keep Sri Lanka, Nepal, Bangladesh, and even Bhutan on its side, and to wean Myanmar away from China.

Pakistan remains critical to India's view of its neighbourhood. It is the country that broke away from India, so to speak, and has maintained consistent hostility towards India. Every Indian prime minister has come into power hoping to leave as his/her legacy the resolution of the conflict with Pakistan. The fact that this has not happened points to the problem having deeper roots than is generally assumed.

For Pakistan, antagonism towards India has become an essential characteristic of its national identity. Until and unless the Pakistani military–intelligence establishment moves away from viewing India as an existential threat and stops using jihad as a lever of foreign policy, there is little hope for normal relations between the two countries.

India, therefore, has to plan on the assumption that Pakistan will continue to be hostile towards India and will act as an obstacle to India's rise. India would have to convince others, especially the

United States, that instead of mediating in some India–Pakistan dispute, their role should be to check Pakistan's implacable hostility and disregard for international norms when it comes to India.

China will continue to bolster Pakistan because Pakistan is China's secondary deterrent. Just as Chinese support enables North Korea to tie down Korea and Japan, Pakistan keeps India militarily preoccupied to China's advantage.[57] But China is also wary that if it pushes India too far, it would join the bandwagon against China and create an effective anti-China alliance with allies such as the US, Japan and Australia. So far, India interacts with these countries without committing itself to a military alliance.

India's relationship with the United States is deeper and multi-dimensional. But there is still a gap in expectations of the other from both sides, and the two countries are still in a process of adjusting and adapting. The Indian elephant takes longer to think and act than Americans are used to. From being a non-aligned country to becoming a partner of the US has taken a few decades, and a military alliance will not happen overnight.

India is also still unwilling to change its policy of non-alignment and strategic autonomy. That it is a member of BRICS (Brazil, Russia, India, China and South Africa), RIC (Russia, India, China), and Asian Infrastructure Investment Bank at the same time as it is against OBOR/BRI (One Belt One Road/ Belt and Road Initiative), supports Japan's Quality Infrastructure Initiative, has again restarted the Quad and sees the US as a natural ally reflects India's pursuit of maximum options in foreign relations.

And this clashes with the American tendency to view nations as allies or potential enemies. India has its task cut out for itself in persuading the US that it can be a partner, including a military one, without being part of a formal military alliance.

⌒

There is no denying India's potential, but the size of its population and a sense of historical greatness alone are insufficient to guarantee that India will fulfil its promise. Just as China's centralized system of governance and its planned capitalism create their own challenges, chaotic democracy and erratic economic liberalization, coupled with a general reluctance to project power beyond its immediate neighbourhood, impede India's prospects.

Already, the country's economic growth has slowed down and double-digit growth rates are not being sustained, it is unable to provide employment to the 12 million people who enter its labour market annually, 29.8 per cent of India's population still lives below the poverty line, 2.5 million Indians die annually from pollution-related deaths, rural India is far from being fully immersed in modern technology, and India's military modernization has yet to take off.[58]

The assumption that India's rise is predestined has led to hubris and an insufficient examination of factors that might inhibit fulfilment of the promise that both Indians and others have often seen as inevitable. That India can rise is not the same as saying that it will do so irrespective of its leaders' policy choices.

The interaction of culture and politics has already hindered many changes that would have accelerated India's ascent. The democratic system has opened India to the manipulation of vote banks, embroiling it in cultural and religious controversies that inhibit serious policy debates.

For India to realize its potential, its leaders would have to single-mindedly focus on economics and building up hard power. They would have to put India's diversity to good use instead of using it to tear the nation apart in pursuit of votes. That is easier said than done, given the temptation, even in developed countries, to rally voter support through demagoguery.

1

Ancient Culture, Modern Times

IN SEPTEMBER 1995, rumours spread across India that statues of Ganesha, the elephant-headed Indian deity, were 'drinking' milk.[1] All across the country people crowded temples attempting to recreate this event.[2] Rationalists offered a scientific explanation, arguing that capillary action – the inclination of liquids in absorbent materials to rise or fall as a result of surface tension – probably created the perception that a statue had 'drunk' the milk placed on it. But many Indians still believe that the elephant-headed deity drank milk only from the hands of the devoted. Two decades later, in October 2018, India's prime minister Narendra Modi claimed that Indians should be proud that Ganesha's elephant head was the first instance of plastic surgery in the world.[3]

How does one reconcile this dichotomy of an India that has the trappings of modernity with a core that practises an age-old culture? Ancient civilizations are replete with epics that play a role in myth-making and shape a people's way of life. But India's pride in its past has led to the conviction that the past, and the mythology that sustained it, contains explanations for every phenomenon that has already occurred or is likely to occur in the future. It is as if the key to the present and future lies in either reliving the past or connecting everything to it.

Modern India's founding generation sought to have one foot in the future and one foot in the past. They wanted to learn from the rest of the world, as well as to teach others about India's rich heritage. India had historically been focused on itself, which left it open to invasion and conquest by outsiders. Post-Independence

Indian leaders seemed intent on ensuring that the country did not turn inward to the point of being isolationist again and remained engaged with the countries and cultures around them. Recovering from colonial rule, they sought to rebuild a sense of national pride by drawing on the glorious past.

There are many material explanations for the success of invaders and for India's lapse into colonial rule, ranging from inadequate focus on military power to neglect of technology. But these were glossed over by Indians in the years immediately following Independence. They chose instead to idealize India's ability to regenerate itself after every adversity. India, the state, may have been ruled by foreigners, including local dynasties of foreign origin, but India, the civilization, has lived on as a continuum. In the words of the former Indian minister of external affairs, Yashwant Sinha, 'India lives in every century of time.'[4]

A sense of exceptionalism lies at the heart of Indian civilization. India is not alone in considering itself a civilizational state or even in viewing itself as unique. But the notion that everything humans are capable of accomplishing has already been attained by ancient Indians is definitely problematic. In addition to claiming that Indian civilization is superior and only needs recognition by the rest of the world, this attitude makes Indians reluctant to look within. It breeds a propensity for living in denial and an unwillingness to acknowledge what may be inconvenient.

THE PAST LIVES ON

In 2018, India was ranked as one of the most unsafe countries for women in the world.[5] The response of many Indians was to castigate the survey instead of examining patriarchal, feudal and chauvinist behaviour among Indians. The same year, India's tech capital, Bengaluru, was paralysed for days over demonstrations against a Bollywood film titled *Padmaavat*. The film, based on a sixteenth century epic poem about a fourteenth century Rajput queen, Padmavati, apparently portrayed Rajputs in a negative light.

That a film made in 2018, based upon a poetic work of fiction written in the sixteenth century, purportedly based on an incident that happened in the fourteenth century, could result in one of the key cities of an aspiring superpower being held hostage by groups that felt their honour was hurt, highlights India's struggle with modernity.

Statistics reveal that, while making slow progress on gender issues, India has seen a rise in rape and sexual assault cases. Instead of debating the social and psychological reasons for this uptick, many Indian leaders attribute negative trends to modern lifestyles and insist that adherence to the traditional way of life would be sufficient to protect and emancipate women. Ostensible plans to combat the increasing number of rapes and sexual assaults have involved patriarchal responses, such as banning Western attire or reducing mobile phone usage and partaking of foreign cuisine.[6]

The belief that rejecting certain foreign foods or attire would immediately restore societal norms or that a film, a book or a painting could dishonour a millennia-old culture reflects not just a refusal to look within but also a broader societal conundrum: is India's civilizational heritage helping it rise or is it slowing down its progress?

In 1926, English writer and philosopher Aldous Huxley, in a travelogue he wrote on colonial India, noted that 'industrious and intelligent men have wasted their time and their abilities in trying to prove that the ancient Hindus were superior to every other people in every activity of life'.[7] He described this as 'one of the evil results of the political subjection of one people by another', which he said, 'tends to make the subject nation unnecessarily and excessively conscious of its past'. According to Huxley, a colonized nation needs to dwell on 'achievements in the old great days of freedom', which 'are remembered, counted over, and exaggerated'.

It appears that even over seven decades after the end of colonial rule, India and Indians still seek to gaze into the past for validation, at the cost of sacrificing investment in the future.

RESPONSES TO CHANGING TIMES

India's 5000-year history bears traces of two distinct traditions. One strand is, for the most part, vibrant, inclusive and open. Indian civilization benefited when its sages, rulers and thinkers were inquisitive and welcoming of new ideas and critical thought. The other strand, however, is an India which is obscurantist, inward looking and believes it does not need to learn from the outside world.

As Rabindranath Tagore (1861–1941), poet, intellectual and India's first Nobel laureate, wrote in 1923, 'Throughout the whole history, India ran a twofold movement, the conservative element seeking order and conformity in social organization and the radical element seeking freedom for its creative energy.'[8] Echoing these views, Jawaharlal Nehru argued in 1946 that India had fallen behind the world because it had replaced the 'creative spirit' with 'imitation' and 'narrow orthodoxy taboos', and rationalism with idolatry and sentimentality.[9] Nehru was, at that time, the prime-minister-in-waiting of a soon to be independent India.

Nehru recognized that the competing strands of openness and closing down built upon each other, neither ever replacing or erasing the legacies of the other. According to him, India is an 'ancient palimpsest on which layer upon layer of thought and reverie have been inscribed, and yet no succeeding layer had completely hidden or erased what had been written previously.'[10]

In his vision, India could embrace the modern without discarding the ancient. But the present must be built with an eye to the future, not with the intent of reinstating the remote past.

By the eve of Independence, the duelling Indian traditions had been reinforced by the chaos and radical change that accompanied colonial rule. Western influence brought upheaval to political power, educational curricula, employment, and even the spoken language. Schools and colleges opened by missionaries taught ideas emerging from the Western enlightenment. While embracing modern knowledge for advancement of their careers, the Indian elite also needed a set of unique and home-grown ideas to maintain an Indian identity.

The responses to colonialism mirrored India's different traditions, one rationalist and liberal, the other conservative and majoritarian. Among Hindus, some believed that the way forward for Hinduism and Indian society was to eliminate or reform what they perceived as ills within society – sati, the caste system, the subordination and seclusion of women – and thereby modernize Hinduism. Others perceived their way of life to be in danger and sought to reinforce tradition as a means of protecting it. Among minorities, especially Muslims, the fear of siege created a similar defence mechanism. Those seeking to protect their respective communities and traditional way of life ended up feeding off each other's fears, which were undoubtedly reinforced by the colonial masters as a means of maintaining power. Thus, colonialism also accentuated communalism within India's diverse population.

THE BIRTH OF INDIAN LIBERALISM

In the nineteenth century, colonial rule led to religious and doctrinal debates between Indian intellectuals and Protestant Christian missionaries, which had to be conducted on terms deemed rational by Western standards. This resulted in efforts by Indian scholars to 'harmonize religion with a rationalist picture of the world',[11] leading, in some cases, to indigenous critiques of traditionalist Hindu society and Hinduism.

Prominent among these nineteenth century modernizers and reformers were Ishwar Chandra Vidyasagar, Raja Ram Mohan Roy and Debendranath Tagore. Swami Vivekananda travelled overseas to proclaim Hinduism's universality, and a few years later, Mahatma Gandhi and Debendranath's son Rabindranath Tagore attempted to reconcile Indian values with Western democratic and humanitarian ideas.

One of the earliest proponents of Indian liberalism was Raja Ram Mohan Roy (1772–1833), a social reformer and educationist, who founded the Brahmo Samaj. Roy, who was subsequently described as father of the Bengal Renaissance, was fluent in several languages, including Sanskrit, Arabic and English. As a newspaper owner and prolific writer, he produced and published texts dealing with the Indian judicial system, religious tolerance and modernization. Roy was a rationalist to the core, refusing to participate in his father's funeral rites because he thought them meaningless.[12] Most of all, he was civically driven, animated by his conviction to be spokesman for a reformed India.

Roy was passionate to modernize India's cultural and social institutions. At the young age of sixteen, he 'composed a manuscript calling in question the validity of the idolatrous system of the Hindoos' earning him the reputation over the years as Hinduism's Martin Luther.[13] Roy rebelled against India's traditional rigid caste hierarchy; he rejected Brahmanical Hinduism, and referred to Brahmins as 'self-interested guides, who, in defiance of the law as well as of common sense, have succeeded … in conducting [ordinary people] to the temple of idolatry', hiding 'the true substance of morality'.[14]

Emphasizing modernity, he sought to synthesize scientific thought with Indian culture and religion. He rejected traditions he saw as an impediment to modernization. He also championed women's rights and worked towards abolishing sati, the inhuman practice of a widow being forced to burn herself on her husband's funeral pyre. It was primarily because of his agitation that the East India Company prohibited this practice of ritual suicide.

Roy also championed Western education to enlighten Indians and modernize a country that he saw as overly dependent on orthodoxy and tradition. He wrote letters to then Governor General Lord William Amherst emphasizing the need for scientific education for Indians and the need to 'employ European gentlemen of talent and education to interest the natives of India in Mathematics, Natural Philosophy, Chemistry, Anatomy, and other useful sciences, which the natives of Europe have carried to a degree of perfection that has raised them above the inhabitants of other parts of the world'.[15]

He even wrote a letter to the Minister of Foreign Affairs of France in 1831 arguing that 'it is now generally admitted that not religion only but unbiased common sense as well as the accurate deductions of scientific research leads to the conclusion that all mankind are one great family of which numerous nations and tribes existing are only branches.'[16] Monier Williams, the Orientalist, described Roy as 'the first earnest-minded investigator of the science of Comparative Religion that the world has produced.'[17]

In 1815, he created the Atmiya Sabha (Spiritual Association) for 'the dissemination of religious truth and the promotion of free discussions of theological subjects'.[18] Roy was the 'first personality to be vocal against prevalent Hindu religious practices and doctrines which were injurious both to the social living of the people as well as to their growth of individuality'.[19] But he did not reject the Hindu element of the Indian personality, seeking only to bend it towards a more contemporaneous attitude.

In several ways, Roy embodied the progressive strain of the modern Indian national identity – a merger of India's historic cultural and religious legacy with liberal values and Western practices. Rather than attempting to turn back the clock to restore a golden age of former glory, he represented the thinking that characterizes the modernizing viewpoint in Indian civil society. Far from some other modernizers who would shun cultural heritage, Roy and his school sought to merge them with the essential and inevitable components of a changing world.

RE-PURIFICATION: THE CONSERVATIVE TREND

There were others, however, who saw Hindu society and Hinduism as under attack, both from what they perceived as centuries of foreign rule (Muslim rule) and now from Christian missionaries. The growth of the Arya Samaj and its use of *shuddhi* (purification or baptism) and *sangathan* (organization) to reconvert Muslims and Christians to Hinduism was representative of this perspective.

The Arya Samaj (society of the honourable ones, the Arya [Noble man]) was a reform movement founded in 1875 by Swami Dayananda Sarasvati. Like the Brahmo Samaj, the Arya Samaj sought to make Hinduism monotheistic to project a counter to the Abrahamic faiths and, thus, prevent Hindus from converting to Christianity. The Arya Samaj opposed idolatry and rituals, but it introduced baptism into Hinduism, in an attempt to bring back Hindus that had been 'lost to the fold.' Unlike the Brahmo Samaj, the Arya Samaj viewed the Vedas, ancient Hindu scriptures, as critical. It also used symbols like the protection of cows to bind Hindus together by setting up cow protection societies (*gaurakshani sabha*s).

It is interesting to note the consistency in conservative thought over the decades: even today, reconversion (*ghar wapsi*) of non-Hindus to Hinduism, protection and reconversion of mosques to temples (Ayodhya's Babri Masjid–Ram Janmabhoomi controversy), and cow protection remain the dominant issues for rallying the Hindu community.

The intellectual ferment of the time also gave rise to the question of 'who is a Hindu?' and generated debate about whether Hinduism ought to be defined as a religion and culture or as a vast civilization capable of subsuming many religions. Indianness defined by religion would exclude Muslims and Christians, as well as Parsis and Jews. The notion that India's purity has been tarnished by a millennium of alien influence led to the concept of rebuilding it as a uniform nation, with one single culture, one language and one religion. It was championed by the conservative strand, which at Independence included organizations like the All India Hindu Mahasabha, but over the decades has encompassed many others.

On the other hand, the vision of civilizational India represented a big tent. According to this view, everyone who lives in the Indian subcontinent, irrespective of his or her caste, religion or language, is from Hind, is a Hindu, and an Indian. Being Hindu or Indian is about being from India, not about worshipping specific gods in specific ways. By embracing other religions, Indians do not stop being Indian, nor can the Indianness of those whose forefathers made the country their home centuries ago, while retaining their religion, be questioned.

CONTENDING IDEAS OF INDIAN-NESS

The Indian national movement was primarily an elite-led movement, at least until Mohandas Karamchand Gandhi took over. The elite that was part of this movement was largely Westernized, even though it reflected various strands of thought: conservative, modernist and secular. Gandhi, with his insistence on non-violence and consensus-building, took politics to the Indian masses. In the process, he became recognized as Mahatma (the great soul) and the Indian national movement reconciled several contending ideologies and visions under his leadership.

Many intellectuals, such as Tagore, and political leaders including Gandhi and his protégé, Jawaharlal Nehru, insisted on the idea of India's essential unity. They rejected the significance of religion as a determinant of national identity and instead championed the idea of a broad Indian nationalism, which advocated unity in diversity. As a deeply religious individual, Gandhi frequently invoked religious symbols and idiom in his political life. But he was emphatic in his belief that India was not just a Hindu land but a home to many other religions, each of which deserved respect.

Tagore's idea of India was open and pluralist. This was a vision rooted not only in his moral worldview but also in his vision of India's past. He argued that contrary to being a society first and foremost for Hindus, India had a long history of pluralism and tolerance. He believed that India's strength came from social unity which was created through respect for difference, and ties which were 'as loose as possible, yet as close as the circumstances permitted'.[20]

Gandhi and Tagore shared views on patriotic nationalism, both desired an Indian nationalism that was universal and positive, but feared it might turn xenophobic, racist and communal. Gandhi once remarked, 'For me patriotism is the same as humanity. I am patriotic because I am human and humane. It is not exclusive, I will not hurt England or Germany to serve India. Imperialism has no place in my scheme of life.'[21] Gandhi's was a vision of positive and inclusive identity, which guided the Indian National Congress into making effort to maintain support from Muslims and other religious minorities for a unified, independent India.

Members of the All India Muslim League, formed in 1906 to protect Muslim interests, were allowed to remain part of the Indian National Congress for over three decades, and the Congress worked closely with the regional parties in most of British India's provinces. It was understood that minorities needed a voice of their own, but that voice had to be incorporated within the larger national movement. Still, the idea of India being Hindu, dating back to the nineteenth century, had not lost the support of at least some political leaders and businessmen.

In his 1925 tract, *Hindutva: Who is a Hindu?* Vinayak Damodar Savarkar, attempted to lay out a vision for the land of the Hindus, very different from the one offered by Gandhi and his disciples. According to Savarkar, 'A Hindu means a person who regards this land of *Bharatvarsha*, from the Indus to the Seas, as his fatherland as well as his holy land, that is the cradleland of his religion.'[22] In other words, it was not enough to belong to India; it was equally important to believe in India as the holy land. This definition rigidly separated Hindus from their Muslim or Christian neighbours, whose religion originated in the Middle East – not India.

In an effort to deny that the words Hind, Hindu and Hindustan have any Persian or Muslim influence, Savarkar argued that Hind comes from the ancient Prakrit language,[23] even though most historians note that the word Hind is the Persian name for the river Sindh or Indus that flows through the subcontinent. Further, he argued, '... although the root meaning of Hindu and Hindi may mean only an Indian, yet it would be straining the usage of words too much if we call a Mohammedan a Hindu because of his being a resident of India.'[24]

The same year Savarkar published his booklet, Keshav Baliram Hedgewar, a doctor from Maharashtra, founded the Rashtriya Swayamsevak Sangh (RSS – National Volunteer Corps) as a Hindu nationalist ideological organization. Hedgewar and his Sangh were deeply influenced by the writings of Savarkar. The RSS also shared the ideology of the All India Hindu Mahasabha (All India Hindu Grand Assembly), a political organization formed in 1907 – one year after the Muslim League's creation – to pursue a Hindu *rashtra* (a homeland for Hindus). But the conservative current of Hindu thought was not strong enough at the time to forestall the momentum of the unified struggle for India's independence.

Indian unity was breached by Muhammad Ali Jinnah's insistence on recognizing the separate identity of Muslims and the demand for a homeland for Muslims in areas of India where they constituted a majority. Once India was partitioned and Pakistan was created, there was some argument that India should be a Hindu state. For proponents of a unified India, this amounted to accepting Jinnah's two-nation theory. After all, he had demanded an Islamic Pakistan for Muslims and described Hindustan as the land of Hindus. Gandhi pushed back against the notion of India as a Hindu state with full force, at the risk of antagonizing radical conservative Hindus, one of whom eventually took his life.

In a prayer discourse six months before his assassination, Gandhi said, 'How can my religion also be the religion of the rest of the Indians? It will mean coercion against those Indians who are not Hindus. We have been shouting from the housetops that there will be no coercion in the matter of religion.' Reiterating that India had not only Hindus but also Muslims, Parsis, Christians and other religious groups, Gandhi argued that the '... assumption of the Hindus that India now has become the land of the Hindus is erroneous. India belongs to all who live here.'[25]

India's first prime minister, Jawaharlal Nehru, was secular, bordering on being an atheist. Born into a family of Kashmiri Pandits, he learned Farsi and Urdu along with English and Hindi. His view of the role religion should play in one's life has, in many ways, defined post-Independence Indian secularism. Nehru understood that most Indians were religious, and that religion mattered, but he was against its use in politics – whether it was by Gandhi or by the Hindu right wing or the Muslim League. As Nehru once noted: 'Religion as practised in India has become the old man of the sea for us and it has not only broken our backs but stifled and almost killed all originality of thought or mind.'[26]

An idealist, Nehru hoped that he would be able to teach and convince his country folk about the need to relegate religion to the personal sphere. As Gurcharan Das writes, Nehru '... united a nation out of the most heterogenous people on the earth. He nurtured democracy. More than any other individual, we owe him our present-day attachment to democratic institutions. He respected minorities and made us secular in our temperament. Most important, he injected in us the modernist ideas of liberty and equality. He gave us youthful hope and optimism.'[27]

And yet, the baggage of the past was so strong on all, even Nehru, that the modern Indian state on the one hand was Western and contemporary and yet, on the other hand, there was a strong desire to let the world know about Indian traditions and culture, to claim their universal relevance. Over the years, the pull of conservative Indian religious identity proved resistant against top-down attempts to modernize Indian culture.

∽

During debates in India's Constituent Assembly between 1946 and 1949, some members reflected the conservative strand of Indian identity by insisting on tying Indian citizenship to religion. P.S. Deshmukh, a Constituent Assembly member from Maharashtra, argued that the creation of Pakistan demanded that the Indian

Constitution have '… a provision that every person who is a Hindu or a Sikh and is not a citizen of any other State shall be entitled to be a citizen of India.'[28] This vision of India not only envisioned the state as built around a particular religious identity, it also notably excluded Muslims.

Prime Minister Nehru, Deputy Prime Minister and Home Minister Sardar Vallabhbhai Patel, and the draftsman of the Constitution, Dr Bhimrao Ramji (B.R.) Ambedkar, argued vehemently against the use of religion in defining citizenship. Nehru stated that 'all these rules naturally apply to Hindus, Muslims and Sikhs or Christians or anybody else. You cannot have rules for Hindus, for Muslims or for Christians only.'[29] Patel spoke about the need for citizenship to be based on *jus soli* '… whereby citizenship is acquired by birth within the territory of the state, regardless of parental citizenship', opposing those who championed *jus sanguinis* '… whereby a person, wherever born, is a citizen of the state if, at the time of his birth, his parent is one'. Together, these leaders ensured that the Indian Constitution, and many early government institutions, reflected the liberal vision of Indian identity.

Modern India's founding generation did not think that transformation was impossible in postcolonial India. Their exertions ensured that India became a democracy even though it lacked a literate population and strong economic foundations – a rare accomplishment for a postcolonial developing country. In the decades following Independence, India chose to educate its people, pull them out of poverty, grow economically and build its military, all at the same time. But even as India built a modern political and economic systems, it has found it difficult to transform society. The element of Indian society, which embraces a conservative attitude towards identity and community, has stood firm and gained ground at the expense of the liberal component.

The struggle between two contending imaginings of India, one modern and secular and the other conservative and religious, continues into the twenty-first century. The contradictions bred by this struggle are there for everyone to see: India has had women as prime minister and president, but fewer women are in the labour force today than in the 1990s. Despite outlawing caste-based discrimination through its liberal and socially progressive Constitution in 1949, untouchables and members of lower castes still face discrimination daily. Notwithstanding guarantees of religious freedom in the Indian Constitution, there have been reports of members of minority communities being lynched and killed in the name of protecting cows, a sacred animal for many Hindus. India is still far from bridging the divide between contending ideas of what the country should become and what it means to be Indian.

LIBERAL DREAM, SCIENCE, AND HISTORY

Sunil Khilnani, in *The Idea of India* (1997), argues that contemporary India has been shaped by a 'wager' of the country's educated urban elite on modern ideas and agencies. 'It was a wager on an idea: the idea of India', Khilnani notes, adding that India's '... nationalist elite itself had no single, clear definition of this idea'. According to him, 'One of the remarkable facts about the nationalist movement that brought India to independence was its capacity to entertain diverse, often contending visions of India ... Indian nationalism before Independence was plural even at the top, a dhoti with endless folds. ... It contains people from markedly different backgrounds yet whose trajectories were often parallel.'[30]

The liberal version of secular Indian nationalism absorbed its diversity. Its advocates hoped to build a modern India inspired by the past, but connected to the present and looking towards the future. Indian secularism was not the American form of strict separation of church and state or the French Jacobin kind that subordinated religion to the state. As English journalist and author, Edward Luce notes, the Indian type of secularism '... is less militant. The state happily promotes all religions rather than disdaining them equally.'[31] It represents a common appreciation for the many faiths which make up India's diverse cultural identity.

In his inaugural speech to the Constituent Assembly of India on 9 December 1946, its temporary chairman, Sachchidananda Sinha, had called for 'a broad and catholic vision' as the basis for independent India's Constitution. He asked his compatriots to seek inspiration from Constitutions around the world: the Swiss, the French, the American, the Canadian. Sinha praised the French and American Constitutions for their embrace of secularism and individual liberty. To drive home the point that Islamic and Christian traditions were part of India's fabric, he ended his speech marking the beginning of Constitution-making with a quote from Muslim poet Sir Muhammad Iqbal and a proverb from the Bible: 'Where there is no vision the people perish.'[32]

This 'catholic vision' was also echoed in the speeches given by the first and second presidents of India, Rajendra Prasad and S. Radhakrishnan, extolling the virtues of an inclusive civilization. Prasad spoke of the need to frame '… a Constitution for an independent and free India' that would '… satisfy all our people, all groups, all communities, all religions inhabiting this vast land', ensuring '… to everyone freedom of action, freedom of thought, freedom of belief and freedom of worship'.[33]

A key drafter of the Constitution, B.R. Ambedkar, expressed his concern about the challenges India faced '… in our own country which is so orthodox, so archaic in its thought and its social structure' and yet he was '… quite convinced that given time and circumstances nothing in the world will prevent this country from becoming one. With all our castes and creeds, I have not the slightest hesitation that we shall in some form be a united people.'[34] But the founding fathers of modern India firmly believed that unity could only be achieved by recognizing, even celebrating, India's diversity.

Although most of the country's founding leaders were Hindu and the majority of the Constituent Assembly comprised Hindus, they did not seek a state which only reflected their religion. One of the first resolutions passed by the Constituent Assembly of India on 3 April 1948 pushed for secularism by prohibiting communal organizations from engaging in coordinated activities other than their religious or socially stated purposes. Coming in the aftermath of Partition and the assassination of Mahatma Gandhi, the resolution reflected an early recognition of the divisiveness of religion-based politics.

India's founding elite spoke of secularism as being Indian in essence, drawing upon the diversity and pluralism within Hinduism. They hoped to contain communalism and religious divisions through constitutional guarantees implemented by courts and through non-discriminatory state institutions. But the alternative visualization of India, one which was Hindu and where Hinduism would guide government policy, contested this approach.

For conservatives, secularism put the majority at a disadvantage by protecting the minorities and by insisting on equality between various communities. In their view, the majority had the right to define how things should be run and while the minority could co-exist, it had to do so on the majority's terms. The two opposing ideas of India conflicted in every space of the social and political fabric of the new country. From how history is taught in schools to the role of women in society, to debates about caste, these opposing strands of thought defined fault lines across society.

Education and history are critical to the different ideological projects, which have sought to define Indian identity since Independence. Historically, Indian education has embodied the liberal ideals of many of its early founders. But conservative attempts to influence and reshape India through education are just as long-standing as liberal ones. Nehru noted that over the centuries in India '... a rational spirit of inquiry, so evident in earlier times, which might well have led to the further growth of science, is replaced by irrationalism and a blind idolatry of the past. Indian life becomes a sluggish stream, living in the past, moving slowly through the accumulations of dead centuries.'[35] In 1926, he noted that 'no country or people who are slaves to dogma and dogmatic mentality can progress,' and lamented that 'unhappily our country and people have become extraordinarily dogmatic and little-minded.'[36]

Just as the modern West is a product of the Enlightenment of the seventeenth century that followed the Renaissance and Reformation, India's liberal current emerged from the Bengal Renaissance in British colonial India during the nineteenth and early twentieth century. The cultural ferment of the Renaissance and the reforming of Christianity were important prerequisites for the Enlightenment, emphasizing the importance of reason and individualism over tradition. Similarly, the Bengal Renaissance began with questioning of religious tradition and involved modern science, history, literature, and western education.

The Bengal Renaissance had challenged perceived societal inequities and some religious beliefs, including the caste system and the burdensome dowry system. It had opened the way for women's participation in society as men's equals, something traditionalists were loath to accept. Stalwarts of the Bengal Renaissance, such as Roy, Tagore and Vidyasagar, paved the way for pioneering work by Bengali intellectuals in the fields of biology, botany, science fiction, physics, and archaeology. Some high-calibre individuals included Satyendra Nath Bose (the theoretical physicist known for Bose–Einstein statistics), Meghnad Saha (the astrophysicist, known for Saha ionization equation), and Upendranath Brahmachari (medical doctor, inventor of Urea stibamine, the medicine for treating the deadly illness Kala-azar) were all products of the Bengal Renaissance.

That spirit manifested itself in India's post-Independence educational curricula, which emphasized English as the medium of communication, taught an inclusive nationalist version of history, and informed children from elementary school onwards about science, including the Darwinian concept of evolution. This progressive bent of Indian education precluded discussion of the universe resulting from 'intelligent design' or evolution being contradictory to science.[37] In any case, the Biblical and Quranic notion of the world's creation by one God is not part of Hindu religion, making it easier for Indians to understand evolution and embrace science alongside their pantheon of gods.

However, a modern curriculum was insufficient to get rid of the pedagogical system that valued learning by rote and by imitation of the teacher. Although India produced doctors and engineers by the thousands, it did not succeed in fully cultivating an inquisitive spirit or critical thinking. Indian conservatives challenged the primacy of the English language and questioned science where it contradicted traditional mythology. Over time, there has also been a rise in revisionist historicism by champions of Hindutva, who have sought to rewrite Indian history to emphasize India's 'Hinduness' and diminish the significance of 1000 years of Indo-Islamic culture and history.

Just as Indian liberals had sought to fuse education with openness and rationality, conservatives hoped to build it with tradition and Hindu specialness. Meera Nanda, a historian of science, argues that India's project of modernity was marked by 'counter-Enlightenment'. Instead of 'bringing religion within the limits of scientific reason, the Indian counter-Enlightenment has tended to subsume or co-opt scientific reason within the spirit-based cosmology and epistemology of "the Vedas".'[38]

Thus, Nanda points out, modern India on the one hand 'embraced the end products of the scientific revolution and the Enlightenment in the West – namely, modern technology and a liberal-secular framework of laws encoded in the Constitution'. Yet, it did so 'without challenging the cultural authority of the supernatural and mystical world view derived from the idealistic strands of Hinduism.'[39] Hence, '… modernity in India has this feel of incompleteness, superficiality and even schizophrenia.'[40] The two contradictory ideas of India have generated an attitude towards education, which is at odds with itself.

The ideological conflict manifests itself across India's many educational institutions. For instance, India has an indigenously built space programme, it has launched satellites into space and Indian scientists, engineers and doctors are sought the world over.

Yet, in 2019, at the 106th annual gathering of the Indian Science Congress, a scientist claimed that the country's epics proved that ancient Indians had knowledge of test-tube babies, aircraft design technology, and guided missiles.[41] Each of these was a reference to different stories from Hindu mythology. This would be akin to Greeks claiming that Icarus and not the Wright brothers were the first to fly in the air or that Athena – Zeus' daughter, who is believed to have emerged intact from her father's head – was an example of brain surgery.

This runs contrary to the liberal and secular vision of Jawaharlal Nehru, who referred to India's schools, hospitals, laboratories, industries and cities as the 'temples of modern India' – places that would build the future generations. He believed in a pure fidelity towards the sciences and hoped that education would instil scientific consciousness and a spirit of inquiry within Indians that would take the nation forward.

As the first non-scientist to preside over the Indian Science Congress in 1937, Nehru had declared, 'It is science alone that can solve the problems of hunger and poverty, of insanitation and illiteracy, of superstition and deadening custom and tradition, of vast resources running to waste, of a rich country inhabited by starving people.'[42] Nehru would have been appalled by deities or dogma slipping into his temples of modernity. But there is no dearth of reports of scientists in India performing religious rituals before launching a space satellite or amidst the conduct of a scientific experiment. The liberal desire for a scientific temperament has failed to win against the conservative agenda of embracing technology without conceding ground on the ancient philosophical foundations of Indian life.

Apart from science, India's liberal and conservative visions also collide over history. Unlike many other postcolonial societies, especially India's neighbour Pakistan, Indian educational curricula and its textbooks had initially sought to create an inclusive national identity that did not whitewash history or deny what happened in the past. Its history textbooks started from the pre-historic era and covered every period until Independence in 1947. If ancient Indian empires like the Mauryas and Guptas had pride of place, so did the Mughal empire and the southern empires like the Cholas. Not only political history but cultural, social and economic history was also taught to children from elementary school all the way to university.

The conservative counter-narrative of India as a Hindu country required significant historical revisionism. Even during Nehru's period there were always those who believed that Indian history had to be rewritten to erase anything that did not bring glory to Hindu India. For example, archaeological evidence suggests that civilization in India began in the Indus Valley, followed by a Central Asian invasion, which repopulated most of northern South Asia. Accepting this would imply that all of India's inhabitants, except very few, have foreign origin or at least some foreign blood. That, in turn, would take away the argument about India's Muslims being lesser Indians because they are descendants of foreign invaders.

Instead of accepting that Aryan Hindus in northern India came from outside some 4000 years ago, just as some Muslims arrived from Afghanistan and Central Asia a thousand years before our time, Hindu nationalists insist that Hindus are descended from the oldest inhabitants of the country. These arguments about genealogy and heritage matter to Hindutva votaries because their claim that India ought to be a Hindu *rashtra* (nation) rests on Hindus being the original people and Hinduism being the indigenous religion of the subcontinent.

As early as 1924, Swami Shraddhananda, an Arya Samaj missionary, wrote a text, 'Hindu Sangathan: Saviour of the Dying Race', in which he argued that 'the ancestors of the present day Hindus, the ancient Aryans, who gave their name to our motherland (the ancient Aryavarta) were a highly civilized organized race.'[43] In 2017, the government led by Prime Minister Narendra Modi set up a committee of such scholars to attempt to use archaeology and DNA evidence for the explicit purpose of identifying Hindus as the direct descendants of India's original inhabitants.[44]

In addition to redefining the origins of India's populace, the country's conservatives also want to erase the significance or achievements of Muslim rule in India, in addition to rewriting the account of India's national movement. For example, textbooks in the state of Rajasthan have altered the outcome of a 1576 battle in which Mughal emperor Akbar defeated the Rajput ruler of Mewar, Maharana Pratap, to project the defeated Hindu general as the victor. Similarly, Rajasthan textbooks do not talk about the assassination of Mahatma Gandhi by Nathuram Godse, a Hindu who was a member of the Hindu Mahasabha and totally avoid mention of India's first prime minister Jawaharlal Nehru.[45] In Odisha, a two-page booklet 'Aama Bapuji: Aka Jhalaka' (Our Bapuji: A Glimpse), published by the school and mass education department of the state on the occasion of Mahatma Gandhi's 150th birth anniversary, makes the astonishing claim that Gandhi's death was due to an 'accidental sequence of events'.[46]

The project of rewriting history often involves outrageous claims and outright fabrication. The objective is to discuss history, not as the record of events in previous times, but as an account of Hindu greatness. For instance, in 2017 India's minister of state for human resource development, responsible for higher education, Satyapal Singh, stated at a public gathering that 'the first working plane was invented by an Indian named Shivakar Babuji Talpade eight years before the Wright brothers',[47] even though there is no evidence to support that assertion. The line of reasoning, if it can be called that, seems to be that the accomplishments of Hindus such as Talpade were deliberately concealed by non-Hindus, who were conspiring consistently to keep the Hindus suppressed.

In April 2018, the chief minister of the northeastern state of Tripura, Biplab Deb, made the stupendous assertion that the Internet existed during the time of the Indian epic Mahabharata, which is reckoned to be around 400 BC. 'Many may decline the fact', Deb insisted, 'but if the Internet was not there, how [could] Sanjay see the war in Kurukshetra and describe it to Dhritarashtra?' According to Deb, the poetic references to certain actions of mythical characters implied the existence of the Internet and satellite technology.[48]

MISPLACED PRIORITIES

India has been at the heart of global discussions about containing a potentially aggressive China. But while officials debate India's role in the Indo-Pacific and the Quad – a maritime military partnership between India, America, Japan, and Australia – religious vigilantes in India have continued to attack their countrymen in the name of protecting the cow. Indian leaders have done little to point out that nationalist energy should be focused on economic productivity and military preparedness, and not on attacking others over religious symbols.

According to a February 2019 report released by Human Rights Watch, between May 2015 and December 2018, over 100 attacks by cow protection Hindu vigilante groups resulted in the deaths of forty-four people – thirty-six of the dead being Muslims – and over 280 people were injured.[49] The government has done little to stop the cow protection vigilantes and even less to change the national discourse away from such issues towards substantive matters affecting India's international stature or power.

Other countries around the world are watching to see how much India invests in strategic planning and defence. But not only has India witnessed a reduction in military spending, it still manages to divert resources for placating cow protection sentiment. In the 2019 Union Budget, funds were allocated to create an authority – the Rashtriya Kamdhenu Aayog (National Cow Commission) – to implement laws and initiate welfare schemes for cows.[50] For most of the world, such choices represent misplaced priorities, even as they pander to certain vote banks in the northern Indian states often referred to as the cow belt.

Admittedly, the role of the state in religious matters has always been problematic in South Asia as well as the Middle East. Cultural and social practices are important parts of the fabric of Indian society. Empires came and went, but social structures such as caste and community remained. Through much of history, India's rulers, whether Hindu or Muslim, avoided interventions directed at vast moral and social restructuring. The British colonial Raj inherited this legacy and continued the practice. The British segregated Indian society along community lines and thus exacerbated the differences between various religious communities. But they also instituted laws that governed each religion through its own codes of law.

The British instituted a few changes, which encouraged liberal secularization. For instance, they banned sati, legalized remarriage by widows, and raised the age of consent for marriage and consensual sex. But they were reluctant to address issues that might have reshaped values or altered traditions drastically. The Indian national movement, on the other hand, was not about ruling India along the path of minimal resistance. It was a political struggle for independence from colonial rule, as well as a movement for societal change. Gandhi championed gradual reform from within society. Nehru, on the other hand, and the drafter of the Constitution, Ambedkar, believed that legal changes would speed up social change. Otherwise, it would take too long for Indian society to change its attitudes on caste, women's status and various superstitions.

Debates over whether the state should be secular or confessional, or the extent to which it should implement laws in the personal sphere and protect religious minorities, consumed much time and energy around India's independence. They still have salience today and are at the heart of the different ideas of India, which shape the core of the state's character under different leaders and political parties.

For the first several decades, Indian secularism meant that the state would treat all religions as equal and ensure, through laws and the Constitution, that there is no discrimination based on religion. The writers of the Constitution also wanted to assure religious, ethnic and linguistic minorities that they have an equal stake and say in India, leading to constitutional provisions allowing minorities to establish educational, cultural and religious organizations supported by the state.

In the Constituent Assembly, Nehru had argued that declaring itself secular, India had 'only done something which every country does except a very few misguided and backward countries in the world'.[51] This concept of 'benevolent neutrality towards all religions',[52] as French historian and author Christophe Jaffrelot defines Nehruvian secularism, had an added dimension: the need to 'reduce the ascendancy of religion in society'.[53] From Nehru's perspective, the presence of 'many faiths and religions' meant that 'no real nationalism can be built except on the basis of secularity'.[54] A multicultural country like India simply could not embrace a monocultural form of government, if it was to survive, prosper and avoid conflict.

Nehru's India was an especially permissive time for the secular vision of the Indian government. In this context it is important to note that 80 per cent of the Constituent Assembly of India seemed to recognize the need for a liberal nationalism; Hindu majoritarianism had not yet entered politics in full force.[55] This allowed India's founding fathers to write a Constitution that embraced a broadly liberal interpretation of individual rights and the state's attitude towards religion. Article 25 of the Indian Constitution ensures the right to practise and proselytize one's religion, and Article 29 guarantees the rights of minority languages and cultures. The early leaders of India were able to create a state, which mirrored their vision of inclusive nationalism.

However, the liberal project of state building was never complete. Luce notes, 'Nehru permitted each religious community to retain its own civil laws, or "personal codes", which govern marriages, divorces, births, deaths and inheritances. It was probably not ideal since it sat uneasily with the principle of equality before the law, which is also enshrined in the Constitution. But in the wake of the horrors of Partition it seemed a necessary concession to the millions of Muslims who had ignored Pakistan and remained in India.'[56] This, and other protections for minorities, led to charges by Hindu nationalists of 'Muslim appeasement', which in turn became an important rallying cry for reversing the entire liberal endeavour. Over time, the minorities became a vote bank for the Congress and other left-wing parties, making it even easier to polarize society between 'Hindu nationalism' and what was derisively called 'pseudo secularism.'

Nowhere in India is the conflict over the state's role in religion more evident than in the treatment of women. Indian society has a strong patriarchal and feudal mindset that views women as property, as critical to family honour, and as something to be controlled. The notion that the control of women – their attire, their education, their marriage – is critical to ensuring the future of a community that is perceived to be constantly under threat from others has been persistent in debates. It was invoked during deliberation of the Hindu Code Bill in the 1950s and continues today amidst discussion of khap panchayat (local village caste council) rulings and honour killings.

Many Indian leaders understood the need to improve the situation of women. Roy, Vidyasagar, Tagore, Nehru and Gandhi had recognized the need to change the reality of women in Indian society. Tagore held strong views on women's role in society and the need for reforms. Like his views on caste, his writings show the evolution of his views from 1881 to 1941. He spoke about the social injustices against women, wrote admiringly of educated and urban Indian women who fought for human rights and equality, and challenged social evils like untouchability, the rigid caste system, denying widows the right to remarry, and patriarchy at large.[57]

These issues have plagued India for decades without resolution and the conservative vision, some would argue, wants the government to give up on pursuing reforms that run contrary to tradition. There seems to be a constant effort to dismiss what liberals might describe as social ills and to insist that adhering to traditional culture is the only honourable way of life for women. In 2012, a khap panchayat in the northern state of Haryana blamed the rise in rapes and sexual assaults on women on the consumption of noodles.[58] Another khap panchayat just outside the national capital, mandated that any female above the age of ten years would not be allowed to wear jeans or use a mobile phone so that they 'do not attract the male eye'.[59]

These councils – khap panchayats – are considered illegal assemblies by the Supreme Court of India, but that has not prevented them from attempting to enforce their diktats.[60] Conservative nationalists tend to side with the khap panchayats' world view. In 2018, the department of labour of the state of Rajasthan mandated that jeans and T-shirts were 'against the dignity' of their office. Further, women studying at all state-run colleges in Rajasthan were informed that they could no longer wear jeans, though the order was later rescinded when students protested.[61]

India's founding liberals saw the state's role in religion as to both support pluralism and intervene when the rights of the individual were at stake. The Hindu Code Bill was Nehru's way of pushing religion into the private sphere and casting the state as an agent of modernization.[62] While Nehru was able to eventually reform the Hindu family code, he faced tremendous backlash from the conservative elements within Hindu society and politics.

The history of this bill dates back to January 1941 when the British colonial government appointed the Hindu Law Committee headed by B.N. Rau, a judge of Calcutta High Court to 'revisit the Hindu Women's Right to Property Act, 1937 and to suggest amendments and clarify rights of the widow; and remove any injustice that may have been done by the Act to the daughters'.[63]

The 1941 Hindu Code Bill 'introduced two types of marriage: the sacramental and civil and promised a great deal of freedom and flexibility in marriage and divorce', and denied the right to Hindus of polygamous marriage. This provoked conservative and religious elements within Hindu society to push back against the Bill and it was allowed to lapse until it was taken up once again by the Constituent Assembly.[64] This time, too, there were concerted efforts by various groups, ranging from lawyers' associations to organizations like Sanatan Dharma Sabha, and All India

Hindu Mahasabha, to present the Hindu Code Bill as a threat to Hinduism itself.

The All India Hindu Mahasabha referred to the Hindu Code as 'suicidal folly' as it would result in the wiping out Hindus.[65] The argument was that through polygamy and higher birth rates, Muslims would shift the demographic balance in South Asia against Hindus.[66] That this has not happened yet, and over 80 per cent of Indians remain Hindu, has not changed the views of social conservatives. Fertility data as recent as 2019 shows that Hindus and Muslims have roughly the same number of children on average,[67] but Hindu nationalists continue to raise the spectre of Hindus being outnumbered over time.

The anxiety that continues to persist was even more widespread at the time of Partition. Nehru even faced pressure within his own party and government to roll back the legislation. The president of the Constituent Assembly and first president of India, Dr Rajendra Prasad, wrote a series of letters to Nehru urging him to drop efforts to alter or, as Nehru saw it, reform the Hindu way of life. Prasad wrote, 'We have to weigh how it will be received by the vast bulk of Hindu public against what foreigners outside India and those who call themselves "progressive" would say.'[68]

Although Nehru was keen to pass the reform package, he waited until after the 1952 elections, when the Congress party swept the polls. Armed with a fresh mandate, parliament passed four separate acts based on the reformist Hindu Code Bill. Nehru skirted the controversy over the original bill by breaking up its contents into separate laws – the Hindu Marriage Act of 1955, the Hindu Succession Act of 1956, the Hindu Minority and Guardianship Act of 1956, and the Hindu Adoptions and Maintenance Act of 1956 – all of which were critical in providing basic legal rights to women.

Chitra Sinha refers to the Hindu reforms as the 'single most important legal initiative in Indian history' because it was an attempt to 'frame a uniform set of rules that could govern all Hindus through the length and breadth of India'.[69] The Bill's legacy was 'the distribution of rights and allocation of resources within the Indian family and enabled Indian society to align with its development model of planned economic progress and modernization. In the process, it endeavoured to give significantly greater rights to Indian women. At the same time, it was a celebration of notions of freedom and individualism over the structured sense of destiny propagated for many centuries in the name of religion.'[70]

For liberal reformers, the amendments of the Hindu personal and family law were the first step towards a uniform civil code for all Indians, irrespective of religion. This did not happen for multiple reasons. In Nehru's calculus, the Muslim minority felt under siege immediately after Independence, and any effort to change Muslim marriage or divorce laws would have added to their sense of insecurity. In later decades, social reform was just not considered a political priority. That enabled Hindutva supporters to become advocates of a uniform civil code, which in turn transformed liberal and secular elements, who should have supported the idea, into its opponents.

WOMEN, COWS AND CASTE

The broader debate over the treatment of women continues in India to this day, alongside discussions about protecting cows and preserving the caste system. In some ways, these three social questions, coupled with the fear of Islam and Christianity, or westernization eliminating Hindu culture have been the defining issues for revivalist, conservative Hindus.

Opponents of amendments to the Hindu family laws had argued that reform went against 'the pristine purity of the Hindu shastras and the exalted position given to Sita, Savitri, Damayanti' – women from Hindu mythology who have been viewed as representing the ideal in womanhood.[71] Nehru had pointed out that these arguments were 'echoes from the past' invoked 'chiefly to hide our present deficiencies and to prevent us from attacking the root cause of women's degradation today'.[72] But the notion that the onus is on the woman 'to be the flag bearer of morality, purity and chastity'[73] remains prevalent in Indian society.

India has witnessed an upsurge in reports of sexual assaults and rapes in recent years. The response of India's leaders, transcending political divides, has been to attribute it to the non-traditional behaviour of women. In 2012, soon after a heinous gang rape of a twenty-three-year-old young woman in New Delhi, a sitting member of parliament referred to women who were protesting the rape as 'pretty women, dented and painted' who 'have no contact with ground reality'.[74] Congress MP, Abhijit Mukherjee, the son of the then president Pranab Mukherjee, later apologized for his remarks after widespread condemnation, including by his own father.

Two years later, the former chief minister of the largest Indian state of Uttar Pradesh, Mulayam Singh Yadav, a socialist, opposed capital punishment for rape on grounds that, 'First girls develop friendship with boys. Then when differences occur, they level rape charges. Boys commit mistakes. Will they be hanged for rape?'[75] Although opposition to Hindu nationalism is an essential element of Yadav's politics, on this social issue, his response was not different from those with a traditionalist point of view.

Tradition and religion have also been at the heart of debates about cow protection and banning cow slaughter, which have raged on since the nineteenth century. In the Constituent Assembly of India, some members, including Rajendra Prasad, sought to enshrine the banning of cow slaughter in the Constitution's chapter on Fundamental Rights. The chairman of the Drafting Committee of the Constitution, B.R. Ambedkar, vehemently disagreed as, in his view, 'rights' properly applied only to citizens and cows were not citizens. 'The "cow-savers" begged to disagree', according to a scholar's account of the argument. '"The cow [in India] takes precedence [even] over the children of the family because she is the mother ... the mother of the nation," averred Raghu Vira. "It is my fundamental right to protect my mother," echoed R.V. Dhulekar.'[76]

But Ambedkar did not agree and refused to include fundamental rights of cows in the constitutional enumeration of citizens' rights.

The result of the passion on both sides was a compromise. On 16 November 1949, India's Constituent Assembly approved a motion for the inclusion, in the chapter of the draft document devoted to Directive Principles of State Policy, of an additional clause on agriculture. It read: 'That the State shall endeavour to organize agriculture and animal husbandry on modern scientific lines and shall, in particular, take steps for preserving and improving the breeds, and prohibiting the slaughter of cows and calves and other milch and draught cattle.'[77] The motion was 'carried, re-renumbered and designated'[78] as Article 48.

The passing of Article 48, which allowed state governments to enact cow protection laws, resulted in new legislative acts being proclaimed in many northern states. As of 2019, twenty-four out of twenty-eight states have laws that criminalize cow killing and, in some cases, even bullocks. As recently as 2005, the Supreme Court has upheld their validity. Ironically, notwithstanding the enthusiasm of some to protect cows and even extend constitutional protection to them, the idea that Indians – even among Hindus – hold a uniform consensus against cow slaughter or on vegetarianism is fiction.

According to several studies, India has many non-vegetarians and there are many Hindus who eat meat, including beef. In a March 2018 article, Balmurli Natarajan and Suraj Jacob use three data sets – National Sample Survey, National Family Health Survey and India Human Development Survey – to argue that India is a 'meat-eating majority nation' and only 23 per cent to 37 per cent of India's population is vegetarian.[79]

India has also for years been one of the leading exporters of beef and has a thriving leather industry. As of 2017, India was the third largest exporter of beef, according to data from the Food and Agriculture Organization (FAO) and Organization for Economic Cooperation (OECD). The OECD–FAO Agricultural Outlook for 2017–2026 report stated that India exported 1.56 million tonnes of beef in 2016 and 'was expected to maintain its position as the third-largest beef exporter, accounting for 16 per cent of global exports in 2026'.[80] The idea that there is a broad-based societal consensus against cow slaughter is fiction. But the rhetoric and symbolism of the cow, which has been used to mobilize Hindutva nationalists in northern India, is very real.

India's conservatives and liberals disagree on handling caste diversity as well. It has been close to seventy-three years since Independence and seventy years since the Indian Constitution abolished discrimination based on caste, sex or creed, but India is still grappling with the realities of caste discrimination. According to national crime statistics, the number of caste-based crimes 'has increased 25 per cent since 2010, reaching nearly 41,000 cases in 2016, the last year on record'.[81] The Constitution and law have not sufficed to end battles over caste, which has been part of Indian social and political history for millennia.

The father of independent India, Mahatma Gandhi, fought for years against untouchability. At the Round Table Conference in 1931, Gandhi described the state of the untouchables by saying, 'They hold no land; they are absolutely living at the mercy of the so-called higher castes, and also, let me say, at the mercy of the State. They can be removed from one quarter to another without complaint and without being able to seek the assistance of law.'[82] Gandhi argued for the need for the state to 'continually give preference to these people and even free them from the burdens under which they are being crushed'.[83]

Still, Gandhi's views on caste were complicated. On the one hand, he believed in the core religious and cultural elements of the caste system, and on the other, like Tagore, he argued that the current system needed repair and reform. Gandhi contended that the supporters of untouchability defended the foul practice on the grounds of religion by twisting scriptures in their favour. 'This religion if it can be called such, stinks in my nostrils', he wrote, adding, 'This certainly cannot be the Hindu religion. It was through the Hindu religion that I learnt to respect Christianity and Islam.'[84] In Gandhi's view, untouchability was an 'immoral and evil custom'.

Nehru believed that the caste system 'brought degradation' and 'is still a burden and a curse'.[85] Gandhi's pronouncements and Nehru's efforts through legal measure proved insufficient to erase casteism from Indian society. Under socially conservative leaders, emphasis on caste is returning in ways that the liberal founders of the country might not have anticipated. In October 2018, in Tamil Nadu, a fourteen-year-old Dalit girl was beheaded by an upper-caste man because of her caste.[86] In May 2018, the video of a Dalit scavenger being tied up and fatally whipped outside a factory in Rajasthan was broadcast across India.[87] In March 2018, in Gujarat, a Dalit man was killed by higher-caste men for riding a horse (traditionally, Dalits are prohibited from riding a horse).[88]

೧

All of this runs contrary to Article 17 of the Indian Constitution, which abolished untouchability and forbade its practice in any form. As with the notions of an Indian persona encompassing all religious traditions, recognizing women as social equals of men and ensuring that all languages and cultures flourish equally, the desire to eliminate caste differences is also floundering against the rise of a conservative Hindu identity. It can be argued that India's embrace of modernity may have been too quick and somewhat contrived. Ancient societies are resistant to change. Moreover, religious fundamentalist movements feed off one other. Hindutva sees Islam, and to a lesser extent Christianity, as existential threats, which justify drastic state action, aimed at undoing what an earlier generation considered modernizing reforms.

Many majoritarian Hindus see the spread of radical Islam, the rise of the Islamic State (ISIS), and Pakistan's role in terror attacks within India as an existential threat. This has mobilized many Indians around an insular and rigid form of a majoritarian identity. Christianity is the second threat, primarily because of conversions among tribal communities and the belief that foreign Non-Governmental Organizations (NGOs) and churches convert these individuals by offering money, jobs and opportunities to study abroad.

In confronting what they see as existential challenges, India's Hindutva conservatives seem to be paving the way for a more traditional India. They deem it more authentic than the pseudo-secular, liberal India of Gandhi and Nehru. But hyper-nationalism is often accompanied by xenophobia, which in turn runs the risk of diminishing the quality of India's interaction with the rest of the world.

India's desire for global pre-eminence and recognition by others of its great-power status requires that the rest of the world be comfortable with India's sense of self. The quest for authenticity through pre-Muslim and pre-Western Hindu traditions, turning back the clock on the status of women, minorities, and lower castes, and an excessively inward focus – though popular at home – may not sit well with India's plans for global greatness.

2

Human Capital

IN JANUARY–MARCH 2019, the Kumbh Mela, one of the largest religious gatherings in the world, demonstrated India's potential for mobilizing and executing complex logistical feats. Around 150 million people, primarily Hindus, attended this ritual, which takes place at regular intervals.[1] For the 2019 gathering, a temporary city was constructed, special trains and planes ferried pilgrims and tourists, and a special police force and district administration were mustered. In total, over forty police stations, 1,22,000 toilets, 15,000 sanitation workers, 20,000 beds, 1000 CCTV cameras, primary health centres, ambulances and special trains were conscripted for the event.[2] The *New York Times* marvelled at the mega organization costing US $600 million that resulted in the creation of 'nine new highway flyovers, 22 pontoon bridges, 150 miles of roads, 20,000 trash cans, 40,000 LED lights, 122,500 toilets and one new airport terminal'.[3]

The Kumbh Mela is held every six years. Each time, states across northern India are able to ensure that millions of pilgrims and tourists attending the religious assembly have access to food, sanitation, water and electricity. Yet, India struggles in providing basic goods and services to its people under normal conditions. Although traffic flows and public order are maintained during the pilgrimage, India is unable to overcome its reputation for bad traffic management and law and order. This begs the question: how can India ensure excellent arrangements for millions of people for a once-in-six-year religious gathering, while it fails to provide the same basic amenities to its citizens on a regular basis?

It all comes down to determining priorities and executing plans effectively. Indians have, for thousands of years, demonstrated their capacity to build and maintain functioning cities. Archaeologists have found evidence of well-laid-out and planned cities from the Indus Valley Civilization, one of the oldest in the world and the oldest in the Indian subcontinent. Harappa and Mohenjo-daro, built around 5000 years ago, had public as well as private bathrooms, covered drains, streets arranged so that they could be regularly cleaned, and storage facilities for food for their residents. If a country inheriting that civilizational legacy now has an abysmal record on these fronts, it reflects poor governance, not an inherent incapacity for organization and discipline.

India has underinvested in its cities, its institutions and, most of all, its people. Unlike many of India's challenges, the failure to invest in human capital is not a product of the liberal–Hindutva ideological divide. It is the function of petty political division, legacies of big government, lack of foresight, and the type of simple mismanagement that is common to developing countries. For India to achieve its promise, it must not only figure out a way to navigate its ideological divide; it must also engage in the type of smart but difficult statecraft, which is necessary to pull it out of developing country status.

For instance, the Indian civilization always valued education. There has always been an emphasis on knowledge and learning, a consensus across ideologies. Although there are differences in pedagogy (as discussed in the previous chapter), the provision of resources for literacy and basic school infrastructure should reach across the ideological spectrum. Yet, more than seven decades after Independence, Sri Lanka's literacy rate is higher than India's. Even in Bangladesh, which was liberated with India's help and started out with a literacy rate of 16 per cent in 1971, an estimated 72 per cent can read and write, close to India's 74 per cent. In the words of leading author and public intellectual, Gurcharan Das, 'The Indian state's biggest failure has been in building human capabilities.'[4] This failure was not predetermined or thrust upon India by circumstance; it is the product of misgovernance.

HUMAN CAPITAL CRISIS

Encyclopedia Britannica defines human capital as the 'intangible collective resources possessed by individuals and groups within a given population'. These resources include knowledge, skills, intelligence and experience. Cumulatively, the human capital of a population represents a civilization's greatest asset, its ability to solve complex problems and organize effectively. Human capital confers direct economic benefits by enabling higher-skilled work and attracting foreign investment. Beyond money, human capital translates to healthier lifestyles and a more civic-minded population. Higher human capital scores are associated with an increased desire to participate in democracy and concern for the environment.[5]

Thus, human capital is a prerequisite for modernization and growth of a country. Climbing the ladder of economic development requires that poorer countries invest in training their workers, gradually increasing their skills, until they are able to attract higher paying jobs and more lucrative forms of investment. Without human capital, countries cannot sustain economic growth or prepare for the highly skilled jobs of the future. Entire sectors of the economy, such as information technology and high-level services, cannot exist without strong human capital to draw from. A World Bank study on 'The Human Capital Project' argues that 'between 10 and 30 per cent of per capita gross domestic product (GDP) differences is attributable to cross-country differences in human capital'.[6]

It goes without saying that countries that have attained long-lasting growth have invested heavily in building their human capital. The United States, South Korea, Japan and Germany are all examples of nations which invested in education and saw massive economic expansion as a result. By contrast, countries which underinvest in human capital languish in low-skilled industries. Unfortunately, India is a leader in that category.

Investment in education is a major driver of human capital. The World Bank study on human capital also found that replacing a low-quality teacher in an elementary school classroom with an average-quality teacher raises the combined lifetime income of those students by US $250,000.[7] Education is especially relevant for building the types of human capital necessary for developing countries today, because the jobs of the future will require more advanced knowledge of technology and science.[8]

Similar is the impact of investing in health, an important component of human capital. Investing in health outcomes is associated with increased lifetime earnings. Studies of malaria testing and deworming in African countries show dramatic gains in the economic productivity of treatment recipients.[9] By contrast, underinvestment in health can cripple a country's productivity. Evidence suggests that failing to invest in nutrition and health stunt a country's ability to grow. Studies from Southeast Asia suggest that inadequate nutrition lowers IQ scores and hurts classroom learning.[10]

India's development of human capital has lagged behind other countries in the region. Half of its adult population is either illiterate or not educated beyond the primary school level.[11] Total adult literacy stands at 74 per cent, which is far below 86.3 per cent for the rest of the world.[12] Comparatively, India is thirty years behind China, which attained a literacy rate of 97 per cent in 2010, in educational attainment.[13] The issue of developing and maximizing human capital will only become more acute as India's population expands.

In 1951, India's population stood at 361 million, but by 2030, India's population will hit 1.5 billion. Some progress has been made, illiteracy has dropped by over 50 per cent. Yet, even seven decades after Independence, hundreds of millions of Indians cannot read or write, functionally excluding them from the modern economy. India's low level of educational attainment, even compared to peers, points to failures in policy to build human capital.

Many developing countries such as South Korea and China successfully spent on education and raised literacy rates. India's spending of roughly 3.5 per cent of GDP on education for an increasingly younger population falls far below the world average of 4.8 per cent. Education was originally a state subject in India, but since 1976 it has been added to the concurrent list. Most of the funding for education comes from state governments, supplemented with Central government money. This has helped exacerbate educational inequalities, especially in poorer states. In the 1980s, only 10 per cent of state funds went to education, a proportion well below other developing countries.[14]

India's population is rapidly growing and 53 per cent of the population is under the age of twenty-five.[15] India has one of the fastest growing working age populations in the world, with over 66 per cent of its population between fifteen and sixty-four. By 2030, over 80 per cent of its population will be of working age.[16] Having a large working-age citizenry could be what some call a 'demographic dividend' if all young people can be put to work for a higher national output. To reap that divided, India needs more than just numbers; it needs to invest in making its populace more productive.

Without serious development of human capital, India's youth bulge will only translate into more unskilled workers who are underequipped to participate in the modern economy. The 'demographic sweet spot' – the abundance of young, working-age people with a potential to enhance productivity – will not last for long.[17] Unless they are trained and put to work, too many unmarried and unemployed young people could become a strain in society. In the short run, countries benefit from younger populations as they are more productive, boost savings, and provide the additional revenues governments need to finance expensive development programmes. India's demographic dividend is expected to peak by the early 2040s,[18] after which it would have to cope with the challenge of an ageing population. India would then have to keep up economic growth with fewer and fewer workers.

This transformation is already happening in some parts of India. The country's size and regional divergence has led to the creation of two Indias. The states of peninsular India (Kerala, Karnataka,

Tamil Nadu, Telangana and Andhra Pradesh) and to a lesser extent the state of West Bengal, economist Arvind Subramanian points out, are closer to East Asian countries, with sharp rises and declines in the working age populations.[19] The hinterland states (Madhya Pradesh, Rajasthan, Uttar Pradesh and Bihar), with a younger and rising working-age population, will only plateau by the middle of the twenty-first century. Peninsular India also has higher literacy rates and performs better on most social indicators than the Indian hinterland.

This means that, on the one hand, India may be able to benefit from the demographic dividend for a longer period but, on the other, the government will need to adopt different policies for the two diverse regions. Half of India may soon face problems associated with ageing, as greater attention will be needed for elderly citizens, and tax revenue will plateau. The other half will need greater investments in education, health and skill development, otherwise the country cannot count on the demographic advantage in expanding prosperity.

That India has not been able to develop its human capital represents a major failing of its contemporary elites. Otherwise, Indian civilization has always valued education, going back to ancient India, which managed an advanced system of learning. The *gurukul* system was aimed as a life learning, or life building, institution. Hindu boys, only from the two upper castes, would be sent at a young age to the ashram (hermitage) of a well-known rishi (sage), where they would spend the next 8–10 years learning life skills. Religious education formed a vital part of their studies, but so did life lessons.

The guru was teacher, mentor and parent all rolled into one. Along with studies, the students learned to cook, clean and take care of the hermitage as well. It was a primarily oral, rote-based system of education that emphasized memorizing and recitation from memory rather than developing a questioning spirit. The oldest university in the Indian subcontinent was a Buddhist *mahavihara* (monastery), at Nalanda (in the present-day state of Bihar).

When Buddhism developed as an organized religion in India, education was focused on training missionaries for proselytization. Nalanda was founded around the fifth century BC as a training monastery for Buddhist monks. During the medieval period, there were parallel systems of education for Hindus and Muslims, with the latter going to *maktab* (elementary school) and *madrasa* (higher-education school). The aim of these was to impart religious education, basic reading and writing skills. The colonial era brought the modern schooling system – primary, secondary and tertiary – and many schools and colleges were set up by Western missionaries across India. These schools have co-existed alongside the traditional institutions of learning.

By 1765, the British East India Company was the ruling power in Bengal. Initially its directors had no incentive to take on the responsibility for the education of the Indian masses. However, there were some attempts by those referred to as 'Orientalists' within the company to foster oriental learning. The first Governor General of India from 1774 to 1785, Warren Hastings, helped found the Calcutta Madrasa in 1781 for the study and learning of Persian and Arabic. In 1791, the efforts of Jonathan Duncan, the British Resident at Benares, led to the foundation of the Sanskrit College at Benares.

The East India Company Act of 1813 passed by the British parliament allocated Rs 1 lakh annually for the 'revival and improvement of literature and the encouragement of the learned natives of India and for introduction and promotion of a knowledge of the science among the inhabitations of the British territories in India',[20] while renewing the company's charter. Within twenty years, 12,498 schools had been established in the Madras Presidency, providing education to 1,88,650 students, 1705 schools with 35,143 students in Bombay Presidency, and around 1,00,000 village schools in Bengal Presidency, which included Bihar and Orissa.[21]

The purpose of education under colonial rule was to create functionaries for the government, as well as for economic activity. After Independence, Nehru viewed education as important for the transformation he envisioned for India.[22] He, along with India's first education minister, Maulana Abul Kalam Azad (1888–1958), laid the foundations of India's current education system. Azad was one of the founders of the Jamia Millia Islamia, originally founded in Aligarh in 1920, conceived as the first modern university set up by Indians under colonial rule.

As education minister from 1947 until his death in 1958, Azad championed the cause of education as the 'birthright of every individual' and voiced his belief that without at least a basic education, people cannot fully discharge their duties of citizenship.[23] Azad can be credited with streamlining modern Indian education, setting up of the University Grants Commission in 1953, establishing science and technology institutes and centres around the country, including the first-ever Indian Institute of Technology (IIT) in India in 1951.[24]

Nehru and Azad trusted India's state governments to take care of primary and secondary education, while the Central government focused on higher education. That expectation has been unevenly fulfilled. India has witnessed a thirty-fourfold increase in the number of universities operating across the country since Independence. In 1950, there were twenty universities in all of India, a number which had increased to around 677 by 2018. But all of India's states could not always keep pace with the basic education needs of their rising populations. The universities and colleges could help produce teachers and that they did with varying quality. From 3,86,169 in 1951, the number of available primary school teachers in India rose to 5,816,673 in 2009.[25] India's progress in scaling up its education infrastructure was not always proportionate to its requirements.

Much of India's human capital gap can be traced to underinvestment in primary education. India has created impressive secondary and tertiary institutions, but at the expense of neglecting basic competencies. While investment in higher education has helped the country create the world-class institutes and the growth of its services sector – especially information technology – not enough attention and investment in primary education has also meant that India lacks a literate work force. In order for the nation to unlock the potential of its massive population, it needs to make meaningful contributions towards foundational education.

Indian primary schools are plagued with overcrowded classrooms, absent teachers and unsanitary conditions, and often lead parents to decide it is not worth their child going to school.[26] According to a report by the National Council for Teacher Education, an autonomous organization set up by the Government of India in 1961, 40 per cent of government-run primary schools have over thirty students per classroom, and 60 per cent lacked electricity. Twenty-one per cent of teachers were not even professionally trained.[27]

Private schools in India have better learning outcomes than government schools at a much lower unit cost.[28] Private sector education has more freedom to innovate and design effective curriculum than public sector education. They also have a strong profit incentive to provide quality education, lest they lose their students to government schools. There is certainly inequality in private schools, which are only available to those who can pay, but government vouchers and incentive programmes can help make these institutions affordable for the masses.

India's research space also has suffered from underdevelopment. The country's firms lag behind the rest of the world in future-seeking investments and are considerably less innovative than even peers in developing countries. The government has failed to create a culture of innovation and an economic climate which prioritizes research. In most countries, research and development (R&D) investment comes from a combination of the government, the private sector and universities. In India, however, the government is not just the primary source but also the primary user of R&D resources.

India's spending on R&D as a percentage of GDP is well below what other countries spend – the US (2.8 per cent of GDP), China (2.1 per cent), and South Korea (4.2 per cent). All these countries witnessed an increase in R&D as they became richer. India has yet to do that.[29] India's research sector falls badly behind many of its peers. Only twenty-six Indian companies are in the top 2500 global R&D spenders compared to 301 Chinese companies. And while Chinese firms are in each of the top ten R&D sectors, there are no Indian firms in five of the top ten sectors.[30] India spends 0.6 per cent of GDP on R&D and has only one active researcher per thousand workers. In comparison, Israel spends 4.27 per cent of its GDP on research and has over twenty-three researchers per thousand workers.[31]

India's relatively poorer human capital has resulted in it lagging behind other leading countries in start-ups. Ninety per cent of Indian start-ups fail within the first five years, the main reason being lack of innovation. In a survey, 77 per cent of venture capitalists stated that Indian start-ups lacked 'new technologies or unique business models in addition to lack of skilled workforce and funding, inadequate formal mentoring and poor business ethics'.[32] Jugaad – an Indian concept of emulating ideas to adjust a model for local needs – has dominated the Indian start-up economy. India has Ola (for Uber), Gaana (for Spotify), OYO Rooms (for Airbnb) and Flipkart (for Amazon). However, India has never come up with equivalents of Google, Facebook or Twitter. By contrast, China created Baidu (to counter Google) and Alibaba (to displace Amazon).

If a yardstick of innovation is the patent, India compares poorly on global patent rankings even when compared to its Asian counterparts. In 2015–16, according to the World Intellectual Property Organization (WIPO), India filed 1423 international patents, while Japan filed 44,235, China 29,846 and South Korea 14,626. Even this number is inflated, as over 70 per cent of the patents filed in India were by foreign multinational companies. India ranks sixty-sixth on the Global Innovation Index (GII), forty-one places lower than China.[33]

Another crucial capacity for the Indian workforce is skill development. A skilled workforce is necessary for productivity gains, economic growth, and attracting higher quality jobs. On the individual level, a skilled workforce increases income, health and civic engagement.[34] Developing skilled labour is also key to having a workforce that is less susceptible to the challenges that come from automation. Skilled jobs are more likely to benefit from automation, as technology increases the productivity of skilled workers. While artisan manufacturers may find themselves replaced by robotic production, workers in information technology or research professions will find more jobs available to them than ever. These jobs also have positive societal benefits. They attract foreign investment and create downstream demand for local goods and services.[35]

A good example is Singapore, which has coupled economic and skill development with courting of foreign investment and finance in vocational schools. In Singapore, unlike most developing countries where the education ministry is responsible for the development of education and the human resources ministry for skill development, the Economic Development Board is 'at the centre of the effort in that it is responsible for both economic development as well as skills development'.[36] The board takes an innovative approach by tailoring education funds to areas which are most in need of skill development, in order to ensure a steady and reliable supply of workers to attract foreign investment.[37]

India's lack of skills infrastructure is massive problem for a country with a rapidly growing population. Every year, 12 million Indians enter the labour market, but the Indian economy created only 3.8 million jobs between 2014 and 2017. This means the market is unable to absorb more than one-fourth of the 12 million new workers looking for jobs on an annual basis.[38] Only 6.8 per cent of India's entire labour force has received any vocational training, compared to 59 per cent in China. Further, according to surveys, 95 per cent of Indian engineers 'are not fit to take up software development jobs'. With such a low skilled population, India is an undesirable location for more high-skilled jobs, even with a growing young labour force.

India's healthcare is another area where misgovernance has undermined the development of human capital. Healthcare is important for developing human capital, because a sick population loses productivity and drains resources from the healthy to care for the ill. Unfortunately, India has failed to invest in the type of healthcare infrastructure needed to support its population.

K. Sujatha Rao, a former top healthcare official, points out that seven decades after Independence, 'two-thirds of Indians do not have access to tap water and a clean toilet, over a third are malnourished, while a million-and-a-half children die before they turn five'.[39] Infant mortality rate (IMR) is high in India standing at 40.5 deaths per 1000 live births, even higher for female children than for males (female infanticide is still practised widely).

The Indian government has been slow in providing its people with serious preventative care – immunization, access to safe water, decent sanitation and nutritional support for children.[40] This shifts a disproportionate amount of healthcare costs onto the individual. Less than 10 per cent of health expenditures go to traditional public health, an area which most directly focuses on preventative care.[41] This is why, even though India spends 4.1 per cent of GDP on health, it has one of the world's lowest shares of public spending in total health spending (29 per cent) and one of the highest shares of private spending (71 per cent) and out of pocket private spending (61 per cent) in total health spending.[42]

The Indian government regulates healthcare tightly, but the Centrally administered health networks are grossly dysfunctional. If we look at the supply side, even though the government spends money on primary care infrastructure and personnel, it delivers care that is no better in competence and much more labour intensive than the private sector. The Indian government exercises significant influence over all major health programmes, creating labyrinthine bureaucracies and administrative processes.[43] Turning to the demand side, surveys show that patients often prefer to go to a fee-charging doctor who will treat them with more consideration even when private doctors are less qualified than doctors in government hospitals.[44]

According to a *Lancet* survey, more than half of all Indian medical graduates are not adequately trained to work in the primary healthcare setting, and students are not taught enough about even basic health issues like common infectious diseases or maternal health.[45] As a result, India faces a shortage of trained doctors. According to a 2015 study, India needs at least 4,00,000 physicians to fit its needs, but barely has 90,000 qualified professionals.[46] Further, the same study notes that while the country needs 10,000 medical teachers, most medical colleges are working with only 45 per cent of their needs. Moreover, India also suffers from brain drain in the healthcare sector. High-skilled medical talent is in global demand, so skilled doctors are often tempted by offers from Western developed countries with higher pay to emigrate.

TEEMING CITIES, PARALYSED POLICY

According to Gilles Duranton of the Wharton School in the US, 'the city is not only the place where growth occurs', it is 'the engine of growth itself'.[47] Cities are places of common learning, where economies of scale bring together industry, culture and education. They are essential for developing human capital. For India, cities hold enormous potential, but all too often are held back by poor governance and a lack of civic amenities.

Cities are powerful drivers of economic growth in the developing world. They provide the necessary locus for factors of production to come together, moving labour into higher productivity activities and powering growth. Cities also reallocate labour from lower productivity activities, such as agriculture, to higher productivity activities, such as manufacturing.[48] This advantage is particularly acute in the developing world, as a 2014 study of 125 global metropolitan areas in China, India, Southeast Asia, Africa and South America found that many cities in emerging and developing nations have higher relative productivity advantages than those in developed countries.[49]

Cities have also been particularly important for India's economy. Thirty per cent of India's population lives in urban areas; this share will rise to 40 per cent by 2030.[50] Soon, five of India's largest states will have more population living in cities than in villages.[51] According to a study by McKinsey Global Institute in 2010, India's cities could generate 70 per cent of net new jobs created until 2030, in addition to producing around 70 per cent of Indian GDP and contributing to a near fourfold increase in per capita incomes across the country.[52] India's future, thus, lies in its cities.

Indian politicians, on the other hand, still believe in the notion that 'real India lives in its villages'. This is the legacy of the Indian freedom struggle and an extension of Gandhi's belief about India being a land of the simple living, high thinking and moralistic farmer. Gandhi promulgated the idea that villages should occupy a place at the centre of the Indian state. This view persists to this day and, at least at the ideational level, diverts time and money from urban planning.[53]

In Gandhi's age, the divide between the materialistic urban individual and the salt of the earth peasant may well have been stark. But in changed circumstances, it is important to acknowledge that a larger proportion of Indians now live in cities and the country's economic growth will be generated in its urban centres. The result of neglecting the cities has been chronically poor governance and mismanagement. India's cities lack clean water and adequate sewerage. Without federal assistance, the required capital investment for infrastructure upgrades is far beyond what urban local governments can afford.[54]

India also lacks adequate affordable housing for its massive low-income urban populations. There is a huge disconnect between demand for affordable housing and supply, as government-run housing schemes often fail to provide enough volume for the urban poor. India has a deficit of over 18 million affordable housing units.[55] India's cities rank poorly against their peers. The 2019 liveability index of the Economist Intelligence Unit ranked New Delhi 118 out of 140 cities, while Mumbai was ranked 119.[56]

These unliveable conditions have hurt India's ability to take adequate advantage of its cities. In 1950, the nation was more urban than China – 17 per cent of Indians lived in cities compared to 13 per cent Chinese. Between 1950 and 2005, however, China's urbanization rate was 41 per cent compared to India's 29 per cent. By 2025, 64 per cent of China's population will live and work in cities, as opposed to 38 per cent of India's.[57] Not only has India urbanized at a much slower rate but China has invested more in its cities.

China has fostered a set of practices to develop its cities rationally. From funding to governance, the Chinese government has taken an active and enthusiastic role in urban investment. India, on the other hand, has under-invested in its cities. According to a McKinsey study, China spends US $116 per capita on capital investments in urban infrastructure annually compared to India's abysmal US $17.[58] India is a long way off from providing the infrastructure to meet this urbanization challenge.

The Indian government has acknowledged that it requires approximately US $1.1 trillion capital investment in urban infrastructure to successfully manage and grow its cities. It needs to build more than 700 million square metres of residential and commercial space every year and construct over 350 kilometres of metro transportation systems. This would involve construction at a pace twenty times more rapid than the highest pace of development achieved by the country in the last decade.[59]

Successive Indian governments have failed at urban planning. Other developing countries, such as China, have successfully created liveable and vibrant cities which contribute substantially to economic growth. India's urban expansion has been unplanned and haphazard. Reforms to increase affordable housing would have to include easing of the permitting process, reductions in stamp duty and service tax, and reforms to make it easier for low income individuals to access mortgages. Investments need to be made in infrastructure development, as well as in sanitation and transportation. Cities have the potential to lead India's economic growth, but that requires supportive public policy.

India's struggle with itself over identity – the two ideas of India at odds with one another – has been reinforced by poor governance and vice versa. The ideological divide affects the vision and direction that India chooses for itself, and sometimes results in electing leaders who are unable to execute rational policies. Together, these problems paralyse India, making it unable to plan and carry out ambitious national strategies. From the relationship of the state and religion, to the proper allocation of funding to healthcare, the country often stands still or moves too slowly to meet the demands of a burgeoning populace.

Ideological divisions and poor governance often feed into one another. Bad government policy and execution creates poor economic outcomes and dissatisfaction with the status quo. Poverty and inequality breed resentment and the desire to find scapegoats, reinforcing majoritarian conservatism or hostility towards the more prosperous. This, in turn, feeds into poor governance by drawing attention and resources away from critical concerns such as urban planning and education reform. Populist pandering helps win elections at the expense of discussions about difficult but necessary reforms.

Conflicts over identity and poor governance do not need to exist at the same time. Many countries struggle with one but not necessarily the other. There are countries with an iron-clad sense of self, which is widely shared amongst the population but have decrepit institutions, while others have functioning institutions that make up for the lack of strong national identity. In India, however, both issues layer on top of one another and present a special challenge.

Its demographic boom, rapid urbanization and ageing health infrastructure demand that the government move quickly and decisively. Yet, the machinery of government itself is torn between competing visions of the country's future. At the same time, inaction pulls India further behind, and reduces its ability to modernize and achieve its goals, whatever they may be. At such an important point in India's history, the country cannot afford to but often finds itself in a state of policy paralysis.

3

Economic Potential

'WHATEVER YOU CAN rightly say about India', observed British economist Joan Robinson, 'the opposite is also true.'[1] India is indeed a land of economic contradictions. It is a country that has sent satellites into space and has an indigenous nuclear programme, but does not have a brand of razor or fountain pen associated with it.[2] Even after seven decades of state-driven poverty alleviation programmes, enormous subsidies and populist welfare economic policies, millions of Indians still live below the poverty line.

Although the country has reduced poverty significantly, the estimated number of Indian citizens living in extreme poverty in 2018 stood at 73 million. Another 365 million lived in more moderate poverty.[3] At the same time, more than half of Indian economic growth in the last decade has come from the service sector, which is typically higher skilled and higher paying than manufacturing. Economists cannot help but wonder how a society capable of massive feats of engineering and innovation can have such poor economic outcomes.

India's problem with economics seems to be cultural. As a society, India has a generally hostile attitude towards the free market. Neither of the major political parties is pro market, and India's right wing is distinguished by cultural and social issues, not by its economic stance. It is ironic that even India's conservative leaders describe themselves as 'socialists', implying that Hindu culture has an inherent aversion to market and liberal economics.[4] Public opinion polls show general scepticism of the power of market forces to generate socially desirable outcomes. One need not believe that markets always operate socially optimally to notice that Indian society demonstrates a hostility to the principles of market economics that depresses innovation and growth. Laws are passed without serious concern about distorting economic activity, bloated state-owned enterprises choke off competition, and protectionism scares off foreign direct investment.

It can be argued that Indian civilizational attitudes are skewed against the generation of wealth. Its society elevates pure, but not applied, intellectual pursuits above commercial interests. Commercial pursuit, making money, or being a businessman is thus viewed as 'impure' or 'dirty'. This deeply ingrained philosophical outlook is historically animated and goes back to ancient India. The fourfold Hindu *varnashram* (caste system) that has pervaded Indian social thinking for millennia accords the highest ranks of society to priests and warriors. Economic productivity depends on the entrepreneur and the worker, but Brahminic tradition is contemptuous of manual labour and does not accord a high status to the trader. Merchants – *vaishya* or *bania* – are accorded third place in the fourfold Hindu caste hierarchy, just above the caste of manual labourers.

Modern India's political development has also biased it against wealth generation. In India, the development of a robust democracy before industrialization created a political architecture which constrained capitalist institutions and practices. Pressures on the government for redistribution of wealth built up in India before enough of it had been generated. Foundationally, modern economies require economic growth before gains of that growth can be distributed through pro-poor welfare policies. India embarked on major redistribution efforts without the jobs and growth created by unconstrained markets. It has been a case of trying to divide the little the country has more fairly, instead of attaining higher levels of wealth creation and expansion necessary to sustain major redistribution efforts.

Wealth generation in the West arose in a certain culture and was based on a certain philosophical outlook. The Protestant work ethic, a bourgeoisie that demanded rights, rule of law and limits on state power led to a liberal democracy. The Renaissance, the Reformation and the Enlightenment all helped create the environment for both liberal democracy and free market capitalism. India, on the other hand, embraced democracy without the accoutrements of free-market capitalism. Its civilizational foundation does not value wealth generation, leading to a culture where even talking about being wealthy or making money is looked down upon. The caste structure restricts professional mobility, at least philosophically, and families tend to dictate the life paths of their children, instead of encouraging passion and innovation.[5]

The country's lack of innovation can be attributed to the fact that Indians never developed the intellectual institutions prioritizing economic growth. The Indian educational ethos never developed a scientific method that would encourage citizens to rationalize and conquer the natural world. Caste prejudice led well-off Indians to shun manual labour and technology, even among merchant castes. Consequently, India's industrial landscape has grown to fit its parochial, anti-collaborative mindset. As such, India produces far fewer large industrial firms than its size would suggest.

Even though the nation has over the last few decades moved towards a form of free-market capitalism, it is far from building a facilitating environment for sustained economic growth. Indian society has followed an economic dogma, which, true to its past, does not prioritize wealth generation or growth. Indian government leaders made the choice, for the people, that slower, stable levels of economic growth are preferable to higher, albeit more turbulent levels. India still retains significant elements of Central planning, and government policies do not encourage entrepreneurship or investment beyond planned levels.

With the exceptions of the high-tech and IT sectors, where entrepreneurs benefited from an absence of previously written regulations, India remains an over-regulated economy. Most significantly, aspirations of competing with China notwithstanding, the gap between the Indian and Chinese economies is far from being bridged.

PERFORMANCE BELOW EXPECTATIONS

By 2050, India is slated to be one of the three largest economies in the world. Its economic growth has been high over the last three decades, especially since market liberalization reforms were introduced in 1991. According to the World Economic Forum, India has grown steadily over a five-decade period, from 4.4 per cent in the 1970s–80s, to 5.5 per cent during the 1990s–2000s and 7.1 per cent in the last decade.[6] India touched double digit growth in a couple of years, raising high hopes, only to slide back, and it is unclear whether Indian economic growth will continue at its aggressive pace.

To understand where the country is going, one needs to appreciate both the successes and failures of the present. There is much that Indians can be proud of. The country has eliminated famines encountered in an earlier time and now has substantial food reserves. Life expectancy has more than doubled, from thirty-two in 1947 to 68.8 in 2017.[7] It is hard to contest that the quality of life for the average Indian has grown tremendously. Its economy also looks considerably more modern than it did in the past. India's growth has stabilized with its economy's diversification and transition toward services.

The service sector makes up an outsized part of the economy, and knowledge sectors such as information technology have grown dramatically. By 1980, the share of agriculture in GDP fell to 36 per cent and, by 2013, it was only 14 per cent. By contrast, the share of service sector workers rose from 18 per cent to 24 per cent. This indicates considerable development in high-growth sectors of the economy, and a gradual shift away from lower productivity sectors.[8] Moreover, India's growth has been remarkably resilient to economic downturns.

Largely due to India's massive size and diversified economy, it has not been subject to the volatility and shocks of much of the rest of the world economy. India's geography also positions it to have a wide basket of trading partners, helping insulate it from economic downturn in any one part of the world. Even political risk, which disrupts economic growth in many other parts of the world, appears not to cause massive shocks in the Indian economy. Over much of the last two decades, the country has achieved impressive levels of economic growth, despite parochial economic institutions and onerous government regulations.[9]

Still, India requires higher levels of economic growth if it is to ascend above its developing-nation status. Based on current GDP figures, achieving consistent 8 per cent growth for three decades is required to elevate India into the global middle class. The nation's future growth potential is dependent on structurally reforming its economic policies. Between 2004 and 2008, when India witnessed a durable period of economic growth above 8 per cent for five consecutive years, it benefited from important reforms undertaken in the 1990s and early 2000s, which liberalized the economy and opened it up to foreign investment. India's growth was also furthered by a stable global macroeconomic climate.[10]

Many economists doubt India's ability to maintain such high levels of economic growth going forward. India is the poorest large national economy, and until 2014, it had a lower per capita income than Zambia and Laos. Indian economic growth has relied on the country's size, its massive population, to catapult it by sheer force onto the global stage. For it to achieve per capita incomes necessary to make it a prosperous nation in the next quarter century, it would need to proceed at a breakneck pace of growth of over 6 per cent each year.[11] This appears difficult considering that India's current economic growth rate has dropped to an official figure of 5 per cent with some economists speaking of it hovering around 3 per cent.

A look into India's past provides reason to be sceptical of a high-powered economic future. Through much of its history after Independence, between 1950 and 1980, economic growth was poor. The poverty ratio did not substantially fall during this period, and the overall number of people in poverty rose dramatically.[12] With a closed economy and an overbearing state presence in most key sectors, India failed to create a climate conducive to economic growth and poverty alleviation.

Even in the context of recent economic growth numbers, it is difficult to be optimistic about India's economic picture. Only three countries have ever sustained high levels of economic growth for three decades – China, South Korea and Taiwan – and India's growth already appears to be running out of steam. The reforms of 1991 were effective in liberalizing capital markets and some sectors of the economy, but were radically incomplete.[13] For India to realize the full potential of global supply chains and foreign capital, it requires further market liberalization reforms. The economy still suffers from inefficient public sector industries, tight banking regulations, and poor delivery of public services.[14]

India's challenges on the jobs front are enormous. A snapshot of the wide gap between the number of jobs available and the number of people looking for them is provided by periodic reports about job applications, especially for much sought-after government jobs. In May 2017, 2.5 million Indians appeared for a competitive exam for 6000 jobs – approximately 400 people competing for each position – as Group D employees in the West Bengal government. In January 2018, the job of peon in the Rajasthan government attracted 12,453 applicants for eighteen vacancies – 700 candidates for each of the relatively low-paying slots. Among those hoping to become a peon were 129 engineers, twenty-three lawyers, a chartered accountant and 393 postgraduates in arts.

Similarly, on 31 March 2018, over 20 million people applied for 90,000 jobs in the Indian railways through an online exam. There were at least 300 applicants for each job as the railways sought 26,502 train drivers and 62,907 gangmen, switchmen and trackmen, cabin men, helpers and porters. On 8 April the same year, Mumbai police sought to fill 1137 vacancies for constables. Among the applicants were 167 MBAs, 423 engineers, 543 postgraduates, three law graduates and 167 graduates in business administration.

Engineers, with BTech and MTech degrees, 150 of them, have become constables in the Haryana police.[15]

Not only are there fewer jobs for more people, the jobs that are available do not match the academic qualifications of large numbers of applicants. India seems to have trained many more engineers and college graduates in other fields than its economy is currently able to absorb. The inability to create more jobs follows a historical pattern of under-employment and inadequate productivity: more people are employed to do work that could easily be done by fewer individuals, and collective effort disguises the lack of some people's effort and productivity. It reinforces doubts that a culture that looks down on economic activity can ever reach its potential for economic expansion. India's civilizational heritage may be its biggest burden when it comes to its economic aspirations and ambitions. Without enlarging the economy, it is unclear how the country might find the resources invariably needed to become a global great power.

THE HISTORICAL PATTERN

Indians take pride in the data amassed in Angus Maddison's *Contours of World Economy 1 – 2030 AD*, which states, 'From year one to year 1000, India had the largest economy in the world controlling nearly a third of the world's wealth.' According to Maddison, India was 'the world's leading economy in the year 1700', which fell into manufacturing decline by 1900 due to colonial rule and the destruction of India's textile industry at Britain's hand. Moreover, under the Mughal emperor Akbar (1556–1605) '15 per cent of India was urbanized', but by 1872, colonial rule resulted in 91.3 per cent of Indians living in villages.[16]

Senior economic journalist and author T.N. Ninan points out that arguments about India accounting for a fourth of the world's total income of GDP in the first half of the eighteenth century forget that this 'compares with about one-fortieth today'. During that era, Ninan explains, national income 'was merely a matter of the size of the population. In the pre-industrial age, incomes did not vary hugely across countries; if you had a larger share of the population you accounted for a greater share of world GDP.'[17] Thus, the wealth of nations in that era did not reflect entrepreneurship or innovation and comparisons with it are not sufficient for planning future economic growth.

The Mughal empire was indeed one of the richest empires of its time. In 1750, India accounted for 25 per cent of the world's industrial output. The Mughals encouraged trade 'by developing roads, river transport, sea routes, ports and abolishing many inland tolls and taxes. Indian handicrafts were developed. There was a thriving export trade in manufactured goods such as cotton cloth, spices, indigo, woollen and silk cloth, salt, etc.'[18] But these numbers alone are not indicative of a thriving commercial culture. India's economic heft was largely due to its massive population. As global industrialization kicked off, the country's economic advantage deteriorated quickly.

According to Maddison's calculations, India's per capita income was US $550 in 1500 while China's was US $600. However, with the Renaissance, Europe jumped ahead. Italy had a per capita income of US $1100 and the Netherlands US $761. By 1600, Dutch per capita income was US $1381, while the UK's jumped from US $714 a century earlier to US $974.[19] In the eighteenth and nineteenth centuries, India experienced a prolonged period of deindustrialization. GDP per capita fell from US $638 in 1650 to US $526 by 1871. The share of agriculture as part of the Indian economy grew, while manufacturing dwindled. This last shift was a function of colonial policies, but the larger share of India in the global economy earlier was a function of its population size rather than a sign of its inherently higher productivity.

The colonial era left a scar on the Indian view of foreign investment. The East India Company came to manufacture and trade but took over the country and established foreign rule. As a result of that experience, Indians have become suspicious of traders and foreigners, breeding an anti-business attitude. There is also fear that foreign multinationals seek to enter India solely to take over the Indian market, fostering the desire for economic self-sufficiency or 'make in India.' Together, these factors have inhibited openness to foreign direct investment (FDI) and dampened purely economic decisions based on economies of scale and comparative advantage.

Gurcharan Das contrasts what he refers to as India's 'absurd attachment to swadeshi'[20] – the desire to produce everything possible at home – and Chinese 'ambivalence' to the West with the reaction in Japan. 'Instead of tiresomely proclaiming their own superior past' the Japanese 'were not ashamed to throw out what did not work and adopt what did' from the West. In the end, the Japanese became 'so good at copying that they eventually beat the West at its own game'.[21] Japan's advantage in embracing that attitude is obvious. For a relatively small island nation with a modest population size, Japan has been one of the more productive nations of the twentieth century and continues to be a major economic power.

On the other hand, India's aversion to Western ways has acted as a brake on the realization of its economic potential. The Indian national movement was anti-imperialist, anti-colonialist, and anti-racialist, but in its economic underpinnings, it was anti-capitalist because capitalism was associated with imperialism. The freedom struggle also had a strong moral dimension championed by Mahatma Gandhi, who saw the pursuit of wealth as wrong and championed 'simple living and high thinking' as the true path. This, combined with the anti-imperialist and anti-capitalist dimension of the national movement, influenced the modern state's views on generation of wealth. International trade was perceived as a 'whirlpool of economic imperialism', and to avoid falling into it, economic nationalism, self-sufficiency, and import-substituting industrialization was emphasized.[22]

Economic journalist Swaminathan Anklesaria Aiyar refers to the Indian scepticism of capitalism, and especially the belief that capitalism led to imperialism and colonialism. Fearing that colonialism would return to India 'in the guise of economic domination through trade and investment', India pushed for 'economic independence' and sought economic self-sufficiency.

While borne of noble intentions, this philosophy had disruptive consequences for India's economic growth. In the first few decades after Independence, India's socialist leaders hailed India's declining share of global trade – from 2.2 per cent to 0.45 per cent – as a triumph.[23]

India's first prime minister, Jawaharlal Nehru, laid down not only India's foreign and security policy but also the foundations of India's economic policies. For Nehru, socialism within a parliamentary democracy was the only way to ensure economic development along with social equality. He was influenced by Fabian socialism and believed that the commanding heights of the economy should lie with the state, as the market could not be trusted. This paternalistic approach towards the market, disdain of commercial enterprise and the belief that the state needs to protect the individual from the market has underscored economic policies for over seven decades.[24] While Nehru was a devotee of science and a rationalist, he was a creature of his age and also embraced mega planning and heavy-handed government intervention.[25]

Gandhi's economic vision for India was similarly anti-capitalist. He advocated for an India which was a republic of small, self-sufficient villages, and shunned urban development.[26] His ideas of 'sharing' and 'trusteeship' lay at the core of modern India's paternalistic policy, whereby government regulations were implemented to prevent large firms from producing many basic goods.[27] The Gandhian legacy is visible in many economic arenas, but none more so than in India's industrial sector.

Indian regulations incentivize textile companies to remain small – 'cottage industry'. They favour cotton over synthetic fabrics, even though the latter are more in demand globally. They are structured so that a smaller enterprise that does not grow and does not make profits, but receives state support. The regulatory framework effectively penalizes companies that seek to grow big and are profitable.[28] Gandhi's vision of 'self-reliant villages, with a reinvigorated agriculture and craft production' have been combined with Nehru's 'democratic socialism, with the state leading the process of industrialization'. Gandhi 'distrusted technology but not businessmen', whereas Nehru 'distrusted businessmen but not technology'.[29]

Indian capitalism has thus grown under the shadow of a strong bureaucracy. Investments were made in India's industrialization, but certain areas were reserved only for the small-scale sector. This prevented economies of scale or the style of mass production that would boost labour-intensive manufacturing. While capitalism was routinely criticized, 'it was the system India's economy was based on' and in truth socialism 'was never practised but the rhetoric of socialism was the norm, with a burgeoning bureaucratic system acting as the surrogate for socialism'.[30] According to Das, India ended up with contradictory 'holy cows': 'small companies are better than big ones (Gandhi), public enterprises are better than private ones (Nehru), local companies are better than foreign ones (both).'[31]

Economic policy following Independence involved harsh government intervention, ignoring the problems of political self-interest, populism and insufficient state resources. There were, however, several plans or ideas thrown up around Independence that represent paths not taken. These include the Bombay Plan, the Vakil–Brahmananda plan and the Sarvodaya Plan. The Bombay Plan refers to a document titled 'A Brief Memorandum Outlining a Plan of Economic Development for India' signed by eight leading Indian industrialists offering a series of proposals for building independent India's economy.[32]

The plan aimed at doubling agricultural output and achieving a fivefold growth in the industrial sector. According to P.S. Lokanathan, editor of *The Eastern Economist*, the objective of the plan was 'to achieve a balanced economy and to raise the standard of living of the masses of the population rapidly by doubling the present per capita income'.[33] Critiqued by many for seeking to keep foreign ownership out of certain areas, supporting limited nationalization, and backing state regulations and control, the Bombay Plan nevertheless offered a far more pro-market vision for India than anything proposed by leaders in government.

India has only once in its history had a right of centre conservative party with a proper capitalist vision. This was the Swatantra Party during the 1950s and 60s. The party was supported by corporations, businessmen, princely rulers and some influential thinkers and writers. Unfortunately, it could never gain mass support. The Bharatiya Janata Party (BJP) and its earlier offshoots are right wing in the religious ideological sense, but not in the sense of support for capitalism. The BJP's lower-middle-class, or petite bourgeois base is, at its core, protectionist and averse to integration in the global economy.

⁓

Modern economies require decades of work and political effort to reach their high-output levels of efficiency. Over time, modern economies foster norms and culture that promote hard work, innovation and risk taking. According to Swedish economist Gunnar Myrdal, India suffers from 'poor work discipline, contempt for manual work ... and superstition'. He continued that decades of education and exposure to the rest of the world have been unable to attack these pre-modern attitudes and centuries of culture and tradition. The Indian government has never been able to marshal the force necessary to break through and modernize India's attitude towards work.[34]

Independent India inherited many strong institutions. Namely, it benefited from a strong bureaucracy which ensured good governance, an independent judiciary and a relatively free press.[35] For a young developing country, these institutions could hardly be taken for granted. Nevertheless, during most of its time after Independence, India grew at a sluggish 3.5 per cent. Indian economist Raj Krishna called it the 'Hindu rate of growth', which was slower than the world average for developing countries.

Much of the blame for such poor economic performance can be attributed to the Indian government's paternalistic attitudes towards its people. A maze of regulations and regulatory bodies smothered innovation and investment. The government set up a narrative of self-sufficiency, which virtually eliminated competition and investment from new firms and shut out imports necessary for economic growth. For decades, industrial licensing covered production, diversification, imports and expansion. Industrialists needed approval from a bureaucrat to set up, expand and run their industries.

The desire to 'Make in India' dates back to the 1950s, and defined India's trade policy, restraining and regulating foreign direct investment. In 1991, India's foreign investment inflow was barely US $100 million, something 'hard to believe for an economy of India's size'.[36] According to leading economists Jagdish Bhagwati and Arvind Panagariya, India's inward-looking trade policy combined with a hostility to foreign direct investment (FDI) meant that 'India turned away from integration into the world economy, forgoing important gains from taking advantage of such integration.'[37]

India's colonial legacy led to a distrust of business and hostility towards international trade.[38] What was unique to the country was the 'heavy industry strategy' adapted from the Second Five-Year Plan onwards that was 'used to justify the physical allocation of investment'.[39] India's policymakers took it for granted that government intervention was needed to hit the targets of five-year plans, and that market forces alone would never be able to create economic progress.[40]

This resulted in growth of rent-seeking. Indian regulations led to dozens of permit and licensing requirements, which dominated every sector of the economy.[41] The firms and individuals who were able to navigate these barriers were able to shut out foreign competition and limit the number of domestic start-ups they would need to compete against. The dominant role bestowed upon the public sector hurt India.

Public sector enterprises were not limited to public utilities – electricity, water, power – but extended to the manufacturing industry, consumer sector, and even transport and the hotel industry. There was a misplaced belief that these enterprises would be profitable and would 'spearhead' investment. What happened instead was that these businesses became 'sick' – an Indian euphemism for bankrupt – and keeping them afloat imposed a huge burden on the exchequer.[42]

Further, these public sector enterprises hindered innovation and entrepreneurship within the system. Import-substitution meant Indian businesses chose to reinvent the products which had already been perfected elsewhere, resulting in the manufacture of poor-quality, high-cost goods.[43] Well-intentioned governments sought to balance growth and welfare, but state intervention only led to poor capital-output ratio and massive corruption.[44]

Successive administrations continued to promote the failed vision of government intervention. India's industrial growth fell from 7.7 per cent a year between 1951 and 1965 to 4 per cent between 1965 and 1980. Rakesh Mohan, head of National Council of Applied Economic Research, places 'the economic cost of [Prime Minister Indira] Gandhi's follies at 1.3 per cent lower per capita GDP growth per year'. Under Indira Gandhi in the late 1960s, India withdrew further from world trade and continued to raise tariffs unsustainably.[45]

Indira nationalized banks, the insurance sector and even the mineral resources sector. While the motive was to ensure that everyone obtained access to banking services, public sector banks went down the same path as their other public sector colleagues. The nationalization of banks also created a deep nexus between the political class and the business sector. These banks thus became saddled with 'bad loans' – money given to certain businesses or public sector enterprises – and to this day, India's banking sector is smarting from this legacy. The system discouraged talent and merit in hiring and did not promote efficiency or profit.

Indira Gandhi's legacy lies not just in the policies that were implemented but also in the battle of ideas or rhetoric. Her ability to combine electoral power to economic populism has been used and adopted by every successive prime minister. Economic reforms are always presented to the Indian public as welfare-oriented and pro-poor. It has proven impossible for an Indian government, irrespective of its political ideology, to argue for reforms as being pro-capitalist, pro-free market, and aimed at making Indians wealthy.

The economic vision of Indira's son, Rajiv, was a 'half-way house' according to I.Z. Bhatty of National Council of Applied Economic Research.[46] Rajiv 'nudged India out of its moribund systems' and sought to change 'the terms of economic debate'.[47] He made economic policy part of his foreign policy endeavours. He lowered taxes on the technological industry, sought to attract foreign investment, and improved bilateral economic and scientific ties with the United States. Yet, Rajiv did not alter the fundamentally state-oriented direction of India's economy. In 1990, an incredible 70 per cent of the employees in India's organized sector (firms that employed more than ten workers) still received pay cheques from government.[48]

1991 REFORMS AND THEIR AFTERMATH

The First Gulf war of 1990–91 led to a drastic decline in remittances, which at the time constituted the largest source of foreign income for India.[49] Years of fiscal profligacy and high foreign debt meant that when Narasimha Rao's government took over power in June 1991, India had only enough foreign exchange for thirteen days of imports.[50] India appealed to the International Monetary Fund (IMF) for money and breathing space to calm the markets and, as part of the IMF programme, the Indian government agreed to implement a series of reforms for economic liberalization and the opening up of the economy. The crisis helped India significantly overhaul the government in a way that would have been difficult to do otherwise.[51]

At the helm of India's 1991 economic reforms, Prime Minister Rao was not a free market evangelist. Rather, he pursued a middle path, making concessions to international creditors and the IMF, while struggling to retain India's paternalistic structure. Initially,

India's opposition parties attacked Rao and Finance Minister Manmohan Singh's reforms as a betrayal of Indian values and culture, but as the economy grew, the objections melted away.

These reforms, despite being incomplete and unevenly distributed, represent the best effort at modernization put forward by any Indian government thus far.[52] The aim of these reforms was to move India towards a free market economy, and remove controls on trade. Import tariffs were slashed and investment licensing scrapped in most industries. This resulted in a massive 6 per cent annual growth every year from 1993 to 2003.[53]

The scope of the 1991 reforms was impressive. The reforms cut tariffs in an attempt to open up international trade. Before 1991, India had some of the highest tariffs in the world. In 1991, the peak rate of customs duty fell from 200 per cent to 65 per cent in 1994.[54] In 1990, custom duty collection stood at 30 per cent of imports; by 2014, it had dropped to less than 10 per cent.[55] The highest tariff rates, which applied to manufactured goods, were brought down to 150 per cent in 1991 and to 15 per cent by 2005. The government also removed capacity restrictions on domestic producers, allowing more firms to enter and compete in the product and service markets. Telecommunication and air travel were no longer government monopoly areas.[56]

Reform of India's currency policy and exchange markets improved the country's external position. India eased up on foreign exchange flows, both inward and outward. In 1978, its foreign exchange reserves stood at US $5.82 billion. They went from US $5.83 billion in 1991 to US $300 billion in 2008,[57] and reached a high of US $426.028 billion in 2018.[58] As a result of this restructuring, India became more trade oriented, businesses were encouraged to produce better products for the market, and there was more choice for consumers. Economists observed a decline in inflation, more foreign investment and faster economic growth.

There were additional initiatives in the taxation, banking and public sectors, along with modifications of industrial policy and the stock markets. The *Economist* described the Budget presented by Finance Minister Manmohan Singh, on 24 July 1991, to India's parliament as one 'that would change his country and the world'. Singh 'devalued the rupee, abolished most of the quotas and licences that dictated who could produce what, and opened some industries to foreign capital. His reforms ripped pages out of the Red Book of regulations with which customs inspectors tormented Indian businessmen.'

According to the *Economist*, Singh commended his budget proposals to parliament by paraphrasing Victor Hugo: 'No power on Earth can stop an idea whose time has come.' 'That idea, Dr Singh suggested, was India's emergence as a "major economic power in the world",' the magazine concluded.[59]

Dismantling India's complex licensing system and opening much of the economy to private competition had a salutary effect on the economy. According to former chief economic advisor Shankar Acharya, the 1991 reforms were the reason for 'a swift turnaround in India's external sector', as well as an 'unprecedented spurt in economic growth' between 1992 and 1997. However, Acharya regrets that by 1995, the policy reforms lost their momentum and some of the early successes were reversed by 1996. This was reflected in the slowing down of growth between 1997 and 2001.[60]

Nearly three decades after the 1991 reforms, the full promise of economic liberalization has not yet been achieved. India is still home to a huge bureaucracy and public sector. The 1991 reforms did not change Indian culture, and neither did it change the paternalistic attitude of the Indian state that continued to mistrust the private sector.

Even though India's 'Inspector Licence Quota Raj' (the massive licensing and inspection system that India traditionally operated with) had been largely abolished, many regulations remain and new ones have appeared in recent years in areas as diverse as the environment to the Internet. The Economic Freedom Index of America's Heritage Foundation still places India at just 123 out of 178 countries. Of the foundation's five categories – free, mostly free, moderately free, mostly unfree and repressed – India falls into the 'mostly unfree' category.[61]

India's economic growth after 1991 was strong, but the prevalence of an overbearing government continues to rob it of the benefits of economic freedom. The bubble burst in 2011–12 with the collapse of corporate investment. Many economists blame governance failures for souring the investment climate. High inflation and an unwillingness to let go of onerous regulations turned formerly excited investors away from the Indian market. Investors had been counting on India to deliver more reforms akin to those made in 1991. The longer the government refused, the more worried they became about putting their money in India.

The government's response in the first decade of the twenty-first century was to embark on a massive spending campaign designed to push Indian demand for goods, thereby generating economic growth to meet that demand. The hope was that consumption would encourage investment and productivity, in order to satisfy consumer spending requirements. Their mantra for creating demand was to undertake large-scale infrastructure projects that would create a demand for investment goods.[62]

Some of these policies did not have their intended effect. Individuals were not encouraged to become more productive, and the government's strategy failed to stimulate investment enough to seriously increase economic growth.[63] Instead, there was inflation, leading the Central bank to raise interest rates. As borrowing became expensive, investment declined and caused a slowdown in the growth rate.[64]

The 1991 reforms were undoubtedly a great step forward for Indian economic liberalization. But the steps taken soon after 1991 were not enough. India's reforms focused primarily on product markets but left the key factor markets – land, labour, energy, capital and access to credit – unreformed.[65] India still needs significant reforms to improve ease of land acquisition, increase labour market flexibility and lower borrowing costs if it wishes to improve its manufacturing industry.

According to Chief Economic Advisor Krishnamurthy Subramanian, the 'critical areas' to boost economic growth and the manufacturing sector are land, labour and financial sector reforms.[66] In a series of interviews to Reuters, many Indian business leaders stated that the reason for investor apathy was 'a delay in land acquisition for private factories, decades-old restrictive labour laws and higher borrowing costs' leading potential investors 'to build new plants in countries like Vietnam, Thailand, and Bangladesh'.[67] Land costs have actually gone up in recent years, and hiring costs have risen as well.

Despite three successive decades of rapid growth, India's employment situation remains alarming. While a small number of workers in the organized services sector have good jobs and a good work environment, the vast majority are forced into the 'unorganized sector', doing low-productivity work. India is facing an unemployment problem, with a steady rise in the labour force of around 1 million new jobseekers every month.[68]

India's rigid labour laws are a deterrent to job creation as well as economic growth. According to a University of Kent–Penn State University study by Amrit Amirapu and Michael Gechter, India's labour regulations lead to a 35 per cent increase in firms' labour costs. In November 2019, Prime Minister Modi indicated an interest in finally overhauling India's cumbersome labour laws – something he avoided during his first term in power. The government has tabled an industrial relations bill that empowers the government to change the ceiling on employee count for a company to retrench workers without government approval. While the current upper threshold limit of 100 workers has not been changed, the bill allows the government to amend this number without seeking parliament's approval.

While the government is optimistic that these reforms will boost economic growth, there are those who say that there is a lack of 'scientific evidence to show that a relaxation in labour laws will make much difference in terms of attracting foreign capital'.[69] Moreover, the legal changes will not replace the archaic and stringent labour laws on hiring and firing, but simply give the government the flexibility to relax the conditions through an executive order. In the absence of fundamental change to the legal regime, every investor would have to seek a project-specific exemption to benefit from the proposed flexibility in labour laws. Most investors would find this almost as cumbersome as the obtaining of licences and quotas in the past.

Amidst the slowing of the Indian economy to almost 4.5 per cent growth, from a high of 8 per cent a few years ago, the government decided in October–November 2019 to lower corporate taxes and relax rules for FDI. It also announced privatization of two large public sector conglomerates in the oil refining and shipping services sectors, Bharat Petroleum Corporation and Shipping Corporation of India.[70] The government is also seeking to sell 100 per cent of its stake in India's national carrier, Air India, after failing to find investors for partial divestment of the government's stake in the airline. Investors were 'uncomfortable with the government retaining a 24 per cent stake in the airline as well as the requirement to stay invested for at least three years. Also, Air India's debt of more than Rs 33,000 crore that was bundled with the sale deterred investors'.[71]

⁓

Instead of giving up the paternalistic approach to the economy that keeps the hand of the government in most economic activity, officials have tried in recent years to massage the numbers to paint a rosier picture of the economy. Different government agencies have released differing data and the government has changed its starting point over the years to make it seem that they are doing better than they actually are. Data from the Centre for Monitoring India's Economy (CMIE) varies from that released by the finance ministry and the government's policy think tank, NITI Aayog. For example, CMIE stated that only 1.43 million jobs were added in 2017, whereas NITI Aayog put the number at 7 million. Economist and Indian government's representative at the IMF, Surjit Bhalla, claimed that 15 million new jobs had been created, leaving one to wonder about how the hugely different figures of 1.43 million and 15 million were computed.[72]

Additionally, a relatively quick turnaround in the economic managers of India has also contributed to the impression that economic policy is subservient to political or ideological considerations. In his government's initial years, Prime Minister Modi was advised by three world-renowned economists. Raghuram Rajan, professor of finance at the University of Chicago's Booth School of Business and chief economist at the IMF, served as governor of RBI; Arvind Panagariya, professor of economics at Columbia University in New York, became vice-chairman of NITI Aayog; and Arvind Subramanian, senior fellow at Peterson Institute for International Economics in Washington DC, was appointed chief economic advisor. Rajan left in 2016, when his contract was not renewed amidst open policy differences with the Modi government. Panagariya and Subramanian left in 2017 and 2018 respectively. The departure of these economists, all of whom championed free trade and open markets, was followed by the return of government interventionism and protectionist policies. Leading analysts told Reuters after the departure of Subramanian that 'Modi's economic outlook is now a throwback to India's inward-looking policies of earlier years'.[73]

In June 2017, the *Economist* argued that Modi was not an economic reformer as much as a Hindu nationalist and populist. Despite the slogan of 'Minimum Government, Maximum Governance,' his first term in office showed continuation of the Indian reluctance to push through major reforms. The social policies of the government not only caused unrest – like the ban on beef and killing of cows – but also hurt India's leather and beef exporting industries. Subramanian summarized the problem the ban created in the livestock industry: why would one own an asset if there is no terminal value of that asset?

NEXT STEPS

To invigorate its economy and move reforms forward, India will have to change the rules governing land ownership and utilization. As an agricultural economy, India focused on protecting the interests of farmers while increasing farm output. Now, land is needed for industrial and infrastructure projects, and land acquisition for these purposes needs to become easier. The land market in India is severely distorted at the moment. Land titles are unclear, and it is not easy to transfer or sell land, or even to use it as collateral for borrowing money.

India's attempts at modernizing land records through the Land Records Modernization Programme that 'aims to put titles on a clear and secure basis by undertaking cadastral surveys, reconciling entries in various registries and computerizing land records' has lacked support from Central or state governments.[74] Until recently the relevant statute in India was the 1894 Land Acquisition Act, which was only updated by the 2013 Land Acquisition, Rehabilitation and Resettlement Act (LARR).

The newer law has proved no less difficult than the one inherited from over a century ago. According to this act 'land acquired by government on behalf of private companies has to pass four hurdles a) a favourable "social impact assessment"; b) compensation to landowners of at least four times the market price of land in rural areas and at least twice the market price in urban areas; c) consent by 80 per cent of affected families (70 per cent for public–private partnership); d) a relief and rehabilitation package for people affected by the project'.[75] Businesses find the cost of land somewhat exorbitant and the process to acquire it immensely cumbersome.

It takes around 'four to five years to acquire land under LARR even when the effort is successful', which is abysmally slow for a country that seeks to industrialize and grow.[76] In 2014, the Modi government sought to amend the act and 'abolish or weaken the "social impact" and "consent" requirements for specified high priority projects' initially through the parliament, and subsequently through a presidential ordinance. But this endeavour faced opposition from within the ruling party and, eventually, the matter has been left to the state governments.[77] A fresh and comprehensive effort would be needed, possibly with support from other political parties, to make land acquisition easier for projects necessary for economic transformation.

For all the focus on improving the life of India's farmers, the country has so far achieved only one-third the agricultural productivity of China. India's land productivity (measured as yield per hectare) is also low. For example, Indian yields of rice are half that of China and one-third of the United States. Similarly, the median household net farm income (as measured by income from cultivation, net cost and unsold produce valued at local market rates) in India was Rs 1600 per month, not far above the poverty line.[78] The reason might be that Indian agriculture is one of the most regulated private enterprises in the country.

If India aims to become a free market for agricultural produce, it would need to update its agricultural trade regime. According to former finance minister Yashwant Sinha, India's approach to agriculture is 'a whimsy': 'If sugar prices rise, imports are allowed, if sugar prices drop, exports are allowed. Sometimes we permit onion export, sometimes we forbid it. Sometimes we permit the import of wheat, sometimes not. Through these unpredictable import and export restrictions, our agriculture has not been allowed to be linked to the global markets.'[79] India needs to allow market forces to enter agriculture while reserving government action for mitigating only the most severe food-related outcomes, such as famine.

Controls on areas of food distribution, such as storage and marketing, should be abolished, in order to encourage competition.[80] Currently, only one-fifth of public sector spending on agriculture is investment, while the rest is mostly in the form of cash subsidies. This money should be repurposed to drive growth in agriculture, by spending it on rural roads, electrification, irrigation and environmental protection where the market will not automatically invest.[81]

Similarly, India needs to change its politically motivated obsession with producing everything within the country. The nation could reap the benefits of long-term economic growth by ending regulations aimed at prioritizing domestic production. For example, India has not been able to set up a massive solar power generating capacity, because of rules that cells and panels for solar power generation must be made in India. The more expensive locally made cells and panels have impeded the expansion of the solar energy industry. A similar phenomenon has been at work in other sectors too.

In over 800 industries, from manufacture of the likes of shoes and matches to the production of garments, which are under the domain of large enterprises in countries like China, the Government of India tried to ensure 'pre-existing employment' by banning the large organized sector.[82]

Even goods such as air conditioners, which are traditionally manufactured by large companies elsewhere, are made by small firms in India,[83] and the desire to protect small-scale weavers has discouraged economies of scale in the textiles industry. The result is that some Indian-made goods cannot compete with mass produced cheaper products from countries that focus on economies of scale.

Although the 1991 reforms abolished import licensing and foreign companies could sell in India, 'production within the country continued to be reserved for small-scale units', which could not compete and thus imported products dominated the domestic consumer goods market.[84] Indian yarn is the most competitively priced in the world and yet, inefficiencies creep into the system in downstream processes such as weaving. Rigid labour laws and hardly any large-scale operations mean that there can never be economies of scale. India has only three or four garment makers whose turnover exceeds US $100 billion, and none of them have the economies of scale as their Chinese counterparts. However, the Indian garment workers are 20 per cent more productive than their counterpart in Bangladesh, a rising exporter of garments.

The garment export industry employs 7 million people, or about a million for every US $2 billion of exports. This number could grow to 18 million jobs if India reached Bangladesh's export target for 2020 (US $36 billion). This would translate into 2 million additional jobs every year for the next five years. Unfortunately, India's most labour-intensive large industry during the period 2000–2012 only received US $1.27 billion in foreign investment.[85]

For years, small-scale weavers paid no electricity tariffs, just as farmers are exempt from paying full price for electricity and water. These subsidies have not only burdened the government treasury, they have limited India's capacity for large-scale production. The country has also tended to insist that its industries use domestic technology whenever available and to demand technology transfer when foreign technology is deployed.[86] The government also required that factories be set up in backward areas,[87] limiting locational advantages determined by purely economic criteria.

The result of such over-regulation has been the opposite of the desired outcome: for years, India became heavily import dependent and ran large trade deficits.[88] Ninan argues that India's success over the last few decades has demonstrated that its people and markets have delivered. It now needs 'government policy and executive action' to change the investment climate. Corporations should find it easier to enter the Indian market and bankrupt entities must be able to shut down their business and move on. Subsidies that are a burden on the taxpayer must end and inefficient public sector enterprises must shut down.

4

Geopolitics and Foreign Policy

LIKE AMERICANS IN the nineteenth century who believed in 'manifest destiny', many Indians believe that their country has a right to historical greatness. The world may look at India through the lens of its struggles with modernity, its economic obstacles and its demographic challenges. For most Indians, however, India's centuries-old civilization, its geographic location, its population comprising one-fifth of humanity, its growing economic power and military strength, and its history make it inevitable that it will be a great power not only in Asia but the world.

This faith in 'Indian exceptionalism' pervades and defines India's external relations. For Indians, the country is unique and thus deserving of global power status. In a speech in March 1949, India's first prime minister and foreign minister, Jawaharlal Nehru, stated that it was inevitable for India to play an important global role 'not because of any ambition of hers, but because of the force of circumstances, because of geography, because of history'.[1]

Indian exceptionalism rests on the belief that there is something unique about the nation, which enabled it to gain independence without violence, revolution or war. Indian discourse often speaks of an 'Indian character' that will overcome odds and circumvent difficulties. In this case, they are not just 'feel good' avowals, but, rather, reflect a deep-seated way of thinking, similar to the messianic vision of the United States.

As Stephen Cohen, an American scholar who worked for decades on India, wrote, 'Whether a realist or an idealist, almost every member of the Indian strategic community thinks that India's inherent greatness as a power is itself a valuable diplomatic asset. India's ambassadors are expected to persuade foreign officials of the wisdom and moral correctness of the Indian position, say, by stating the Indian case and supplementing political arguments with information about India's great civilization, its cultural and economic accomplishments and its democratic orientation.'[2]

INDIA'S SENSE OF SELF

India's interactions with the world are framed by civilizational and historical imperatives. It is not unusual for countries to argue that their path is unique and specific. But for India, this is more than a platitude. It has always sought to be viewed as an example to the world: India is unique in maintaining a democratic system in a poor postcolonial state; its path of economic growth, emphasizing self-sufficiency, is different from others. India retains a large military without being trigger-happy in deploying its troops beyond its border; it sees itself as having global influence, without viewing power as only the ability to coerce, unlike other regional or global powers.

Indian leaders have often expressed the thought that the country could lead the world, albeit in a different way from traditional hegemons. The moral and realist dimensions of India's foreign policy are often reflected in the same conversation by its diplomats and leaders. In a speech in January 2019, the then foreign secretary Vijay Gokhale spoke about how India's ancient philosophy of *Vasudhaiva Kutumbakam* (the entire world is one family) 'presented the world with a philosophy for uniting mankind and erasing artificial barriers'.[3] And yet, India's top diplomat emphasized how 'at the heart of our global engagement is to make our diplomacy an enabler of the security, development and prosperity for the people of India'.[4]

India's desire to engage with the world, but on its own terms, is part of its five-millennia history as a civilizational entity. Ancient Indian kingdoms also maintained relations with countries and regions beyond the subcontinent, even when their focus was their immediate neighbourhood. There is evidence of diplomatic exchanges between ancient Indian kingdoms and those in China, Rome, Greece, Egypt and Mesopotamia. The Hindu and Buddhist religions that started in India expanded beyond the subcontinent, providing evidence of historic links beyond its shores and mountains. Some Southeast Asian empires were even led by dynasties which practised Hinduism and Buddhism – such as the Srivijaya Empire in present-day Indonesia (Java) and the Khemer Empire which covered much of what today is Cambodia, Thailand, Laos, and southern Vietnam.

The general attitude of the present being guided by the past and the future only reflecting it has also applied to modern India's foreign policy. There seems to be an abiding grip of history and tradition on how India views the world. Indians would argue that modern India is inspired by the past, connected to the present and looking towards the future, but critics see it as overly burdened by philosophies and ideas rooted in the distant past. Inspired by the concept of the eternal cycle of life, Indians remain confident that their tomorrow will be as good as their yesterday, if not better. To them, the republic mirrors the glory of past dynasties and empires, which is sometimes seen by others as reflecting a vanity that does not always indicate the current economic or power realities. India's interaction with the rest of the world continues to be guided by a civilizational sense of the country's self.

Belief in the greatness of Indian civilization lies at the core of Indian nationalism and foreign policy. Its leaders have often voiced the view that India was a 'guide'[5] for the world and had a 'mission to fulfill'.[6] Of late, BJP leaders have been claiming the status of Vishwaguru (world teacher) for India![7] In the decades immediately after Independence, this desire to be a global leader, albeit a moral one, manifested in the preaching overtones of Indian foreign policy.

During the 1950s, India's championing of anti colonialism and anti-racism and its campaign against apartheid in South Africa reflected the tendency to adopt moralistic stances. So was India's demand for reforms not only in the United Nations Security Council (UNSC) but also in the international economic order, including the International Monetary Fund and World Bank.

These positions did not always benefit India materially, but the moral dimension of policymaking has always been incredibly important for the country. India saw the world's major powers, especially the industrialized capitalist nations, as unwilling to cater to the interests of previously colonized, poorer countries.

India's economic growth and its rise in military capability in the last two decades have only enhanced its desire to play a leading role in the world. From being a founder-member of the Non-aligned Movement (NAM) during the Cold War, to being part of the Group of 77 (G-77), and in recent years, the BRICS (Brazil, Russia, India, China, South Africa) economic grouping, India has always been engaged in efforts to create international institutions that are not run by western European powers or the United States of America.

NON-ALIGNMENT AND STRATEGIC AUTONOMY

If any one idea could capture Indian strategic thinking during the early years of independence it would be 'non-alignment.' No other term is so ubiquitously known or so widely used when addressing New Delhi's attitudes towards engaging with the world. Jawaharlal Nehru, who brought non-alignment into prominence, envisioned it as a 'policy of friendship toward all nations, uncompromised by adherence to any military pacts. This was not due to any indifference to issues that arose, but rather to a desire to judge them for ourselves, in full freedom and [free of] any preconceived partisan bias'.[8] At the height of the Cold War, non-alignment represented a commitment to be neither pro-Western nor pro-Soviet, and instead sought to judge foreign policy issues on the merits of each case.

At the core of India's foreign policy lies a desire for autonomy in decision-making, resulting from the impact of British colonial rule when that autonomy did not exist. The colonial experience left an indelible mark on India's collective personality. During the British

Raj, the local populace was kept out of decision-making, and Indian interests were subordinated to the interests of the colonial rulers. The Raj forced Indians to fight distant wars with which they had little to do. While Indians were involved in local government and administration, they had nothing to do with foreign policy, which remained firmly in the hands of colonial officers and administrators. As a result, the key demand of India's freedom struggle was the right for Indians to make decisions that affect their lives and their future, i.e., self-determination.

Its founding elite was adamant that independent India would make its own decisions, even if it resulted in occasionally treading a somewhat lonely path. Standing alone at times or standing up to the dominant superpowers was perceived as a badge of honour by its leaders. Territorial integrity and economic autarky, championing of anti-colonialism, aversion to military alliances, and seeking a South Asia free from foreign influence, were deemed critical to independent India. These, above everything else, are the defining elements of its national interest.

The pursuit of an independent path was always tied to the moral certitude that India ought to be a beacon not only for Asia but also the entire world. India's policies were framed to build a world based on ideals of peace and international friendship. To create this idealized world, it championed non-alignment, encouraged multilateral cooperation through the United Nations (UN) and regional organizations, and supported decolonization and disarmament, including universal nuclear disarmament.

India's championing of non-alignment followed directly from the desire to make decisions without having to take directions from others. Non-alignment meant the country did not need to consider someone a friend or enemy because of the friendship or hostility of a superpower. It also enabled India to safeguard its territorial unity by staying out of external disputes it might be drawn into through alliances. Above all, non-alignment provided a platform through which India could attempt to lead other developing countries at a time when it lacked resources to be a superpower itself. Nehru argued that other countries would respect India only if it was not 'a camp follower'.[9]

Through much of the Cold War, Americans, in particular, criticized India for adopting a moralistic or preachy foreign policy, while ignoring the excesses of the Soviet Union or of newly independent postcolonial countries. But the policy helped India achieve a key goal: being recognized as a world leader without the material resources for such leadership. India wanted to lead Asia and viewed itself as a future great power, but it lacked the wherewithal to achieve these goals through military or economic means. But the preachiness that annoyed Americans worked well with other former colonies and developing nations. India's decision to identify itself with the goals of decolonization, anti-racialism and global disarmament helped the country punch above its weight in a political and diplomatic sense.

Non-alignment also helped India stay out of the major powers' entanglements. As American political scientist Werner Levi explained in 1964, 'For a nation with few effective means and little spare energy to influence international events, the idea of making a virtue of staying out of international troubles is practical and wise.'[10] There was, of course, the downside of not being able to secure critical material support for war and conflict. During the 1962 India–China war, the non-aligned countries remained so, and India had to accept economic and military support from Western countries. Non-alignment clashed with the reality of living in a world where the defence of a country depends on its economic and military prowess.

Moreover, non-alignment set up a subtle confrontation between India and the US, and other Western countries. Non-alignment was more anti-Western capitalism and imperialism than it was against Soviet communism. Some analysts ascribe that to Nehru's sympathy towards Soviet socialism, coupled with his own scepticism and cynicism towards American capitalism. Others attribute this to America's pro-Pakistan policy and Soviet support, especially their veto on the Kashmir issue in the Security Council. The result was a balancing act between the superpowers, trying to secure economic and military aid from both blocs without becoming too dependent on either. Although offers of exclusive security and economic assistance in return for joining a bloc were often lucrative, India's leaders also feared that Cold War alignment could tear their fragile nation apart.

Ensuring India's territorial integrity and unity was, and remains, an important element of the framework within which the country formulates its external engagement. As a country that was colonized piecemeal by a distant power, which initially only sought trading privileges, India has been vigilant about safeguarding its territory against foreign encroachment. The legacy of Partition also reinforced the need for unity and cohesion, lest the country is again divided in the name of religion or ethnicity. Independent India has consistently sought an international environment that would guarantee its sovereignty, safeguard its territory, help build its economy, bolster its military resources, and ensure domestic stability and social cohesion.

Indians have always seen a peaceful and stable global environment as the precondition for the nation's development and evolution in pursuit of its historic place under the sun. Steering clear of blocs confronting each other was India's way of ensuring that it would not be hurt by distant wars or international conflict. Non-alignment was also fitting for the relative youth of India's bureaucratic institutions. Nehru was well aware that many postcolonial states did not remain stable, and could devolve into coups or become embroiled in wars for natural resources. This lesson was especially apparent in its neighbourhood, in the case of Pakistan – which quickly became known for weak civilian institutions and overbearing military involvement in politics after alignment with the United States.

Pakistan's strategic doctrine, which centred on militarily balancing against India, empowered the army at the expense of civilian institutions. By contrast, Nehru's choice of a strategic doctrine which emphasized non-military tactics has long been argued as a deliberate effort to strengthen the relative power of civilian institutions against the military. It helped create democratic norms, avoiding over-reliance on the armed forces, which might have been used to justify military involvement in politics.[11] Thus, in Nehru's mind, non-alignment was a guarantor of Indian democracy, which has flourished over the years against all predictions of its imminent demise.

Since the 1990s, India's expanding economic and military capabilities following the end of the Cold War have diminished the need for the country to emphasize on non-alignment. India is now able to go beyond trying to be a global leader through rhetorical moralizing alone, with the material capacity to engage in a more assertive and actionable foreign policy. Still, it remains averse to joining foreign-led alliances and its desire for strategic autonomy – one of the central tenets of non-alignment – remains unchanged. India wants to deal with the world's major issues without being tied down to a single great power or a set of powers. It does not wish to be in a position where its stance is predetermined by alliance commitments.

INDIA AND GLOBAL ORDER

India has always supported the idea of creating global norms through multilateral institutions. Critics see a dichotomy in its almost zealous insistence on absolute autonomy while simultaneously championing multilateral institutions, where member states have to give up some of their autonomy as a condition of membership. Indian officials would argue that the country fully supports multilateralism, but seeks to keep in check the prospect of global institutions becoming instruments of renewed dominance by major powers. International organizations that promote cooperation between sovereign nations are desirable, but dominance of some over others through the grouping of nations is not.

As a champion of cooperation between sovereign nations, India has sought membership of almost every major global and regional organization possible. In doing so, its leaders insisted that they sought to advance not only India's interests but also to voice the collective interests of developing nations. India has often portrayed itself as an example for other poor and formerly colonized countries, primarily in Asia, but increasingly all over the world. India was one of the founding members of the UN, in 1945, even before Independence and played a critical role throughout the era of decolonization. India's positions in multilateral institutions, from the UN and its specialized agencies to the IFIs (International Financial Institutions), have been somewhat consistent since Independence.

India supports multilateralism, but it also seeks to reform global agencies, which it feels are influenced heavily by the world's major powers. Seeing itself as a future major power, India has positioned itself as the voice of equanimity in international bodies, demanding that more powerful nations voluntarily cede some of their influence for the sake of greater fairness in international affairs. This has positioned the country well as a partner for developing nations even though, unlike developed countries, it does not have vast amounts to give to poorer countries as aid. According to Aid Data, a research lab at College of William and Mary, between 2014 and 2017, India has moved from thirty-first to twenty-fourth rank on the 'most influential development partners list'.[12]

For decades, Indian activism in the UN has focused on seeking change in the composition of the Security Council to reflect contemporary global power realities. Specifically, by enlarging the UNSC – a group which holds veto power over security-related decisions. At the time of the UN's creation, Indians argue, it might have made sense to give a veto to only five major powers. The United States, the Soviet Union, Britain, France and China were allies during the Second World War and, having defeated the Axis powers, were expected to be the key arbiters of global security. But much has changed since that time and those changes need to be reflected in the UN's structure. Otherwise the world body runs the risk of falling behind times just as the League of Nations failed to reflect global power realities at the time it collapsed.

India's case for Security Council reform is backed by the logic of contemporary international relations. Russia no longer wields power like that of the Soviet Union, while Britain and France have also considerably diminished in stature. The powers vanquished during the Second World War – Germany and Japan – have re-emerged as global economic powerhouses, with Germany having the additional advantage of being leader of the European Union. Moreover, at the time of the creation of the UN, economic, political and military power was concentrated in Europe and North America, but now Asia and Latin America have come unto their own. Some would argue that, for the sake of fairness, Africa also deserves a place at the global high table even if no single African country meets the criteria for being considered a world power. Currently, India, along with Brazil, Germany and Japan, is part of the group of four nations (G-4) that see themselves as worthy of permanent membership in an expanded Security Council.

India now possesses demonstrated nuclear weapons capability and has one of the largest standing armies in the world. It is one of the major contributors of troops for UN Peacekeeping Missions around the world – indicating its preference for not stationing its forces outside its territory except as part of a UN Peacekeeping Force. Over the decades, around 1,80,000 Indian troops have served as UN Peacekeepers. The country has participated in forty-four of the sixty-nine UN Peacekeeping Missions mandated by the UN and 156 Indian Peacekeepers have been killed while serving the United Nations.[13] From an Indian perspective, these facts support its claim to greater say in UNSC decision-making.

In addition to playing a key role in peacekeeping, India also remains very active in the UN's functional organizations, contributing personnel and ideas to virtually all of them, including the Food and Agriculture Organization (FAO), World Health Organization (WHO), United Nations Children's Fund (UNICEF), United National Development Programme (UNDP), and United Nations Educational, Scientific and Cultural Organization (UNESCO).

A similar activism characterizes India's role in global financial institutions. India has been a member of the World Bank, since its creation in 1945. One of the twenty-five executive directors on the bank's board is from India. For years, the country was among the World Bank's leading borrowers, utilizing loans for infrastructure development, such as construction of dams and canals or for poverty alleviation programmes. Since 2006, India has also contributed financing for projects in other parts of the world. Its direct lending through the World Bank stands at US $10.5 billion.[14] Also, India is the largest client of the World Bank's government lending arm, the International Bank for Reconstruction and Development (IBRD), having borrowed US $10.2 billion between 2015 and 2018 alone. As of mid-September 2018, the total World Bank lending to India stood at US $27.2 billion, representing 104 projects, of which the share of IBRD was US $18.1 billion (fifty-two projects), while the International Finance Corporation (IFC)'s India portfolio at the end of July 2018 contained 281 projects, amounting to a committed exposure of US $6.4 billion.[15] India also received US $9 billion for forty-six projects from the International Development Association (IDA), which focused on poverty alleviation during the same period.

The country's membership of the International Monetary Fund (IMF) also dates back to its inception. India has drawn on IMF funds on three occasions, once in the 1980s and twice in the 1990s to address balance of payments problems.[16] India has drawn more on technical assistance from IMF than seeking financial bailouts. This has included the training of Indian officials in monetary policy and tax administration, assistance in foreign exchange market reform, as well as in tax and customs administration. Mirroring its stand in the United Nations, India has also sought reform of the IMF quota system, so that developing countries – like India – have a greater voice when voting.

Although deeply involved in international financial institutions (IFIs), Indians are wary of the potential for political and strategic factors in these groups to influence their autonomous decision-making. For example, the Asian Development Bank (ADB), under

Chinese pressure, in April 2009, had turned down Indian requests for financing of projects in Arunachal Pradesh,[17] the Indian state that China claims as its territory. India has sought a greater voice for itself and other developing nations in the Bretton Woods system, while also helping to lay the foundations of new institutions like BRICS Bank and AIIB (Asian Infrastructure Investment Bank), where the developing world might have greater say.

In the initial decades after Independence, India's leaders and its successive governments emphasized security and political dimensions of foreign policy, while economic foreign policy took a back seat. India took time in figuring out its place in the global economy. Nehru and Indira Gandhi spoke of changing the global economic order, but they were more concerned with diplomatic means and hoped to accomplish their goals through participation in organizations like the Non-aligned Movement and the UN. Instead of building India's economic muscle under existing rules of the game, they hoped that it could lead other poorer nations in demanding changes to the underlying structure of the global economy. This, in turn, was supposed to raise India's weight in world affairs and strengthen its economy. But this approach resulted only in resolutions and speeches that did not alter the way the world economy functioned and did little to improve the country's standing on the economic ladder.

It is only from the 1990s that Indian leaders acknowledged the dynamics of global economics and decided to increase its share of global GDP. India's leaders are now acutely aware of the rise of China, which has built its international stature by enhancing its economic prowess. Now, economic foreign policy forms a key part of India's external relations and the nation is more integrated with the global economy. India increasingly depends on external relations for investment, energy and growth.

According to data compiled by the US Energy Information Administration (EIA), India imports approximately 4.3 million barrels of crude oil per day and by 2040, it will need 10 million barrels of oil per day.[18] India is the third largest importer of oil in the world. Two-thirds of its energy needs are provided by the Middle Eastern Gulf countries – including Iran – for many years. In recent years, India has engaged in oil and energy diplomacy with the Gulf states to ensure that the sanctions on Iran do not result in a supply problem for India.[19]

Part of seeing India as a future great power has been the gradual recognition that its interests are not limited to its immediate geographic vicinity, but are spread all over the globe. India's vast diaspora, from Africa and the Americas to Fiji and Australia, is now considered an asset in the exercise of global influence, though, unlike some other countries, it is only in recent years that the Indian government has strengthened ties with and tapped into the potential of these communities spread all over the world.

In 1947, there were 3,410,215 persons of Indian origin in the British dominion and colonies. Indians numbered 7,00,000 in each of the colonies of Burma, Ceylon and Malaya. Additionally, 2,82,400 Indians reportedly lived in South Africa, 1,84,100 in British East Africa, and 2,71,640 in Mauritius, where Indians constituted 64 per cent of the population. The Indian diaspora was also settled in far off places like Fiji (1,25,675 persons, constituting 47 per cent of the population) and the British West Indies, which had an Indian-origin population of 4,06,000. Smaller pockets of Indians existed in other countries: 30,000 in Indonesia, 4000 in the Persian Gulf (Oman, Kuwait, Bahrain), 2500 in Iran, 1000 in Egypt, 700 in Iraq and 200 in Afghanistan.[20]

In its early years, independent India saw the diaspora as members of a cultural and civilizational community, and expected those settled overseas to act only as citizens of their countries of residence. Over time, the diaspora and migrant workers have become important economically as well. As of 2015, the number of people of Indian origin living outside the country numbered 27 million, including temporary migrants, with the vast majority in the Gulf and in Western countries.[21] India receives US $79 billion a year in remittances, the largest for any expatriate group in the world, and this contributes to 3.5 per cent of India's GDP.[22]

INDIA AND ITS NEIGHBOURHOOD

Based on the Rajamandala concept first articulated by ancient India's statesman–scholar Kautilya, India's sense of itself and its place in the world is that of concentric circles moving outward from the subcontinent. India's immediate neighbourhood – South Asia – has remained at the top of the list of priorities for every government, irrespective of political party or ideology. The country seeks the first circle in its immediate neighbourhood to comprise friendly states and remains averse to outside powers aligning with its neighbours, or neighbouring states working in collusion with outside powers at India's expense. Indian leaders may have given varying names – from Indira Doctrine and Gujral Doctrine to Neighbourhood First – to their outlook on the South Asian region, but all of them demonstrate this criticality of South Asia to India's foreign policy.

Every presidential address to the joint session of parliament reaffirms the aims of India's foreign policy as being 'peace and friendship in the world, non-alignment and the building of a just and equitable world order'. Starting with discussion of ties with neighbours in South Asia, these speeches progress outward to other parts of the world: Central Asia, China, East and Southeast Asia, Middle East and the Gulf, Russia, Europe, the United States, Africa and Latin America.[23] Yet, while preaching engagement, the head of state reminds members of parliament that independence in foreign policy decision-making remains the country's topmost priority in external relations.

While India aspires to eventually achieve global great power status, it has always considered itself a hegemon in its immediate neighbourhood. South Asia is India's backyard, where it does not take kindly to the interference of other major powers. The greater neighbourhood, extending from the Gulf to Southeast Asia, is also part of India's sphere of influence, and developments in the region are deemed critical to India's foreign and security policy.

The standard Indian description of itself is that of an ancient land unified by geography and tradition. Five thousand years of continuous civilization nurtured in the vast space between the Himalayas to the north, the Indian Ocean to the south and the Hindu Kush and Arakan mountains to the west and east has bred a sense of exceptionalism. For Indians, the subcontinent represents one civilization and one indivisible historic entity, whose past achievements are a source of immense pride and cause for a sense of superiority. International relations theories originating in the West, based primarily on Europe's experience, may serve as a point of reference in Indian discourse, but for most scholars and politicians from the country, India remains a unique member of the international community. Like China, India is both a civilization and a state, but unlike China, it comes together through tolerance of diversity and consensus rather than by eliminating differences by force.

Geography has played a significant role in emphasizing and defining the importance of India's land and sea borders for its leaders throughout history. Indian empires often incorporated neighbouring territories in order to create buffer states to ensure security. For the makers of India's foreign policy, the subcontinent is one entity, the states neighbouring the country are important for its security, and India's immediate area of interest extends from the Middle East to Southeast Asia. This civilizational sphere of influence protects it from invasion, irredentism, and disintegration.

For every Indian government, security has meant ensuring that the subcontinent remains stable and peaceful. The country's outlook on its immediate neighbours is heavily influenced by the view that they are an integral part of Indian civilization. While the concept of a geographic 'sphere of influence' for a major power is widely understood, Indian philosophers and empires have, over time, also delineated a 'civilizational sphere of influence'[24] for the nation.

Located at the crossroads of South Asia, Central Asia and the Middle East, ancient Indian kingdoms and empires maintained cultural and economic relations with Mesopotamia, Greece, China and Rome. Except for the Chola dynasty (300 BC–1300 AD), which built an overseas empire, Indian armies did not seek conquest of lands outside the subcontinent. Ancient Hindu treatises on statecraft and religion recommended isolation from other civilizations. Kings could conquer territory from neighbouring kings within the subcontinent, but annexing other cultures or peoples was deemed unethical.

Modern India's statecraft draws from that historical experience and it hopes to assure neighbours of its goodwill by invoking ancient history. It does not always work, as has been the case with Pakistan, which considers civilizational subsuming more dangerous than military annexation, and accuses India of harbouring hegemonistic ambitions.

India is sometimes described as the region's 'big brother' with whom several neighbours have border disagreements. Some of India's neighbouring states were once part of an Indian empire, while others emerged as separate kingdoms within a vast Indian civilization. India is the geographical, socio-cultural and economic centre of South Asia. In the words of former diplomat S.D. Muni, India's centricity in the region is because 'there is a bit of India in every other country of South Asia'.[25] As is often the case with smaller neighbours of a large country, it is easy to fuel resentment or fear of domination among the country's neighbours. Yet, concerns of neighbours notwithstanding, India has not pursued a hegemonic or expansionist policy under any government or leader.

After Independence, Nehru focused on Asia, where he sought to act as leader of a vast continent that was just emerging from Western colonial rule. He did not think in security terms, at least until the war with China in 1962. In Nehru's view, bilateral treaties of friendship and peace with the three northern Himalayan kingdoms – Bhutan, Nepal and Sikkim – and an offer of a no-war pact to Pakistan[26] was enough to deal with South Asia, freeing him to seek prominence on the Asian and global stage.

The notion of the subcontinent as India's backyard attained centrality under Indira Gandhi. Under her, India's goal in its immediate vicinity was no longer simply to protect its security and strategic interests; the country would henceforth also be interested in any incidents in the neighbourhood that had or could have an impact on it. The 'Indira Doctrine' was a South Asian version of America's well-known 'Monroe Doctrine'. As writer Ashok Kapur states, Indian leaders beginning with Indira Gandhi wanted the nation to be 'the only security manager in South Asia' and sought to reduce the role of external actors – primarily the United States and the Soviet Union – and their ability to influence regional politics 'to a level of economic and technological assistance that would not encourage Pakistan to pursue its irredentist claims'.[27] India was not always able to achieve this policy as Pakistan continually sought parity with its larger neighbour, drawing the United States into the region as its ally.[28]

Under Indira Gandhi, India also sought acknowledgement as South Asia's pre-eminent power; the nation, was willing to flex its muscles to assert its pre-eminence and did not want outside powers to involve themselves in the region's affairs without India's approval. The 'Indira Doctrine' manifested itself most prominently when, in 1971, India protested against the suppression of democracy in East Pakistan and went to war to prevent the genocide of Bengalis by the West Pakistan army. After assisting in the birth of Bangladesh, Indira withdrew Indian troops from erstwhile East Pakistan relatively quickly to demonstrate that India's assertion of power did not amount to coveting other nations' territory.

More recently, India has tried to use economic diplomacy to strengthen ties with its neighbours. It has offered trade concessions, such as zero tariff or removing non-tariff barriers, and concessional loans and credit to Afghanistan, Bangladesh, Sri Lanka and Nepal, primarily with geopolitical motives. Such initiatives have become possible because of India's economic growth. Any loss that India incurs in trade, lending or investment, is deemed bearable as long as it leads India's neighbours to uphold the country's security interests.

In December 2018, India announced it would give Rs 4500 crore to Bhutan in aid.[29] Similarly, Maldives was offered US $1.4 billion in financial assistance and credit.[30] After the disastrous floods and landslides in Sri Lanka, India stepped in and provided emergency relief.[31] These aid packages serve the dual purpose of fostering goodwill and fulfilling India's civilizational aspirations as the steward of South Asia. Its willingness to expend money in assistance for neighbouring states is also connected to the fear of encirclement by China, which has been investing heavily and lending extensively to these countries. India also spends heavily on aiding Afghanistan, where it is competing for influence with its difficult neighbour, Pakistan – a subject discussed in greater detail below.

As a postcolonial state, territorial integrity and unity are critical for India. Over seven decades after Partition, the Indian state still fears an insurgency that could lead to separation or another partition. Thus, India's neighbours are its first layer of security and, at the same time, they are also potential causes of tensions as the nation shares ethnic-linguistic similarities with all of them. Neighbours are important as they can either support New Delhi or provide safe havens to the insurgents. India's security and interests depend on neighbours that are stable, economically and politically, and do not allow their territories to be used either as hiding places or by powers that are antagonistic to India (e.g., China).

One neighbour with whom India continues to have great difficulty is Pakistan. Since it was carved out of India in 1947, Pakistan's identity and foreign policy have been framed around not being India. A religion-based national identity was constructed based on the view of 'Hindu' India as the 'other' for an 'Islamic' Pakistan. This feeling of mistrust towards India and the insecurity about India's larger size led Pakistan's leaders and strategists to argue that India never accepted the creation of the country and seeks to undo Partition. Pakistan's foreign and security policy is, thus, driven by a fervent desire to check 'hegemonic' India from achieving its nefarious aims in South Asia and beyond.

Although there is no evidence that India seeks to reincorporate Pakistan, the fear of India undoing Partition has informed Pakistani decision-making for over seven decades. For example, in 1971, during the civil war in East Pakistan that resulted in the creation of

Bangladesh, India supported the Bengalis, but withdrew its forces as soon as the war ended. That only led to the Pakistani view that India seeks to divide their nation along ethnic lines and wants to dominate through proxies. Still, every Indian prime minister, from Jawaharlal Nehru to Narendra Modi, has sought to improve relations with Pakistan based on the belief that it will lead to a peaceful neighbourhood.

Traditionally, there was a broad consensus within India's policy community that a politically stable and economically integrated South Asia – including Pakistan – is in India's national interest. In the last two decades, three successive Indian prime ministers – Atal Bihari Vajpayee, Manmohan Singh and Narendra Modi – attempted to restart and rebuild relations with its neighbour, which have been especially fragile since Pakistan started sponsoring jihadi terrorists in an effort to unfreeze the conflict in Jammu and Kashmir.

Although Pakistani civilian leaders have sometimes reciprocated Indian initiatives or even initiated peace moves themselves, a hard core of Pakistan's national security apparatus remains wedded to the idea of India being Pakistan's permanent enemy. Civilian leaders who initiated friendship towards India – Benazir Bhutto, Nawaz Sharif and Asif Zardari – have been targeted by their domestic opponents as 'security risks' or 'Indian agents'. They have also lost influence and power soon after the initiation of a peace process with India, losing power in military coups or military-backed political and judicial manoeuvres.

Throughout the various ups and downs, India's traditional argument was that the two countries must build people-to-people ties and economic relations before resolving outstanding issues like Kashmir. However, in recent years, the rise in terrorism – including the 2008 Mumbai terror attacks – has made it increasingly difficult for Indian governments to consider dialogue with Pakistan without any discussion of terrorism. If terrorism is front and centre for India in any dialogue, it is still Kashmir which dominates Pakistan's agenda.

The Kashmir conflict, a legacy of Partition, has been viewed by Pakistan as the 'unfinished business of Partition' and every Pakistani leader and government has tried to solve the problem; whether through war or negotiations. India has always maintained that Kashmir is an Indian territory and the instrument of accession signed by the Maharaja of Kashmir in October 1947, and successive elections within the province, demonstrate that the people of Indian Kashmir wish to remain with India. Pakistan's argument has always been that as a Muslim-majority area, Kashmir should have gone to Pakistan at Partition.

The two countries have adopted differing policies when it comes to dealing with Kashmir. Pakistan has always sought to internationalize the Kashmir dispute. Its leaders have consistently demanded that a plebiscite should be held in Kashmir in accordance with the United Nations resolutions to ascertain the will of the people about joining India or Pakistan. However, the last of the UN resolutions was voted on in 1957, over six decades ago. India views Kashmir as a bilateral issue, not an international dispute.

For New Delhi, the Simla Agreement of 1972 remains the framework within which the two countries should discuss any problem areas, especially the Kashmir issue. The 1972 Simla Agreement states that both countries 'resolved to settle their differences by peaceful means through bilateral negotiations'. The Lahore Declaration of 1999 reiterated the Simla Agreement 'in letter and spirit'. But Pakistan's military argues that the Simla Agreement was a treaty that was imposed on it after the devastating loss the country suffered in the 1971 war that resulted in the separation of East Pakistan and the creation of Bangladesh. They would prefer to ignore the agreement signed under duress and find a new basis for bilateral relations that denies India an upper hand.

However, Kashmir forms a subset of the broader issue of India–Pakistan relations, and Pakistan's desire for parity with a much larger neighbour. Unable to maintain parity with India on the conventional military front, asymmetrical warfare in the form of terrorism was viewed by the Pakistani deep state as the cost-friendly and yet potent alternative against the larger country, India. Pakistan has nurtured a hardline 'Kashmir bazor shamsheer' (Kashmir by the sword) lobby that portrays India as an existential threat to Pakistan – a view also supported by the country's politically dominant military.

Until a few years ago, India pursued a policy of sporadic engagement with Pakistan even amidst intermittent terrorist attacks. The hope was that these comprehensive dialogues – covering everything from Kashmir to Siachen, and the economy to the visa regime – would help build a mechanism that would resolve both the larger and smaller issues between the two countries. But since 2015, New Delhi has made dialogue contingent on Pakistan ending all support for Kashmiri terrorist groups and giving up the option of using force to gain control of Kashmir.

There has been no bilateral meeting between the Indian and Pakistani prime ministers since the December 2015 visit by Prime Minister Modi to Lahore to meet the then prime minister Nawaz Sharif. Relations have only worsened since. The Pathankot terrorist attack in January 2016 was followed by the Uri terror attack later that year, which resulted in India's surgical strike against Pakistan-based jihadi camps.

In February 2019, after one of the deadliest terror attacks against Indian security forces by a Kashmiri terrorist belonging to the Pakistan-based terror group Jaish-e-Mohammed in Pulwama, India ended its traditional strategic restraint and struck at terror camps deep inside Pakistan in Balakot, in Khyber Pakhtunkhwa.

The two countries are at an impasse now. India, as of now, does not believe it needs to restart a dialogue with Pakistan unless and until it takes actions against terrorist groups that target India. Pakistan believes it only needs to convince the global community to exert enough pressure that will bring India to the negotiating table.

On 5 August 2019, the Indian government amended the country's Constitution, removing Article 370 that conferred special status on Jammu and Kashmir, and divided the erstwhile state into two Union

Territories. The erstwhile state of Kashmir – the one Maharaja Hari Singh acceded to India in October 1947 – now no longer exists. Part of its territory is with Pakistan, which has already ceded a portion to China, and the part that was with India is split, with autonomy less than that of a state under the Indian Constitution.

The decision might face a potential legal hurdle before the Supreme Court of India over whether a state can be downgraded to a Union Territory without the consent of its elected legislature. But the government believes it has changed the reality on the ground, in the hope of resolving the long-standing dual issues of national integration and international legitimacy with respect to the former state of Jammu and Kashmir.

India's leaders believe that since the disputed state itself now no longer exists, the only matters that now require resolution relate to territory of the erstwhile state controlled by China and Pakistan. They think they have resolved the Kashmir issue and presented the world with a fait accompli. The expectation is that at some future time, China and Pakistan will accept a settlement that lets them legally keep the territory they already control, and India can move on by fully integrating the area it controls. As of now, India has benefited from its friends around the world, notably the United States and most Western countries, being willing to give it time to restore the situation in Kashmir to normalcy.

Pakistan has received little support in its attempts to raise the matter of Jammu and Kashmir at the UNSC. There is an international consensus that terrorism is not acceptable as a means of focusing attention on any grievance. But if the internal situation in Jammu and Kashmir, where suspension of civil liberties and severe militarization have accompanied the change in constitutional status, does not change for the better, the problem could come back to affect India's global standing. Like all defining decisions, this solution to a seventy-year-old problem must stand the test of time before being described a permanent triumph.

In addition to Kashmir, India also has a stake in the end of conflict in Afghanistan. India has always seen Afghanistan as its neighbour, and has a deep historical and strategic interest in that country. India's policy towards Afghanistan has been impacted by its relations with Pakistan and how Pakistan has perceived the India–Afghanistan relationship.

Since Independence, Pakistan's leaders, especially its military–intelligence establishment, have always feared that close ties between India and Afghanistan would result in a pincer movement that would dismember Pakistan, given the fact that its ethnic Pashtuns have close ties with their kinsmen in Afghanistan. Much of Pakistan's Khyber-Pakhtunkhwa province and some of Balochistan were ruled from or associated with Kabul and Kandahar before the British took control of the territory and the Durand Line came into existence in 1893.

Pakistan's policy towards Afghanistan has its origins in the policies of the British Raj, which saw Afghanistan as a buffer between Russia's Central Asian empire and their own empire in the subcontinent. Until 1947, Afghanistan's foreign policy was, for all practical purposes, subject to a British veto. In an earlier era, civil servants and generals in British India had even determined who would sit on the throne in Kabul.

Since Independence, Pakistan's leaders have sought influence over Afghanistan like that enjoyed by the erstwhile colonial power. Officials in Islamabad wish to arrogate to themselves the right to decide who wields power in Afghanistan and want their smaller neighbour to the west to subordinate its decision-making to Pakistan's preferences.

Pakistan's leaders cite fears of strategic encirclement by Afghanistan to the Northwest and India to the Southeast. Their support of jihadi groups, like the Mujahideen during the 1970s and 1980s, the Afghan Taliban and the Haqqani network have been based on the desire to install a government in Afghanistan that would be controlled by Pakistan. By installing a pro-Pakistan government in Afghanistan, the country hopes to thwart an Indian-backed effort for a Pashtunistan (Land of the Pashtuns) at its own expense.

Pakistani leaders have sometimes even voiced the belief that they should have the right to decide who wields power in Kabul. Immediately after the end of the anti-Soviet Afghan jihad of the 1980s, then-military dictator General Zia-ul-Haq stated, 'We have earned the right to have [in Kabul] a power which is very friendly toward us.'[32] This belief, rather than any action on India's part, is at the heart of Pakistan's Afghan policy.

The real fear motivating Pakistani leaders is that overlapping ethnicities might lead some of their countrymen to feel greater affinity with Indians or Afghans across the border, rather than with co-religionists of other ethnicities within Pakistan. This is more a psychological fear than a serious likelihood, which is why no substantive policy concession or internationally backed negotiation has ever been able to address it.

Pakistani officials often claim that they cannot forget Afghanistan's vote at the United Nations in 1947 against Pakistan's membership. Few of them acknowledge that Afghanistan later withdrew its objection, recognized Pakistan and established full diplomatic relations with the new country. Similarly, there is no admission that Afghanistan supported Pakistan, not India, during several India–Pakistan wars, and never took advantage of Pakistan's vulnerabilities.

The Pakistani fears about Afghanistan reflect the desire to suppress Pashtun nationalism through Islamic fundamentalism. They have been a major factor in Pakistan's support of the Afghan Taliban and its role in undermining efforts to build a democratic, stable and peaceful Afghanistan. On the other hand, India continues to cultivate goodwill and support among Afghans by deepening economic, cultural and educational ties, based on their treaty of friendship signed in 1950.

Unlike Pakistan, India has avoided taking sides in intra-Afghan disputes. Even during the anti-Soviet Afghan jihad of the 1980s, India did not support any of the Mujahideen groups. It was only during the civil war that broke out in 1992 that India built ties with leaders in the Northern Alliance, including Ahmad Shah Massoud and Burhanuddin Rabbani as a response to Pakistan's backing first of Gulbuddin Hekmatyar and later of the Taliban.

Immediately after 9/11, New Delhi aided the US-led international efforts in Afghanistan. Pakistan's then military dictator General Pervez Musharraf and his advisors had demanded that Indian presence and influence be limited if the US government wanted Pakistan's help in Afghanistan.

India is today the largest regional donor and fifth largest global donor to Afghanistan, with over US $3 billion in assistance. India offers 1000 annual scholarships to Afghan students and has trained over 4000 Afghan military officers. New Delhi has helped construct key infrastructure inside Afghanistan, from roads and highways (Zaranj–Delaram) to dams (Salma dam) and the Afghan parliament building. India has also built hospitals at Farkhor and Kabul, and donated wheat to feed schoolchildren in Afghanistan.

India's influence in Afghanistan comes from soft power. Indian engineers build highways, roads and government buildings, Indian doctors and nurses run clinics across the country, and India provides scholarships for Afghan students to study in India's first-grade schools. For decades, Afghans have studied in India, including former president Hamid Karzai. India has invested in building its neighbour, not on coercing its friendship through military force.

Indian policymakers believe that an economically prosperous Afghanistan would serve the interests of all of its neighbours. A stable Afghanistan could be a bridge between South and Central Asia, linking together to two economic zones. India has worked with neighbouring countries, such as Iran, to plan strategic trade corridors and railroads, which would link the region together and draw in investment from the outside world. One such example is the Chabahar Port project, which seeks to establish a trade route between India and Iran, and create links into Central Asia through Afghanistan.[33] What India wants in Afghanistan, more than anything, is a prosperous partner.

RISE OF CHINA AND INDIA'S SLOW EMBRACE OF THE US

The economic and military rise of China over the past two decades poses a challenge to the liberal international order and American pre-eminence, which has characterized global affairs since the end of the Second World War. The American grand strategy for Asia and the Pacific, since 1945, centred on creating an international diplomatic and security architecture that ensured stability.

China is gradually creating a new Asian order with Chinese primacy at its heart. The US Indo-Pacific strategy thus has been one of renewed engagement with its partners and allies across the region – India, Japan and Southeast Asia – to construct a configuration that will be able to counter the Chinese march.

Among Asian countries, India has consistently viewed China's expanding influence with suspicion. This is partly a function of historical experience. India had engaged communist China as an Asian brother from 1949 to 1962, only to become victim of its military aggression over a border dispute. Since 1962, India has noted China's efforts to build close ties with countries on its periphery, thereby trying to possibly encircle India, as well as its efforts to lay the groundwork for military and naval bases throughout the Indian Ocean. With a population of more than 1 billion, China is also the country with sufficient manpower to match that of India.

The country's competitive relationship with China – its northern neighbour and rival for leadership in Asia – dates back decades, but it is the not-so-peaceful rise of China that lies at the core of what is happening today. After building its economic and military potential, China has over the decades encroached in a region that India has always considered its sphere of influence: South Asia and the Indian Ocean region. India and China consider each other as rivals for the status of the dominant ancient civilization in Asia. They have rarely had good relations in the modern era, barring a few years in the early 1950s. But neither country wants to openly declare the other a sworn enemy.

Both China and India believe their civilizational heritage confers on them a certain right to a position at the global high table. Both are easily provoked by attacks on their national self-respect, both are sensitive to 'loss of face', and both have contended with Western colonial influences that have shaped their foreign policies.

They are neighbours whose colonial-era boundary serves as an 'imperial fault line' – creating a long-standing border dispute, which has led to frequent border frictions and one all-out war in 1962.[34] China has never favourably viewed India providing refuge to the Dalai Lama, the Tibetan leader, and thousands of Tibetan refugees.

China's close ties to Pakistan, which have an economic and military, especially nuclear, dimension, are not viewed approvingly by India. Deepening Chinese influence within other countries in South Asia – like Nepal, Sri Lanka and Bangladesh – are seen by India as part of China's 'string of pearls policy': encircling India by having a presence among its neighbours.[35] China views India's growing ties with the US and its allies, like Japan and South Korea, as a strategic encirclement of its boundaries.

China has used the last four decades of peace with India to create its economic miracle and modernize its military. India's economy, by contrast, has not grown consistently at double digits, and its military modernization is decades behind what it should be. Roughly speaking, China's GDP is four times India's (the latter is US $2.4 trillion, and the former is US $11.2 trillion); their population is approximately the same and China's military budget is three times India's – India spent US $66 billion in 2019, China over US $200 billion.[36]

From the start, the 'peaceful rise' of communist China has been a function of Beijing's savvy ability to convince other countries to give up their own areas of influence. China has achieved this by building economic and strategic relationships with the immediate neighbours of its competitors – in India's case, all its South Asian neighbours – and then egging on the neighbours to push back against perceived hegemony by the country in question. Indian leaders have always resented the presence of any external power in the region unless that power accepted Indian predominance. Beijing's refusal to do so has repeatedly irked New Delhi.

China's rise has forced New Delhi to take a more active stance in containing its rival. Indian analysts have always viewed China's policy as one of strategic encirclement, often called the 'string of pearls' theory, one designed to give the Peoples Liberation Army (PLA) an advantage in a potential conflict, and more leverage in negotiations over disputes. New Delhi views the One Belt One Road (OBOR), or the Belt and Road Initiative (BRI), as a continuation of China's planned encirclement of India.

China's project in South and Southeast Asia has been to build a network of friendly states which rely on it for patronage. Ever since the 1990s, 60 per cent of China's arms exports have gone to three of India's immediate neighbours: Pakistan, Myanmar and Bangladesh.

Starting from the 1950s, China built a close relationship with Pakistan, an alliance which today has a strong military, nuclear and economic component. From assistance in the nuclear arena to protection at the UNSC, China has openly supported Pakistan. In return, Pakistan has become, in the words of scholar and diplomat Husain Haqqani, China's secondary deterrent against India.

The US $62 billion China–Pakistan Economic Corridor (CPEC), the showcase initiative of China's Belt and Road Initiative (BRI), is a prime example. Massive infrastructure projects being built inside Pakistan will provide China with access to the Persian Gulf, via the port of Gwadar. Unless Pakistan's economy grows substantially, the country will only end up further in China's debt under the project's massive high-interest loans.

Sri Lanka is another case in point. Its relationship with China dates back to the 1950s, during the era of Asian bonhomie and non-alignment. The long civil war in Sri Lanka, and India's sporadic support of the Tamil rebels, hurt India's relations with the country, creating an environment of mistrust which Beijing has subsequently exploited. Chinese investment in Sri Lanka under the Belt and Road Initiative (BRI) included building the port of Hambantota. Colombo's inability to pay back the high-interest Chinese loans resulted in Sri Lanka having to lease the port to China for a period of ninety-nine years.

China also has its sights trained on Nepal, which has long been seen as India's buffer with Tibet and China. Nepal is also the only Indian neighbour with whom India has an open border policy, which has helped trade and tourism, but has also created security challenges. In recent years, Beijing has offered to deepen any rifts between New Delhi and the communist–Maoist government in Kathmandu by offering better terms on trade and infrastructure development.

After Pakistan, the South Asian country with the largest Chinese investment under BRI is Bangladesh. New Delhi's level of trust with Dhaka is high and Bangladesh is critical to India's security, especially its northeastern states. Resolving the land border dispute with Dhaka, providing lines of credit for infrastructure and encouraging inter-regional trade between India's northeastern states and Bangladesh has helped New Delhi.

New Delhi is also wary of Chinese bases and ports, especially in the Indian Ocean, from Hambantota in Sri Lanka to Gwadar and Jiwani in Pakistan on the Persian Gulf, as well as potential bases in the Maldives and in Djibouti in the Horn of Africa. India's response in South Asia has been to offer more economic assistance and aid to its immediate neighbours. Its response in Southeast Asia and the Pacific has been to rebuild relationships with countries of those regions.

India's historical and civilizational ties with Southeast Asia go back to centuries of trade ties, the spread of Hinduism and Buddhism from the subcontinent and an ancient Indian empire that extended its presence to Southeast Asia (the Chola Empire). However, it is only from the 1990s when India adopted its 'Look East' policy, aimed at building closer economic ties with the region, that economic cooperation has seriously begun. It is only in the last decade that a security dimension has been added to this relationship.

Reflective of this 'Look East' policy, India's trade with the region stands at US $76 billion. Although it has refused to become a member of the proposed Regional Comprehensive Economic Partnership (RCEP) free trade agreement, India remains actively engaged in the region. It has also deepened partnerships with Southeast Asian countries aimed at bolstering their defence capabilities and making them strategically useful partners.

In 2015, India and Singapore signed defence cooperation and strategic partnership agreements. Indian armed forces helped build the capacity of their Vietnamese counterparts and in February 2017, the two sides held discussions on the sale of the surface-to-air Akash and the supersonic Brahmos missiles. New Delhi has provided over US $500 million in credit to Vietnam to modernize their armed forces and since 2016, India has trained Vietnamese navy submariners at its naval training school.

The Straits of Malacca are as critical for India as they are for China with almost 40 per cent of India's trade passing through this narrow waterway. In mid-May 2018, Indonesia and India signed an agreement as part of which the former has given the latter access to the strategically located island of Sabang, at the northern tip of Sumatra and less than 300 miles from the Malacca Straits. India will invest in the dual-use port and economic zone of Sabang, and also build a hospital. Indian naval ships will also visit the port, which is deep enough to serve as a potential base for submarines.

New Delhi has also boosted relations with the Pacific Islands, again a region with which India shares civilizational ties and is home to a large Indian diaspora. Since 2014, there have been annual conferences of the Forum for India Pacific Islands Cooperation either in India or in the region itself, and New Delhi has offered massive assistance, including annual grant-in-aid to each of the fourteen Pacific Island countries, ranging from US $125,000 to $200,000. India has also set up a fund for adapting to climate change, capacity building of coastal surveillance systems, and technical training and educational fellowships.

In the Indian Ocean region, it has deepened relations with island nations like Seychelles, Maldives and Mauritius, as well as with strategically located countries like Oman and the UAE. In January

2018, India and Seychelles signed a twenty-year pact whereby India would build an airstrip and a jetty for the Indian navy on Assumption Island. In February 2018, New Delhi and Muscat finalized an agreement through which India gained access to the strategically located port of Duqm, on Oman's southern coast.

Many Indians believe their country is China's match in view of their civilizational heritage and potential, but China does not see India as an equal, particularly because of the vast difference in the size of the two economies. India needs to boost its economic growth and modernize its military if it wants Beijing to treat it as a serious rival. In the last two decades, the United States and its major allies have taken an interest in the rise of India as part of their strategic plans for dealing with China's global pre-eminence. Although India and the United States are closer today than they ever were before, the world's oldest and largest democracies have never really been allies and are still trying to determine the future contours of their partnership.

The United States and India have core values in common – democracy, multi-ethnic and multireligious populations and pluralism. They both consider terrorism and the rise of China as threats, and have an identical vision of an open and rule-based global system. But Indians remain wary of depending on the Americans, while US decision makers privately express their exasperation over India's slow and deliberate decision making. From the Indian perspective, an alliance with the US might result in the country losing its strategic autonomy without necessarily securing the guarantee of US support against China. Indians see a strong isolationist streak manifesting under President Donald Trump, exemplified in American policy towards Afghanistan, as well as the rest of West Asia.

The US does not see India's immediate neighbourhood as India itself sees it. For example, the country is concerned that a US military withdrawal from Afghanistan after a deal with the Taliban would lead to Pakistan trying to fill the vacuum. Not only would that amount to rewarding Pakistan for supporting terrorism, it would also deny India access to Central Asia while bolstering China's role in the region. The Americans, who are more concerned about China's naval prowess and the threat that might pose in the South China Sea and the Pacific region, want India to actively check China's growing influence in Southeast and East Asia, without recognizing its priorities in South and Central Asia.

Thus, the India–US relationship remains stuck in a grey area where desire for partnership far exceeds operational and functional instruments of collaboration. Educational and economic exchanges remain the mainstay of the relationship, while political and military ties have advanced very slowly. In some ways, that has been the history of the ties between the two countries. Both have seen opportunities in befriending each other, but fallen short of each other's expectations – going back to 1792, when President George Washington appointed a consul to the British Indian Empire based in Calcutta. Until 1941, the only ties between India and the United States involved minimal economic activity and education through American missionaries in India.

In 1941, President Franklin D. Roosevelt had appointed an envoy to what was still British India, with a view of building relations with a future independent India. President Roosevelt and the United States government were keen for the British government to grant India independence; yet, they were reluctant to hurt the war effort. In 1946, the United States established full diplomatic relations with India, even though the British had not yet granted the country independence. With China facing a civil war between the nationalists and the communists, an independent India looked like a potential ally to the US administration in the decades ahead.

But despite American support for Indian independence, and a common appreciation for democracy between the two nations, Jawaharlal Nehru opted for non-alignment during the Cold War. There were other complicating circumstances that constrained the US–India relationship in the years immediately following Independence. Although the United States provided economic and developmental aid to India, the nation found American military support to Pakistan detrimental to its interests. India's close relations with the Soviet Union was another factor that kept New Delhi and Washington estranged throughout the Cold War.

India welcomed aid from both the US and the Soviet-led blocs, arguing that its priority was its own development and that it could not afford to ally with only one superpower. US development assistance in the form of PL-480 local currency loans and support in the modernizing of Indian agriculture, as well as in the setting up some of India's higher educational institutions was deeply appreciated. But India's unwillingness to commit to the American bloc came in the way of deeper relations.

From the 1990s onwards, succeeding American and Indian administrations have attempted to forge a multifaceted partnership. The success of President Clinton's landmark trip in March 2000, in which he spoke of the need to 'start a new chapter' in Indo-US relations, was continued under President George W. Bush. The United States ostensibly 'de-hyphenated' its ties with India and Pakistan, meaning that relations with one would not come in the way of a partnership with the other. President Bush's offer to India of a civilian nuclear deal in 2006 created the prospect of a more extensive connection. Under President Barack Obama, the United States described the US–India relationship as the defining partnership of the twenty-first century. But at every stage the promise of the relationship that was loudly proclaimed did not always result in specific manifestations of a substantive alliance.

The United States views India as a potential counterweight to a rising China, but cannot help noticing India's unwillingness to exercise hard power or agree to military alliances. As the world's largest democracy, with a multicultural society and expanding military heft, New Delhi has the potential to balance China's expansion westward. As the PLA navy moves into the Indian Ocean and builds a blue water fleet, the United States sees India as a valuable partner in balancing China at sea. India and the United States agree on the need for an open and inclusive Indo-Pacific region and, upholding a rule-based liberal international order. They are just somewhat slow in figuring out how to manage the region's security and what commitments each is able to make towards their shared objectives.

India's growing economic and security relationships, and interest in the Indo-Pacific region, are aligned with its deepening partnership with the United States. Two years after signing the US–India Joint Strategic Vision of 2015, India joined the Quad (a strategic grouping of the United States, India, Japan and Australia) and there is talk about making the grouping something more than an annual talk shop. Three years into the administration of President Donald Trump, India and the United States have a bilateral trade relationship of over US $142 billion and a defence relationship where India is described as a major defence partner by the US.

India lies at the core of the Trump administration's South Asia strategy, as well as its Indo-Pacific strategy. Unlike his predecessors, President Trump has been openly critical of Pakistan, has cut almost all aid to that country, and asked India to play a bigger role in Afghanistan. His opposition to China has been unambiguous, a fact that Indians tend to appreciate.

From being 'estranged' democracies during the Cold War, India and the US today share, in the words of former secretary of state Rex Tillerson a 'growing strategic convergence'. From having almost no military relations during the Cold War, India has become a significant buyer of US military equipment. The United States increasingly also views India as a potential regional security provider, and seeks to build its security capacity through commercial and defence cooperation between the two militaries.

Though India is a virtual American ally, it remains reluctant to be a formal American ally. The US has historically preferred institutional arrangements for collective security, while India is reluctant to cede power to a collective security mechanism. It has always been reluctant to join any formal military alliance or any grouping that appears like a military alliance.

Despite its slow embrace of the United States, India's desire for multiple partnerships in the global arena stands out. It speaks of a special relationship with the US but is, at the same time, a member of the BRICS grouping, the Russia, India and China grouping and the Asian Infrastructure Investment Bank (AIIB) where China is the main investor. India is against the One Belt One Road or Belt and Road Initiative, it supports Japan's Quality Infrastructure Initiative, is a member of the Quad, and says that it views the United States as a natural ally. This reflects the country's pursuit of maximum options in foreign relations. India has warmed up to America's influence, but it has certainly not committed to an exclusive alliance with the United States.

INSTITUTIONS OF FOREIGN POLICY

Even though India's prime minister, his Cabinet and parliament are the major pillars of the country's government, it is the professionally trained civil service that is described as its 'steel frame'. That depiction dates back to a 1922 parliamentary speech by the then British prime minister David Lloyd-George. The Indian bureaucratic system, especially the foreign service, is a legacy of British colonial rule with a history dating back to the British East India Company. Some would argue that institutions created under colonial rule, and sustained in the first few decades of independence, might inhibit rather than facilitate India's rise as a major global power.

India was the engine that sustained the British Raj and a huge bureaucratic establishment was set up to serve it. Schools were set up to train civil and military officials to maintain the empire's interests, locally as well as internationally. Under the East India Company, military officers and civilian administrators were company employees and their roles were interchangeable. The Company used the same personnel for domestic, diplomatic and military work, and British policies in relation to India were framed on the basis of reports by these employees. Even after the Crown took over from the Company, the Foreign and Political Department's function was not purely restricted to the foreign affairs of British India, but also included internal and imperial matters.

At Independence, there were differing views in the Congress party about whether or not independent India should retain the British civil services. Nehru supported abolition of the permanent civil service inherited from the Raj and wanted to replace it with a cadre of political appointees. In his view, this would be a more democratic system and, in addition to removing the vestiges of colonialism, would create a more patriotic governing class. Ironically, it was Patel who argued in favour of retaining the permanent bureaucracy created so carefully over almost two centuries by the British.

In a letter to Nehru dated 27 April 1948, Patel asserted that 'an efficient and disciplined and contended service, assured of its prospects as a result of diligent and honest work, is a sine qua non of sound administration under a democratic regime even more than under an authoritarian rule'.[37] According to Patel, the bureaucracy 'must be above party' and a system should be laid out that minimizes 'political considerations either in its recruitment or in its discipline and control'.[38]

Patel's view prevailed and India's founding fathers were able to rise above the resentment resulting from mistreatment by the bureaucracy during colonial rule. India retained the broad British civil service system though, over time, numerous changes were introduced. Today, the Indian civil services are divided into three broad categories: the Central Services (which comprises forty-three services, including the Indian Foreign Service), All India Services (consisting of three services, including the Indian Administrative Service) and the various state services.

Notwithstanding the changes in the foreign office's organization at various times, the training of civil servants remains as stringent as it was in colonial days. In case of the Indian Foreign Service, J. Bandyopadhyaya, the author of *The Making of India's Foreign Policy*, points out, well-trained professional diplomats are crucial for the country's international relations. 'However rational the broad goals and principles of foreign policy determined by the political executive may be,' he writes, 'there will be a wide gap between theory and practice if the personnel responsible for the various major aspects of policy are not properly selected, trained and utilized.'[39]

Since 1926, recruitment of India's civil servants has taken place through the Union Public Service Commission (UPSC) – formerly Federal Public Service Commission – an independent body that conducts annual examinations for the recruitment for various Indian administrative services, including the Indian Foreign Service (IFS) and the Indian Administrative Service (IAS).

Once selected, new recruits (or probationers as they are called) train first along with colleagues from other services at the Lal Bahadur Shastri National Academy of Administration in Mussourie, before heading to the Foreign Service Institute (FSI) in New Delhi for specialized training. The training period lasts three years, after which each officer is assigned a compulsory foreign language. After a brief attachment to the Ministry of External Affairs in New Delhi, the young IFS officer is posted to an Indian mission based on their language skills. At the end of the three-year training period, officers must pass an examination before being allowed to continue further in the service.

There are approximately 770 IFS officers manning 162 Indian missions and posts abroad, as well as at the headquarters in New Delhi. For a country of its size and the demands of global engagement, India has a relatively small foreign service. The external affairs ministry also has 400 support staff, including interpreters and lawyers who are not foreign service officers. These numbers do not compare favourably with other major developing countries. China has 6000 diplomats, while Brazil's foreign service comprises 3000.[40] 'For every Indian diplomat there are four Brazilian diplomats,' the then foreign secretary Shivshankar Menon told a parliamentary committee in 2007. 'For every Indian diplomat there are seven Chinese diplomats,' he said, adding, 'Now we might be wonderful and very efficient, but we are not that efficient or that good. The strain is telling on us.'[41]

Starting off as a small elite service, the IFS only recruited five to ten people each year for several years after Independence. The exclusivity and small number of Indian diplomats led to the view that they were somehow better than others. Quality was believed to be a substitute for numbers. Over time, the foreign service realized its personnel crunch. Had the Ministry of External Affairs been strategic consistently and added to their numbers on a regular basis, India could have doubled the number of its diplomats in fifty years, keeping pace with demand.

Bad personnel management for decades has led to the difficulties Shivshankar Menon identified before the parliamentary committee sixty years after Independence. The Indian government has now decided to double the number of people working for the foreign ministry to 1500 and recruitment rates have gone up. Thirty-two 'officer trainee diplomats' were inducted in 2014, as against the eight to fifteen some two decades ago.[42]

In an effort to bring fresh blood into the Indian foreign ministry, the Modi-led administration is encouraging lateral entry. In a deposition before a parliamentary committee in 2015, the then foreign secretary S. Jaishankar stated that the Ministry of External Affairs would fill positions in its Policy Planning Division by recruiting from outside the government.[43] In the last year, there have been structural level changes within the Ministry of External Affairs with a move away from the current pyramid-style structure into a more decentralized one. The aim is to create a series of verticals with each one being headed by a policy director of the rank of additional secretary. This is in addition to the rise in lateral entry and creation of new divisions like the Indo-Pacific division, the emerging technologies division and others.[44]

The reluctance of an entrenched bureaucracy to yield space is the reason why India took so long after 1947 to create additional structures for policymaking. For example, the idea of an advisor to the prime minister on foreign and security policy issues is not new and has been around since Independence. Nehru's appointment of a secretary-general at the Ministry of External Affairs was meant to put in position someone having trust of the prime minister and knowledge of the Indian system.

Nehru rarely sought advice and the secretary-general ended up becoming just another tier in the Ministry of External Affairs bureaucracy created by the British. Indira Gandhi created the position of chairman of the Policy Planning Committee to help her formulate foreign policy, while other prime ministers relied on advisors within the Prime Minister's Office (PMO). However, it took several decades before a national security adviser (NSA) could be appointed and the edifice left in place by the British was subjected to any serious revision.

The appointment of an NSA since 1999 is designed as an institutional bridge between the foreign service, intelligence services and the PMO. Now, the Indian national security apparatus approximates the American model. It comprises the NSA, the National Security Council Secretariat (NSCS), led by the deputy NSA and the National Security Advisory Board (NSAB) that enables unofficial voices on foreign policy to be heard by the government.

India's National Security Council comprises the prime minister, the NSA, the external affairs minister, the defence minister, the finance minister and the vice-chairman of the NITI Aayog. The composition of the National Security Council and the Cabinet Committee on Security is the same, except for the addition of the national security advisor and vice-chairman of the NITI Aayog. It is argued that the Cabinet Committee on Security always has three or four issues to deal with and has to make quick decisions. It does not have time for elaborate presentations or brainstorming on any issue. The National Security Council, on the other hand, is designed to discuss one issue at a time in greater detail. In practice, however, the National Security Council meets infrequently, often only once or twice a year, and spends most of its time dealing with strategic issues tied to nuclear command and control.

Organizationally, the National Security Council comprises the Strategic Policy Group (SPG), the National Security Advisory Board (NSAB) and a secretariat represented by the Joint Intelligence Committee (JIC). The national security apparatus too has undergone change. Not only does the NSA now hold Cabinet ministerial rank but there are three deputy NSAs and one military adviser.[45] The JIC, originally set up in 1948, analyses intelligence data from all intelligence agencies – domestic and foreign, civilian as well as military. It was originally headed by an officer of the Ministry of External Affairs and rarely fulfilled its role of collecting, coordinating, processing and evaluating intelligence inputs reports from all ministries. It was reconstituted in 1965, and comprised both civilian officials and uniformed military. When the National Security Council system was set up, along with the appointment of an NSA, the Joint Intelligence Committee was included within it.

Direct and constant access to the prime minister enables the NSA to be better informed about current events than even the minister of external affairs. The creation of the office of the NSA has resulted in the erosion of authority for both the foreign secretary and the external affairs minister, which is what the permanent civil service feared all along. It has, however, paved the way for better coordination between different branches of government and made decision-making as well as implementation easier. Critics argue, however, that the concept of NSA is better suited for a presidential system of government than a parliamentary one.

～

India and Indians know that the country is a great civilization, one of the oldest ones, and that it deserves to be on the global stage and amongst the great powers. They also want the world to recognize this fact. However, civilizational heritage and greatness do not by themselves make a country a great power. India is unique, India is different and India needs special treatment is also part of this belief. The nation's foreign policy institutions and practices reflect its desire to be a great power and conflicting urges to remain alone. This internal conflict means that the country's foreign policy is malformed and misshapen – it is fully committed in neither direction.

The challenge for Indian foreign policy is reconciling its realism with its idealism. India has serious challenges to its national interests – in the form of a rising China and questions over the reliability of America – and claims to a historical lineage which demand recognition. To marry the two, India must find a way to meaningfully engage with challengers such as China in a manner which is acceptable to the sensibilities and historical character of its people. India must find ways to work with the United States, marshal international institutions, and grow its foreign service corps in a strategy which complements and draws from its specific and unique geography and history.

5

Military and Grand Strategy

INDIA IS ALREADY a global power in the minds of its public and officials, who would like the country to be seated at the global high table by virtue of its special status. The rise of China in recent years has led several major powers, including the United States, to support India's rise as a global player. But as Australian scholar and leading exponent of the English school of international relations, Hedley Bull, pointed out, great powers are identified by 'comparability of status', 'rank in military strength', and the ability and recognition to 'play a part in determining issues that affect the peace and security of the international system as whole'.[1]

India is, by that criteria, still not a great power. Not only is its global status and military rank nowhere comparable with that of the US or China, its reluctance to exercise power globally is also all too apparent. While its soft power enables India to win admiration, it remains unable to coerce others into compliance with its wishes.

Admiration can give way to criticism relatively easily when India is seen as not living up to its ideals – something witnessed after a spate of domestic decisions in the second half of 2019 were seen worldwide as negatively affecting the country's minorities.

India's dilemma is best explained through the following quote from Lewis Carroll's *Alice in Wonderland*. The Cheshire Cat asks Alice, 'Where are you going?' Alice replies, 'Which way should I go?' To which the Cat says, 'That depends on where you are going.' Alice's reply is, 'I don't know.' The Cat then remarks, 'Then it doesn't matter which way you go.'[2] Like Alice, India wants to get somewhere, but does not know which road to take because it has not decided where it wishes to arrive. It can be a pacifist nation, but the global environment does not render that possible. As for being a global power, it requires hard power commitments more than generic statements about 'friendship with all and malice towards none'.

This need to choose a direction is made all the more important by India's size and economic strength. Faced with a geopolitical landscape that is radically different from its early post-Independence years and a rapidly changing global economy, India is confronted with both new foreign policy problems and new tools at its disposal. While any state undergoing such transformation would be faced with important choices, as a country that encompasses 17 per cent of the world's population, Indian choices carry unusual gravity. New Delhi needs to undertake a clear-eyed assessment of its intentions, whether it has the capabilities to achieve them, and if not, what it needs to do to build these capacities.

India's sense of self – its status quo orientation, adoption of non-alignment, and later strategic autonomy and preference for strategic restraint – all emanate from its civilizational heritage. But that heritage turns into historical baggage if it leads to paralytic indecision. Those who argue that India is docile and non-aggressive often fail to recognize that there is a fine line between docility and contentment. India is and will always be defined by its sense of being a 5000-years-old civilization. But it should not be content with what went before, if it sees for itself a major role in the times that lay ahead.

India needs to settle on a grand strategy. Grand strategy refers to how a state marshals its resources to pursue its global interests. For leaders, this means choosing a foreign policy that matches the capacity of the country. This may sound simple enough, but finding the right mix has often been difficult for countries. As American historian John Lewis Gaddis notes, 'If you seek ends beyond your means, then sooner or later you'll have to scale back your ends to fit your means.'[3]

Most countries that seek to become great powers build their military strength and seek to project their defence capabilities aggressively. India is an enigma in that for the majority of Indians, its claim for the global high table comes from its unique civilization, its democracy and pluralism, its soft power, its economic strength, its geostrategic location and, only reluctantly, its military capabilities.

India is a status quo power that has no revisionist ambitions in its neighbourhood or beyond. It seeks to be an Asian and a global player but, unlike China, it lacks ideological or territorial ambitions. India seeks recognition as the regional hegemon, but a pre-eminence that is benevolent and status quo oriented. The *chakravartin* (supreme ruler dispensing justice and maintaining peace) legacy means that for India's power projection, both in its immediate neighbourhood and beyond, is for recognition of status, not for aggrandizement of territory or rewriting of any global norms.

In an earlier book, I had laid out the four major strands in India's contemporary foreign policy: Imperialist Legacy, Messianic Idealism, Realism and Isolationism.[4] All of these must be considered in formulating a grand strategy for India.

The 'Imperialist Legacy' school of thought draws primarily from the most recent pre-Independence experience of decision-making known to India, the period of the British Raj. For this outlook, India is the centre and New Delhi knows best. India's post-Independence policy towards its immediate South Asian neighbours exemplifies this policy best. New Delhi, whether under the British or after, has always believed that India's Central government is best suited to make security decisions.

Just like British officers during the Raj, the advocates of an imperial foreign policy for independent India insist that its South Asian neighbours should agree and accept that India's security needs are theirs as well. Even the idealist Nehru reflected this mindset when it came to the subcontinent and India's adjacent states.[5] His daughter, Indira Gandhi, proclaimed what came to be called the 'Indira Doctrine', reserving primacy for India in making security decisions for its neighbourhood.

'Messianic Idealism', reflecting the mantra of global peace, justice and prosperity, has served as the strong moral component of India's foreign policy, inspired by the moral legacy of ancient Indian thought reiterated during the national struggle under Mahatma Gandhi. Proponents of this perspective believe that India is an example for the world and that the country has the duty to proclaim that example for other nations. This element of Indian exceptionalism often forms part of its view of itself and of the world. Every Indian leader, whether Gandhi or Vivekananda, whether Nehru or Modi, has demanded that the rest of the world accord India stature commensurate to its civilizational contribution.

It is a function of India's Messianic Idealism that the populace, whether the general public or their leaders, have always believed in India's heritage as a great civilization and have anticipated the future as a great power. It is almost as if all India has to do is to wait for the world to accept its greatness. The nation has often claimed the moral high ground in international relations and believed that it has the right to preach to other nations about what policies to adopt. During the Cold War, India used multilateral venues, like the annual United Nations gatherings and the Non-aligned and G-77 groupings for philosophical elocutions on right and wrong that others saw as sermonizing.

At the same time, Indians have had no qualms in anchoring external relations in realism. From ancient times, realist and idealist philosophies have coexisted in India and the post-Independence era is no exception. Indians reflect a cultural ability to entertain seemingly contradictory thoughts parallel to each other. Belief in moral principles did not turn its leaders into pacifists.

Notwithstanding Messianic Idealism, New Delhi has always recognized the importance of hard power. Indian foreign policy has woven into its thread the ideas of ancient Indian thinker Kautilya (also known as Chanakya), who is sometimes referred to as India's Machiavelli. Kautilya argued that a state should be willing to use any of the following four means to achieve its goals: Saam, Daam, Dand and Bhed (persuade, buy, punish and divide).

For all its Messianic Idealism, the Indian state has a Hobbesian view of the world where it can depend only on itself. This explains the strong desire for strategic autonomy, the push for economic autarky and the pursuit of military self-sufficiency. Indian leaders, from Nehru onwards, have recognized the importance of all elements of national power, including military power. The emphasis on economic growth in recent years is also tied to the realization that India's great power ambitions would not be realized without having the means to pay for a strong military, among other things.

While desirous of playing a global role, the country has also been reluctant to be drawn into global issues or ideologies. There is a strong streak of isolationism in India's global outlook. It is one of its many paradoxes – that it wants to be seen as a great power and is still often reluctant to do what is required of most great powers. Ironically, the British were the first power/empire in India that had an outward worldview. Until the advent of the Raj, with the exception of the ancient South Indian Chola dynasty, no other Indian empire had sought to extend itself beyond the subcontinent. Indian philosophers too asserted that would-be emperors or sovereigns must build an empire within the subcontinent and not outside. Thus, to many Indians, external entanglements hark back to the imperial outlook of the Raj, instead of representing a genuinely swadeshi (home-made) worldview.

Modern India has consistently been reluctant to involve itself in international conflicts and blocs, though Nehru's non-alignment ideology was a way of being involved in the world without external commitments that would bind it to specific choices. India was trying to get the best of both worlds. Even now, the country wants to be a permanent member of the UN Security Council without building the power potential possessed by other permanent members. For Indians influenced by isolationism, keeping the nation territorially intact, building a strong economy, eradicating poverty and creating a just society have often been more important than playing an active role in global conflicts or choosing between ideologies and blocs. While India wants to be considered a global power, not just a regional one, there are limits to which it will exercise power.

Understanding India's grand strategy requires first evaluating the foreign policy tools which the country has at its disposal. One of these tools is the military. At first glance, India fields a large and formidable military. It has 1.3 million active duty military personnel, in addition to 2.8 million personnel in reserves. The Indian army has 2100 aircraft and 4400 battle tanks. The Indian air force has 2082 aircraft and the navy possesses 295 vessels.[6] India ranks fourth in the Global Firepower Index of 2019. The country ranks as one of the top five high-spenders on military purchases.[7] But under close inspection, its numerically massive military faces an uncertain future as an effective tool of foreign policy.

According to the 2018 Stockholm International Peace Research Institute (SIPRI) Report, India's defence spending had surpassed that of United Kingdom and France, and stood at US $63.9 billion in 2017.[8] But India only allocated 1.5 per cent of its GDP in 2020 towards the military, the lowest allocation in decades.[9] According to SIPRI, there has been a fall in India's defence spending as a share of government revenue and GDP. Twenty years ago, 14.8 per cent of Indian government revenue was dedicated towards defence, representing 3.5 per cent of GDP. In 2017 only, 9.1 per cent of government revenue was dedicated towards defence, which comprised 2.5 per cent of GDP.[10]

Moreover, 63 per cent of India's increased defence spending goes towards salaries and pensions for its over 1 million personnel on active duty and more than 2 million veterans. Only 14 per cent is allocated for the purchase of state-of-the-art equipment. In March 2018, then vice-chief of army staff, Lt. Gen. Sarath Chand, informed a parliamentary committee that the latest budget 'had dashed our hopes', as the 'marginal increase in budget barely accounts for inflation and does not even cater for the taxes'. This meant that there were 'hardly any funds for new schemes in 2018–19'. Considering that 68 per cent of the army equipment is categorized as 'vintage', and only 8 per cent as 'state-of-the-art', India's military capability is not what it looks like at first glance.[11] It might have a large military, but it is far from being a great power military.

COLONIAL LEGACY AND MILITARY STRATEGY

India's armed forces owe their strength as well as their weakness to the colonial legacy. The Indian army of today originated under the British Raj and its institutional framework was first created under foreign rule. The structure of the British Indian army has continued, with some adjustments, for over seven decades in independent India. But it must not be forgotten that the colonial army was built for the sole purpose of maintaining the British empire, whereas the army of an independent India has to fulfil a national purpose. The British Indian army was key to the empire; it served as cannon fodder across the globe and its core strength during both World Wars.

For leaders like Winston Churchill, India represented a vital British interest that needed defending because of its value in protecting other interests.[12] Echoing Churchill's views, General Claude Auchinleck, then commander of British forces in the Western desert, who later became commander-in-chief of the Indian army and supreme commander of all British forces in India and Pakistan, stated: 'India is vital to our existence. We could still hold India without the Middle East, but we cannot hold the Middle East without India.'[13]

This view of the Indian army as being critical to British global policy led to frequent disagreements between the government in London and the Raj's administration in Delhi. The former sought an army which could be deployed globally, while the latter preferred to use the force to curb domestic unrest and maintain its borders. Both the 1938 and 1939 Committees of Imperial Defence argued that India was 'the most suitable area east of the Mediterranean in which to station reserves for the Middle and Far East'.[14] But the Second World War transformed the British Indian army, which became 'the largest volunteer force' during that war.[15] The British were able to recruit 2.5 million men from the subcontinent 'without resorting to conscription'[16] and to deploy them far from home.

The British Indian army fought the three major Axis powers (Japan, Italy and Germany) from Hong Kong in the east to Italy in the west. It 'displayed tactical virtuosity and organizational flexibility while fighting in varying terrains, from the swamps and jungles of Malaya and Burma to the rocky terrain of Eritrea, the sandy desert of North Africa, and the mountains of central Italy'.[17] The Second World War transformed the British Indian army 'from an Imperial Policing force in 1939 to a modern professional army in 1945'.[18] The British had, since their advent in the subcontinent, managed to create an army comprising primarily of Indians that became powerful enough to defeat all local rulers and serve as the backbone of Britain's worldwide empire.

According to Stephen Rosen, the British 'accomplished this by separating their armies from Indian society, not by changing Indian social structures. Having conquered portions of India, the British were then able to institute changes that did have a substantial impact on the indigenous social structures'.[19] The British separated the army from society, and introduced to the subcontinent's soldiers stability of pay, uniforms, promotions based on length of service and a pension system.[20] The army was downsized after the end of the Second World War, but on the eve of Independence, it still consisted of 3,91,000 men, and a relatively smaller navy (8700 personnel) and air force (13,000 personnel).[21]

India's national struggle had a dramatic bearing on independent India's relationship with its military. The early leaders of the national movement shaped not only the struggle for independence but also defined the contours of independent India's policies. The modern nation's view of the role of the military, and its defence policies since Independence, can best be understood by examining the views of the Indian liberals in the early twentieth century. They were especially against the high military expenditures of the army that led to the imposition of taxes on the public and demanded that more money be spent on social upliftment.

Although Indians had little say in policymaking at the time, the formation of the Indian National Congress in 1885 had created a permanent organizational structure for Indians to discuss and debate political issues, including views on international developments. Soon after its formation, the Congress started making pronouncements on all aspects of social, economic, foreign and defence policy through resolutions, notwithstanding the fact that control of all these fields remained firmly in British hands. The Congress demanded that Indians be able to decide the country's policies, whether domestic or foreign, and this included defence policy.

From the Congress's perspective, the British Indian army sustained the empire, whether by suppressing riots or fighting wars. Leaders argued not only for the right to decide where the army should be deployed, but whether it should be sent overseas at all. These leaders resented the use of Indian soldiers to perpetuate British imperialism. In 1903, liberal leader Gopal Krishna Gokhale stated during a speech on the Budget, 'Indian finance is virtually at the mercy of military considerations and no well-sustained or vigorous effort by the state on an adequate scale for the material advancement or the moral progress of the people is possible while our revenues are liable to be appropriated in an ever-increasing proportion for military services.'[22]

The Congress was, in principle, against involvement of Indian troops in any imperialist war or adventure. Still, during the First World War, the Congress supported the allied war effort with medical units and military volunteers. Indian leaders had hoped that the Britain would grant India Dominion status after the war in return for the support provided. They were, however, disappointed as the Raj showed little gratitude for India's support and sacrifices during the Great War. In the subsequent years, the use of the Indian army for imperial objectives became a source of persistent disagreement between India's liberals and the British.

At the end of the First World War, an 'Army in India Committee', led by Lord Esher, spoke of the importance of imperial duties in

Indian defence. In response, a fifteen-member committee of the legislative assembly, led by Sir Tej Bahadur Sapru, tabled a report that argued that the 'purpose of army in India must be held to be defence of India against external aggression and the maintenance of internal peace ... Military resources of India should not be developed in a manner suited to imperial necessities.'[23]

Successive resolutions passed by the Congress over the years repudiated the aggressive policies of the Raj and reassured foreign countries, especially India's neighbours, that upon attainment of self-government, the country's foreign policy would be one of friendship towards all. A resolution passed at the Madras session of the Congress in 1927 declared: 'The people of India have no quarrels with their neighbours and desire to live in peace with them and assert their right to determine whether or not they will take part in any war.'[24]

As the Second World War approached, Congress resolutions opposed Fascism and Nazism: criticizing Japan's aggression against Manchuria, Italy's annexation of Abyssinia and Germany's dismemberment of Czechoslovakia. Not only did the Congress pass resolutions but it also raised funds and sent aid for the Abyssinian and Spanish loyalist causes. As foreign secretary of the Congress party, Nehru visited Spain, Czechoslovakia, Russia and even Chongqing in China.[25]

The Congress's own struggle for self-determination drove many of their foreign policy aspirations. At the 1938 Haripura session of the Congress, a resolution was passed that the 'people of India desire to live in peace and friendship with their neighbours and with all other countries and for this purpose wish to remove all causes of conflict between them. Striving for their own freedom and independence as a nation, they wish to respect the freedom of others and to build up their strength on the basis of international cooperation and goodwill.' This desire for peace and mutual self-determination created a clash with the British Indian army's stated purpose as an appendage of colonial rule.[26]

A few months later, in September 1939, the Congress Working Committee issued a statement declaring: 'If the war is to defend the status quo, imperialist possessions, colonies, vested interests and privilege then India can have nothing to do with it. If, however, the issue is democracy and a world order based on democracy then India is intensely interested in it.'[27] The Congress steadfastly opposed the British war effort and most Congress leaders spent the war years in prison or in exile.

The war strengthened and accelerated the Indian independence movement. The 1942 Quit India Resolution passed by the Congress party in Bombay championed the cause of a world federation pointing out that 'the future peace, security and ordered progress of the world demand a world federation of free nations, as on no other basis can the problems of the modern world be solved. Such a world federation will ensure the freedom of its constituent nations, the prevention of exploitation by one nation over another, the protection of national minorities, the advancement of all backward areas and peoples and the pooling of the world's resources for the common good of all.'[28]

Non-cooperation of the Congress with the British during the war years created space for the Muslim League's demand for the partition of India and had the effect of forcing the British to reconsider their belief in holding on to India indefinitely. By the time the war ended, Indian independence became inevitable. In 1945, though not yet an independent country, India was represented at the San Francisco Conference and signed the United Nations Charter. Two years later, the last British Viceroy partitioned the country into the two dominions of India and Pakistan, transferred power to native governments, and left the subcontinent. The new India inherited a strong commitment to civilian supremacy and anti-imperialism, which had been at the heart of the national struggle for freedom.

After Independence, Indian nationalist leaders sought to reform the army in order to ensure civilian control and restructured civil–military relations. As a result, independent India is one of the few postcolonial countries that was not subject to coups or dominance by powerful military factions. Srinath Raghavan notes that instead of giving the British 'credit for a system of military subordination to civilian authority' it is India's liberal nationalist leaders 'who identified the fundamental flaw in the British system and proposed an alternative – one that was eventually adopted by the Republic'.[29] Indian leaders adopted symbolic and real measures to signal a shift from prevalent attitudes under the Raj, when British men in uniform dominated decision-making.

Soon after the transfer of power in 1947, the commander-in-chief of the Indian armed forces no longer remained part of the Cabinet and instead would have to report to the civilian defence minister. In 1955, the office of commander-in-chief was downgraded to the chief of the army staff and was made equal to the other two service chiefs. The official residence of the British commander-in-chief – Teen Murti Bhavan – became the residence of the first prime minister, Jawaharlal Nehru. It was turned into a museum after Nehru's death. The warrant of precedence for official protocol was also changed to highlight civilian ascendancy.

Indian nationalist leaders also sought changes to the recruitment and training policies inherited from the British Raj. They viewed the 'martial races' policy as well as caste and religion-based recruitment to the army as 'incompatible with their hopes for a new secular nation'.[30] For these leaders, democracy could not 'function in this country satisfactorily unless the basis of recruitment for the army is radically changed'.[31] These priorities had been worked out by Indian nationalist leaders in their minds well before Independence.

On 12 September 1946, soon after he took over as minister for external affairs in the pre-Independence Cabinet (Executive Council) of Viceroy Lord Wavell, Nehru sent a long letter to the commander-in-chief and defence secretary demanding large-scale reforms to the Indian army. He sought a change in the recruitment policies, wanted more Indian officers at higher ranks, and more representation from all communities and provinces across India.

At that time 'not one of the four Lieutenant Generals or twenty Major Generals was Indian'.[32] This process of de-racialization was important for creating an army, which truly reflected the character of India and could act with legitimacy.

American political scientist Steven Wilkinson points out in his 2015 book *Army and Nation: The Military and Indian Democracy since Independence* that European colonial empires adopted a policy of building local armies 'populated disproportionately by minorities: a largely Punjabi and Pashtun army in India, a northerner-dominated army in colonial Togo, Ghana and Nigeria, a Sunni-dominated army in Iraq, an army of Karens, Chins and Kachins rather than the Burmese majority in colonial Burma' and 'recruitment of Ambonese and Minahassans rather than the majority Javanese in Dutch-controlled Indonesia'.[33] The British had used minorities in order to enforce a system of divided rule over their colonies, which allowed the British to exert increased influence over local people by exploiting sectarian tensions.

During decolonization, this pattern made states fragile and politically unstable. Minority-controlled militias took over many of these countries, as most postcolonial states fell under military rule. India was a notable exception. It can be argued that Nehru's concern and preparation for civilian control of the military paid off. In response to his letter, the then commander-in-chief, Claude Auchinleck, reassured Nehru that the British Indian army was strictly subordinated to civilian rule.

'The Armed forces of India,' Auchinleck wrote to Nehru, the Vice-President of the Viceroy's Executive Council (in effect the prime minister), 'understand very well that they exist solely to carry out the policy of the government which is in power, and that officers, whether British or Indian, and men must not allow their political views, if they have any, to influence them in any way in the execution of their duty.'[34] When the first Indian commander-in-chief, General K.M. Cariappa, took over in January 1949 'he immediately sent out orders and made several public statements warning against entanglement in politics – "Politics in the army is a poison. Keep off it", he told his officers' while stressing the importance of civilian supremacy.[35]

India's early leaders saw making the Indian army genuinely representative as one of the foremost military priorities of their day. Over time, India implemented changes within the army and reduced the proportion of ethnic Punjabis in the military's ranks. In 1939, Punjabis were 54 per cent of all troops and 60 per cent of Indian troops. After Independence, Punjabis comprised only 32 per cent of infantry.[36] Only one army chief was a Punjabi between 1947 and 1977 (Gen. Pran Nath Thapar, 1961–62).[37] Still, India has laboured to align its pluralistic philosophical character with the realities of its armed forces. In his memoirs, former army chief J.N. Chaudhuri wrote that 'despite this diversity of background and culture, each one of us was very conscious that we were Indians first and anything else a long way second'.[38]

POST-INDEPENDENCE MILITARY STRATEGY

Although India succeeded in diluting the influence of the colonial era in civil–military relations, it did not manage to evolve a military strategy strikingly different from its past. The Indian army's deployment for imperial objectives overseas bred resistance to sending troops outside the subcontinent. That, coupled with ancient India's reluctance to use force beyond its borders, helped determine independent India's military outlook. Reticence and restraint, which are seen as Indian civilizational traits, came to be reflected in its foreign and defence policies.

According to Stephen P. Cohen, doyen of South Asian studies in the United States and author of multiple books on India, and Sunil Dasgupta, director of University of Maryland's Political Science Program, 'One of the most remarkable attributes of India as an independent nation has been its longstanding restraint in military strategy. Reticence in the use of force as an instrument of state policy has been the dominant political condition for Indian thinking on the military, including military modernization. From the initial delay in sending troops to defend Kashmir in 1948 to the twenty-four-year hiatus in testing nuclear weapons, India has used force mainly in response to grave provocation and as an unwelcome last resort.'[39]

There is an ancient legacy of anti-aggression against states or cultures outside of the subcontinent. According to philosopher K. Satchidananda Murty no ancient Indian writer, whether realist or idealist, advocated or contemplated the extension of Indian culture outside of India by force. In a sense, the country's ancient philosophers were isolationists and 'there was a kind of Monroe doctrine towards states outside India, forbidding aggressive wars on states or cultures outside of the subcontinent. Even though ancient Indian monarchs sought to become chakravartin, the boundaries of his rule were limited to the geographically and culturally defined region of the subcontinent.

Ancient Indians did not like exercising power beyond their shores and could not philosophically accept others occupying their land or ruling over them. When Nehru said, 'India's foreign policy is grounded in the ancient tradition and culture of this country',[40] he also suggested that India's opposition to Western imperialism could be traced back to the ancient Indian world view.

For the British, India was at the heart of their global empire, the jewel in the British monarch's crown. It provided both economic and military wherewithal, as well as manpower for sustaining the empire in Africa, East Asia, the Pacific islands and the Caribbean. As historian Lawrence James points out, for over a century, the Indian Empire had 'underpinned' Britain's global power status by providing it with 'markets, prestige and muscle'.[41] India's founding fathers, however, had a different vision for the country's engagement with the rest of the world.

For Nehru, India, as one of two main Asian civilizations, would symbolize the rise of the continent. A few months before Independence, in March 1947, he championed the Asian Relations Conference that was held in Delhi and was attended by delegates from many parts of Asia, even from countries that were still under colonial rule. Nehru believed that India had been forced to participate in imperial adventures against its will and that independent India would not send its troops out of the country. This reluctance to send its troops, except under UN mandate, is a legacy of a colonial past in addition to being influenced by its ancient isolationist history.

India's classical world view was challenged and changed by its colonial past. The Raj left an entire infrastructure of institutions and personnel, which were inherited by the Indian state. In addition, the country's leaders and strategists were also bequeathed the world view of the Raj that went beyond looking only at the immediate periphery of South Asia, and instead sought India's influence from the Gulf to Southeast Asia and even beyond. The role for the Indian empire envisaged by London left an indelible mark on New Delhi's post-Independence strategic thinking. At the end of the colonial era, there were thus some Indians like K.M. Panikkar, Indian statesman, editor and historian, who championed a larger role for India.

It is under British colonial influence that India's neighbourhood began to be seen as stretching from the Gulf and east coast of Africa to Southeast Asia. Indian strategists often seem to agree with former ICS officer Sir Olaf Caroe's assertion that it is 'impossible' to visualize the Gulf unless that prism includes India, which 'stands at the center of the Ocean that bears its name'.[42] Modern India has always seen itself as a key player in the Middle East. Even before Independence, Nehru built close ties with his peers in Egypt and Turkey, and reached out to Arab and Persian politicians and intellectuals.

However, the relationship that modern India sought with its neighbours and the Middle East was different from how the Raj perceived them. For example, in 1950, when India and Afghanistan signed a treaty, the tribes on both sides of the Durand Line asked if India would continue British Raj policy of subsidy and arms but India declined the offer, allowing Pakistan to sort out relations with the tribes.

Further, while India maintained diplomatic and economic relations with the Gulf states, for many decades, it did not seek to maintain any military relationship. This has changed today with close defence relations and military exercises with countries like Oman and UAE.[43]

India's current role as a regional heavyweight was not always the case. During the two centuries of British rule, Indians had no control over economic, foreign or military policies. Even during the two World Wars, when thousands of Indian soldiers fought as part of the British army around the world, they served as cannon fodder rather than as decision-makers. That experience has led to an Indian reluctance to send its troops abroad under multinational command.

United Nations Peacekeeping Missions have been an exception to this rule. Peacekeeping under the aegis of the United Nations has a moral dimension and it fulfils India's desire to play a global role in addition to demonstrating the country's credentials in helping less fortunate countries. India still insists that its presence in global conflicts remain separate from imperial struggles. It refused to send troops for the wars in Korea (1950 to 1953) or Vietnam (1955 to 1975), or for the first Gulf War in 1991.

Many people were surprised when during the US-led war in Iraq in 2003, the Indian parliament and Cabinet debated an American request for the participation of Indian troops. India did not join the war in the end, but that it even debated such an issue was for many a first and showed the changes in how Indians, and others, view the nation's global role.[44] But India's reluctance to send troops outside its borders does not extend to its immediate neighbourhood.

To demonstrate that India sees its backyard differently from how it sees the rest of the world, the country sent troops to Sri Lanka in 1987–90, to enforce a ceasefire between the government and the Tamil rebel guerillas, and to Maldives in 1988, against a coup attempt. India has also fought four wars against Pakistan, including the 1971 war that resulted in the creation of Bangladesh. In the Indian view, the immediate neighbourhood is still part of the subcontinent and therefore is India's arena for maintaining security. But if the country is to be a global power, it would have to start thinking in terms of preparing military strategy that covers much more than its immediate neighbourhood.

In most countries, especially those that seek to play a bigger role in their region or the globe, there is a sustained focus on long-term defence planning. The focal institute is normally the defence ministry with both civilian and military officials, as well as outside experts being part of this effort. India's Ministry of Defence is often referred to as the ministry of defence acquisitions and purchases, as the main action that it undertakes is purchase (or the lack of it) of equipment.

Comparing the Ministry of Defence and Ministry of External Affairs, we see a clear difference in priorities by successive prime ministers. For seventeen years, Nehru was the minister of external affairs and since then, his successors have taken direct interest in international affairs even when they have had senior colleagues as external affairs ministers. While Indian prime ministers have temporarily held the defence portfolio, it has never been for long, as it has never been one that they have relished holding.

Defence has traditionally been viewed as one part of foreign policy, and the only aspect of defence that the government has paid attention to is salaries and pensions of soldiers and officers. Upgradation of military infrastructure, modernizing military equipment, constant training and retraining of defence personnel, factoring in newer technologies, and peer competition have not been the priority and not much attention has been paid to them until quite recently.

Under Nehru, the military and intelligence apparatus were treated as tactical executors of policy and kept away from decision-making. This ensured civilian supremacy, but did not create vertical and horizontal integration in planning for national security. The Ministry of Defence, manned by civilians, kept the three uniformed services – the army, navy and air force – out of policymaking. Most of the proposals considered by the highest defence body – the Defence Committee of the Cabinet – dealt with procurement proposals for necessary supplies or issues relating to soldiers' emoluments, not with real strategy.

At the time of Independence in 1947, the Indian military's officer corps was unacquainted with national security management. The British started giving commissions to Indians as officers in the military only in 1920, having reserved officers' ranks exclusively for persons of Caucasian descent until then. This meant that the Indian officers' corps was only twenty-seven years old at the time of Independence. India had inherited an army from the Raj, but with inexperienced junior generals – some of whom were excellent field commanders, but lacked proficiency in leading a larger force. Only three Indian generals had experience of commanding a brigade during the Second World War. Nehru refused to retain British generals, pushing Indians into senior command positions without adequate preparation.

The situation was exacerbated when generalist civil servants, with little knowledge of security issues and international relations, came to dominate the Ministry of Defence. Diplomats at the Ministry of External Affairs soon insinuated themselves into all aspects of national security. In an interview, a former head of the defence department noted that for decades even the introductory chapter of the annual report of the defence ministry was traditionally written by the foreign secretary, not the defence secretary.[45] Thinking on defence and national security were the prerogatives of civil servants and diplomats, not of the uniformed military. Moreover, while Nehru was interested in economic planning, defence planning really started only after 1964, under American insistence against the backdrop of India's military defeat in 1962 at the hands of China.[46]

Long-term planning is critical for defence and that is something that has been missing in India. Most countries that seek to become great powers have, over the years, created expertise in long-range planning. The United States has the national security council and empowers the heads of executive agencies, such as the Secretary of State, to engage in full-spectrum planning for long-term strategy. Similarly, China's ascendancy is backed by its planning infrastructure; its 'Made in China 2025' initiative,[47] and Belt and Road Initiative provide two examples of policies guided by long-term strategic plans. India has traditionally not invested in this. The Policy, Planning and Research division (PPR) of the external affairs ministry traditionally served as a resting place for bureaucrats, not the place for planning. That has changed in recent years, but still has a long way to go. The Ministry of Defence, which in most countries is where grand strategy is undertaken, has been slow to understand this.

Despite nominally understanding the need for strategic planning, India has failed to put words into action. Reforms recommended by committees on Indian strategic planning are routinely ignored.[48] If India wishes to chart a course for the country, it needs to actively dedicate itself towards strategic planning and be willing to pursue reforms which may sting in the short term.

Over the years, India has tried to modernize its strategic planning with internal audits, to varied success. In 1998, the K.C. Pant Committee was appointed to figure out a national security management system. The committee's recommendations eventually led to the creation of the National Security Council (NSC), Strategic Policy Group (SPG) and the National Security Advisory Board (NSAB). These groups began the process of formalizing India's long-term military and strategic planning.[49]

Further efforts at planning were made in 1999 with the Kargil Reform Committee, which set out to modernize India's planning structure after the Kargil War with Pakistan. It concluded that India needed a more formal planning infrastructure and to put an end to 'ad hoc' strategic vision. Yet, much of the Kargil Committee's findings are still classified and thus cannot inform the continued public discussion over defence reform. And despite these efforts, the country's strategic planning is still generally understood as reactionary and plagued with a short-term mentality.

The Indian parliament has long understood some part of the need for reform and successive committees of parliament have spoken out for the need for reorganization, modernization and upgradation. As early as 1958, the Estimates Committee of Parliament, headed by Balwantrai Mehta, issued a report on the 'Organization of the

Ministry of Defence and Services Headquarters', stating, 'The existing system was inefficient, not [made] for economy or speedy decision-making, ridden by considerable duplication with various segments functioning in a compartmentalized manner instead of moving jointly towards achieving common objectives.'[50]

The Mehta committee noted the 'drastic imbalance in the distribution of responsibility and authority' between the Ministry of Defence, and the various services, and recommended more delegation of power to the latter. It is ironic that five decades after this report, one could still make the same observation. The 1958 Committee's recommendation was to propose the establishment of the British council system that would result in the 'amalgamation of the finance and accounts systems to bring about economy and efficiency.'[51]

The 1962 India–China war provides insights into the world of Indian strategic planning and little seems to have changed significantly since then. After the military defeat, where Indian soldiers were largely routed by the Chinese, the government commissioned the Henderson Brooks–Bhagat report to study why it had lost to its neighbour. Though classified for years, large sections of the report were recently leaked and made available to the public. The report was scathing, indicting Indian intelligence as 'haphazardly collected, badly processed, unimaginatively put across and inefficiently disseminated.'[52] Overarchingly, it highlights a military posture which was woefully underinformed by a serious strategic architecture. Instead, individual personalities and visions dominated, without institutional checks or guidance.

In 1999, after the Kargil conflict, a review of India's national security was undertaken under the Kargil Review Committee, headed by one of India's leading strategists, K. Subrahmanyam. The Kargil Review Committee issued a stinging indictment of the system when it stated, 'An objective assessment of the last 52 years will show that the country is lucky to have scraped through various national security threats without too much damage, except in 1962. The country can no longer afford such ad hoc functioning.

The Committee therefore recommends that the entire gamut of national security management and apex decision-making and the structure and interface between the Ministry of Defence and the Armed Forces headquarters be comprehensively studied and reorganized.'[53]

The committee recommended reforms in all areas, from the country's nuclear deterrence to management of national security, intelligence reforms and border management. The committee also spoke of the need for a higher defence budget, the need for an integrated manpower policy, more funding for defence research and development, better understanding and use of air power, more investment in counter-insurgency operations and much better media relations.[54]

GRAND STRATEGY AND STRATEGIC CULTURE

India's sense of self and threat perception are tied into how its populace has traditionally viewed power, what is the country's role, what should it do, and more importantly, what should India not do in the world. As a subcontinent, protected by the Himalayas to the north and the Indian Ocean to the south, India's perception of strategic culture and sense of security has always been different and somewhat inward looking.

The question, 'Does India have a tradition of grand strategy or not?' has always led to diverging views. There are those who argue that it has lacked strategic culture and others who trace the country's grand strategy back to the ancient era. Thus, India's vision of its place in the world, its historic civilization, the writings of its ancient philosophers and actions of its medieval kings, as well as the policies of its Western colonizers has bequeathed a uniquely Indian strategic culture.

According to critics, for several years after Independence, India's leaders saw external relations as being mainly about diplomatic stature, not about competing interests and strategies. Nehru waxed eloquent about India's special position in the world, but as

Subrahmanyam points out, 'the much-needed synergy for effective national security management', involving interaction of different components of the security establishment, was totally absent.[55]

Most of the institutions currently engaged in shaping India's foreign policy are built on the edifice of the British Raj. They function with varying degrees of efficacy in different situations, but cannot be said to represent an Indian strategic ethos. K. Subrahmanyam argued that the key reason for this was the absence of a strategic culture from the pre-British era. Prior to British rule, various princely states focused on their own security in an ad hoc manner and there was little emphasis on global strategy. Since the princes saw a threat only from one another, they did not care to think about a strategy for the defence of the subcontinent. During British rule, the Raj framed its interests in terms of what benefited the empire and no Indian took part, or was allowed to be involved, in formulation of strategy.[56]

According to Subrahmanyam, while Nehruvian non-alignment was a grand strategy, Indians did not 'think through the strategic consequences of non-alignment'. He goes on to argue that after 1947, India saw itself as a status quo–oriented, non-expansionist power. It, therefore, did not have the 'paranoid sense of insecurity' that leads to serious strategic planning.[57]

The country's early leaders assumed that if India does not threaten others, others will leave it alone and refrain from threatening its security. In addition, civilian control of the military under domestic policy–oriented politicians prevented the development of a large military–industrial complex. India was thus denied the post-Independence institutional structure that could encourage strategic thought, which, in its essence, is about national security. More than strategic security, it is national pride that defined India's external affairs policy in the immediate aftermath of Independence.

High-sounding oratory has been a strong feature of India's approach to international relations. The 2003–04 annual presidential addresses to parliament talked about India forging ahead in the world by 'drawing on the strength of our civilizational and historical ties with countries across the globe'. Ignoring the large number of the poor in the country, the huge gap in GDP and other indicators with China, and the serious lag in maintaining a modern military force, India's president declared the twenty-first century as 'India's century', and insisted that strategic autonomy and independent decision-making were the hallmark of Indian foreign policy.[58]

Using poetic language, the then President K.R. Narayanan described India's foreign policy as 'alchemy' of 'the thirst for Independence, the desire to safeguard our national interest, the desire to pursue peace and cooperation in our environment and in the world as a whole'.[59] In reality, however, India's approach was one of maintaining the status quo, while, in the words of a retired Indian official, 'preaching to others what we don't practice ourselves'.[60] Over the years, critics point out, the country has generally only reacted to whatever the rest of the world does, instead of taking many initiatives. Leaders and diplomats take pride in India being 'one of the few countries that is able to talk on reasonably friendly terms with everybody in the world',[61] a reflection of policies designed to muddle through, instead of charting a new course.

Certainly, India's civilizational heritage must bring with it some sort of common understanding of strategic culture. Arvind Gupta, former deputy national security adviser, argues that the high degree of consistency in India's 'policies, views and behaviour', irrespective of change in governments over the last seventy years, 'indicates the presence of a shared strategic culture'.[62] According to academic and analyst Kanti Bajpai, while Indians may not refer to it as 'grand strategy' when they talk about 'national security', that is what they mean – in effect, India has a unique way of practising grand strategy. 'Indians do indeed think about grand strategy even if they don't use the term "grand strategy" to describe what they are doing and that at any time India does have a set of policies that in aggregate amounts to a grand strategy.'[63]

For Bajpai, Indian grand strategy comprised six schools that he divides into three major and three minor schools, with some overlapping amongst them. The three major schools are Nehruvianism, Neoliberalism and Hyperrealism. The three minor schools are Marxism, Hindutva and Gandhianism. Noting that no one in the Indian strategic community or foreign policy and security apparatus would describe Indian foreign policy along these lines, he argues that they in fact define India's grand strategy. Yet, it would be equally difficult to say that Indians hold no differences about strategic culture. If strategy is the convergence of capabilities and ideals, then the diverging ideas of India must be associated with diverging strategic visions. And indeed, we can see that Hindutva and Indian liberalism offer different nuances to the discussion of strategy.

For Hindutva, rivals are seen in civilizational terms – Christian West, the Muslim World and China.[64] Further, 'civilization states are seen as both external adversaries and internal "fifth" column enemies'.[65] For Hindutva proponents 'the more powerful civilizations and states will always use whatever means at their disposal including violence to maintain their position in the world'. 'Violence has to be used to achieve complete victory over an opponent.'[66] In earlier years, Hindutva proponents viewed Pakistan and China as the main threats. Contemporary Hindutva proponents 'argue that India should be internally resilient particularly in a cultural sense, that it should be militarily strong against Pakistan and China but should also attempt to use its cultural capital with both to improve relations and that it should be wary of the US without becoming anti-American'.[67]

The philosophical conviction in the power of reason and pre-eminence of the individual inform the preference of Indian liberals towards cooperation and membership in the comity of nations. By contrast, at the heart of the Gandhian worldview 'is the individual and his conscience'. 'Truth and nonviolence' must guide the individual.[68] For Gandhians, the greatest threat is the industrial civilization, and violence is anathema. Finally, for Gandhians while India must defend itself, its attitude towards Pakistan and China 'must be negotiation and principled compromise'.[69] While both groups share many common values, they also differ in important ways.

Of course, identifying a problem is easier than constructing a solution. Real reforms to create strategic infrastructure are difficult and costly. Part of the problem is a lack of starting resources and institutions, which could guide the development of grand strategy. In a 2013 piece titled 'Know Your Strength', the *Economist* argued that as a wannabe superpower, India showed a lack of major investment in strategic culture. The article noted that 'strategic defence reviews like those that take place in America, Britain and France, informed by serving officers and civil servants but led by politicians, are unknown in India. The armed forces regard the Ministry of Defence as woefully ignorant on military matters, with few of the skills needed to provide support in areas such as logistics and procurement (they also resent its control over senior promotions).'[70] Instead, Indian strategy consists largely of piecemeal responses to events as they occur, without any overarching strategy.

This ad hoc style of planning has created an attitude towards grand strategy which is insular and not forward thinking. Institutional reform will require the cultivation of a more long-term style of thinking and a more careful assessment of Indian interests. The challenge of strategic planning will be framed by the increasingly competitive geopolitical landscape which India is a part of. From the previous chapter, we know of at least one threat that this ad hoc style of planning will be insufficient to address. The rise of China situates one of the world's most powerful countries as a rival on India's doorstep. China's rise is hardly a single conflict; instead it is a clash between two civilizations which intersects on political, social, security and economic levels. As such, rather than individual policies or quick fixes, the contest with China is fundamentally a question of grand strategy.

More than any other single factor, China's ascendancy presents problems which cannot be remedied with merely tactical fixes – new weapons or augmented troop deployments. China demonstrates a full spectrum of threats to India: troops on the border, access to international finance and regional instability. As such, India's response must include a full suite of responses on all levels. These are issues which require a clear and concerted effort at strategic planning. The country needs to develop infrastructure and institutions which can choose between the many avenues for action in containing China, and harmonize the efforts of economic, political and military actions.

The same factors which contributed to the success of the non-alignment doctrine make its continued future applications infeasible. As the world changes around India, the pillars which uphold New Delhi's grand strategy rest on shakier and shakier foundations. Non-alignment highlighted the importance of legitimacy, clear national aspirations, and proportional tactics to achieve those goals. But shifts in the geopolitical landscape threaten to alter all three of those principles. Like Alice speaking to the Cheshire Cat, India needs to pick a direction in which to move.

Conclusion

'Oh! would some power the gift give us,
To see ourselves as others see us.'[1]

Robert Burns

IN JULY 2019, while presenting the annual Budget for the Central government, Finance Minister Nirmala Sitharaman, chose to carry the Budget documents in a '*bahikhata*' (traditional Indian accounting ledger) instead of carrying them in a 'red box,' as previous ministers had done. The finance minister arriving in parliament with Budget documents in a red briefcase is one of the many British traditions maintained by India after Independence.

Sitharaman's bahikhata was a fourfold red cloth, with the Indian national emblem on it. It was wrapped with a ribbon. Minister of State for Finance Anurag Thakur explained that the abandoning of the briefcase would somehow demonstrate that India was 'moving in the direction to becoming a superpower'. According to him, '*Angrez chaley gaye, angrezon ki paramparyein bhi chali jani chahiye* (The British have left; their traditions should also come to an end).'[2]

The notion that replacing the British briefcase, known as the ministerial 'red box,' with a traditional Indian ledger is somehow a step in the direction of becoming a superpower is more than just naive. It demonstrates confusion about India's desire to be a great global power and the means to get there. Instead of focusing on building economic and military strength, the country's leaders seem to believe that symbols and slogans (like bahikhata and an international day of yoga) demonstrate India's great power, or soon to be superpower status.

Indians, both laypeople and leaders, believe that the nation deserves to be on the global stage as an important and powerful actor. The US, Japan, Europe and Australia, along with many other countries, are also rooting for India's rise. This is an advantage. At no other time in history have so many countries wanted another country to rise to big power status and play more of a role on the global stage. But there is insufficient reflection in India on what holds it back. There is an assumption that a 5000-year-old history of unbroken ancient tradition is somehow enough to make a nation a great power. But if that had been the case, other ancient civilizations would have an equal claim to great power status.

There is a strong belief among Indians, irrespective of where they might stand on the ideological spectrum, that there is a unique way of doing things in the country, and that their way will somehow and in some way overcome any challenges that may arise. While belief in a sense of exceptionalism is important, and predictable, for a five-millennia-old civilization, it can also impede self-awareness. To be a great power in this day and age requires not a harking back to past glory but acquiring and developing contemporary instruments of national power.

The experience of others in expanding their economies and reducing poverty should guide Indians in their path ahead. Great Britain 'took 58 years to double per capita output (after 1780), the US took 47 years (after 1840), Japan took 30 years (after 1965), South Korea took thirteen years (after 1970) and China ten years (after 1978).'[3] In Indonesia, the percentage of people below the poverty line fell from 58 in 1972 to 17 in 1982. In Malaysia, it fell from 37 per cent in 1973 to 14 in 1987. In Thailand, it fell from 49 per cent in 1962 to 26 per cent in 1986. In Singapore, it dropped from 34 per cent in 1972 to 10 per cent in 1982.[4] India, on the other hand, has been slow in implementing economic reform and reaping the benefits that come from it.

There are many examples of economic transformation for India to emulate. Japanese political leaders worked with the business sector to develop their economy. In twenty-three years, from 1950 to 1973, Japan's gross national product (GNP – the total value of goods and services produced in a year) 'expanded by an average annual rate of more than 10 per cent with only a few minor downturns'. Japan also invested in technology and became an export-oriented economy.[5] From the 1980s, China shifted from self-sufficiency to an export orientation.[6]

According to American historian Doris Goodwin, in the United States during the Second World War, '17 million new civilian jobs were created, industrial productivity increased by 96 per cent, and corporate profits after taxes doubled'. This expanded productivity 'ensured a remarkable supply of consumer goods to the people as well'. Thus by 1944, 'as a result of wage increases and overtime pay, real weekly wages before taxes in manufacturing were 50 per cent higher than in 1939. The war also created entire new technologies, industries and associated human skills. The war brought full employment and a fairer distribution of income.'[7]

India's slow and halting progress is the cumulative result of several factors. At Independence, its founding leaders understood the need for social, economic and political transformation, but sought to retain a link with the past. Over the decades, India built a vibrant democracy, an open pluralist society and a mixed economy with insufficient investment in its military and defence. While there were many who thought India would play a role in global security during the 1950s, that ambition was all but abandoned in later decades.

From the 1990s onward, India's economic reforms once again rekindled the nation's promise. The end of the Cold War and collapse of the Soviet Union, the growing India–US relationship, and the economic and military rise of China have only increased the number of those around the world – and in India – who believe that this time round the country will rise and achieve its promise. But key policy changes have remained on the drawing board. India has indeed moved forward, but its accomplishments have fallen short of its greater potential. India takes several steps forward, only to stop and argue with itself every few years about whether to advance into the next century or turn back towards its magical past.

Over the past half century, over a billion people have been lifted out of extreme poverty due to sustained economic growth.[8] In India, extreme poverty has declined gradually and is set to reach an all-time low of 15 million by 2022.[9] Much of the rise in living standards in India can be attributed to economic reforms and an increase in labour productivity brought by the globalized diffusion of technology.[10] For India, the history of economic liberalization has been associated with cheaper goods and services, higher quality products and economic growth.

A stronger middle class and a more robust economy create new avenues to pursue New Delhi's strategic interests. Such changes alter the profile of options available to the government, which can now afford more expensive spending projects and investments. But there is cause for concern over India's long-term ability to grow to the point where it can help shoulder the burden of global challenges. The country's short-term macroeconomic situation seems to be moving towards slowing growth. Experts have noted a 'clear evidence of economic activity losing traction', and the growth numbers from early 2020 point towards a slow growth rate of 2.5 per cent – far below the 7 per cent required for rapid economic expansion.

Labour force participation, especially among women, remains low, which is a cause for concern in a developing economy such as India's. Here, traditional patriarchal mores serve as a brake on higher potential productivity. Religious, ethnic and caste conflicts are another distraction from higher growth rates. At the same time, that growth is slowing down; many experts worry that lacklustre political will, parochial incentives and too much bureaucracy will prevent India from mustering the serious policies necessary to catapult the country forward.

There are strong reasons to be hopeful of India's future, provided economic reform and modernization can be speeded up. A strong democratic foundation provides the political stability and ability to adapt to changing circumstances, which many other developing nations lack. A burgeoning youth population promises a demographic dividend, so long as India can muster the educational resources to raise the human capital levels.

China's slowing economic growth also provides the opportunity for foreign direct investment and manufacturing, which had traditionally gravitated towards China to migrate to India. If it can muster the political will to reform its industrial and investment policies, it could stand to receive a windfall from the producers moving out of China, where higher wages are increasingly deterring investment. Economic globalization also carries implications for the Indian psyche, and the legitimacy of New Delhi's strategic doctrine. Countries that experience the vast economic changes that India is currently wading through seldom remain content with their pre-growth ambitions.

The United States, for instance, spent over 100 years practising a grand strategy of virtual isolation – a tactic which worked well while it was underdeveloped and young. But the twentieth century saw a dramatic change of course for American foreign policy. The country grew larger and more economically prosperous than the former great powers. As the domestic situation changed, American attitudes towards what constituted legitimate foreign policy changed as well. This shift in values called into question the doctrine of isolationism and precipitated an overhaul of US foreign policy to better reflect American values.

Eventually, the United States embraced its role as an active part of the international system. Perhaps, a similar fate of economic growth precipitating political change awaits India. The growing Indian middle class has access to more information about the world and is far more reliant on international commerce than previous generations. This middle class has increasingly become the kingmaker in Indian politics due to its ever-increasing size – over 250 million voters today, and a projected 500 million voters by 2025.[11] As economic growth swells the ranks of India's white-collar electorate, the country's political process will inevitably grow to mirror middle-class values.

Until the advent of satellite television, generations of Indians made do with a single television network. Now, there are over 300 separate channels dedicated to news alone, showcasing a variety of political leanings and values.[12] The rise of a large cadre of politically informed, market-oriented voters seems to be on the horizon. Significantly, it is likely that the next generation of voters will hold different principles than the previous generation, and will, therefore, view different foreign policy goals as legitimate. These changes have already begun to manifest themselves in departures from traditional Indian foreign policy doctrine.

From non-alignment, which meant avoiding involvement in global conflicts and maintaining a safe distance from the United States, in the last decade India has sought to play a greater role both in its neighbourhood and beyond. Relations with the US have also grown. India signed a civil nuclear deal with the United States in 2005, leads joint military exercises with other maritime powers, and has massively expanded its foreign aid budget.

Such changes illustrate the growing Indian willingness to play a part on the global stage, the basis for legitimacy for a new type of strategic doctrine. At the same time as India's aspirations seem to be undergoing an overhaul, the post-Cold War geopolitical landscape threatens to make the stated goals of non-alignment incoherent. Non-alignment rested on the idea that the conflict between Cold War adversaries was not an integral part of the Indian experience; New Delhi could afford to forge its way forward without picking a side. Great power rivalry in the twenty-first century will likely be far more relevant to India's immediate interests.

India's front-row status in tomorrow's great power politics, and the growing irrelevance of the goals of non-alignment, is largely a result of one of the most important shifts in the global landscape: the rise of China. A geopolitical rivalry between China and India is inevitable. As professor of politics and international relations John Mearsheimer writes: 'This is Geopolitics 101: great powers are always sensitive to potential threats near their home territory. After all, the United States does not tolerate distant great powers deploying military forces anywhere in the Western Hemisphere, much less on its borders. Imagine the outrage in Washington if China built an impressive military alliance and tried to include Canada and Mexico in it.'[13]

China's legacy of conflict with India, including the border dispute and the 1962 war, violent expansionism in the Indian Ocean region, regarded by India as its sphere of influence, and overtures to all of India's neighbours, not only Pakistan, make the prospect of rivalry all the more likely. India prefers the post-Cold War multipolarity to the Cold War bipolarity. If bipolarity returns, with US and China as the two poles, India's preference would be for American pre-eminence rather than Chinese dominance.

New Delhi wants to be a part of every international and regional organization, but only if exceptions are made for India and its uniqueness. The underlying principle and belief have always been that the global economic and trading arrangements have favoured Western nations and are skewed against developing countries, and thus, it needs to ensure that favourable terms are achieved not just for itself but for all developing countries.

In international trade negotiations, India has always wanted the World Trading Organization (WTO) to keep Indian interests in mind. Similarly, at the United Nations, India has long fought – along with like-minded countries Brazil, Germany and Japan (G–4) – for an increase in the membership of the UN Security Council based on the argument that the current council reflects the end of the Second World War world and not current-day reality. India is positively disposed towards the Indo-Pacific concept because the concept is open enough to be acceptable to almost every country in the world. It is also principle-based (upholding the liberal international rules-based order) and aligns with India's vision of the Asia–Pacific (an open security architecture). It helps build connectivity and capabilities in countries that are part of India's extended neighbourhood.

It has to end its one step forward, one back approach to partnerships. Working with other democracies in the Indo-Pacific (Japan, US, Australia, and South Korea), India's limited resources could go a longer way. It could help the country deliver on some of the expectations the world has of India, and it does not directly confront China, even as it counters a Chinese-led global order. Understandably, India is a status quo power. But it must build the institutional wherewithal that would lead to long-term planning. Currently, its responses to long-term threats are to partly build capabilities and partly hope that in the long run issues will be resolved. As any democracy, India is more likely to respond to issues when a crisis occurs, whereas it needs more than a crisis-management approach to act as a great power.

The rise of China poses a tremendous amount of uncertainty for India's future. While New Delhi's economic heft has been growing, China's is still far larger by comparison, giving it substantial room in funding its foreign policy ventures.[14] China has double the number of modern fighter aircraft as India, and three times the naval capability.[15] This lack of balance between India and China underscores the need for a re-evaluation of Indian grand strategy – especially when the interests of the two countries clash.

China is routinely aggressive against countries which disagree with it; for instance, enforcing massive boycotts of South Korean goods during diplomatic standoffs regarding North Korea.[16] The simple reality that a massively powerful state with a penchant for aggression exists on India's borders should serve to justify another look at the historic strategic doctrine, in order to emphasize goals that address this modern threat.

China's rapid economic growth, and resultant political and military strength, have redefined India's strategic choices. During the Cold War, India could work with the Soviet Union in balancing US influence because the Soviets did not seek to undermine India's position in South Asia. Beijing's engagement in the neighbourhood, however, is far more active, and collided directly with Indian visions for regional order and primacy. One of the assumptions that surrounded the goals of non-alignment was that by standing back from great-power rivalries, India could independently develop without interference. Now, the country has to worry about China entering and dominating its backyard.

China pours billions of dollars in loans into India's neighbours, attempting to bring them into the Beijing's sphere of influence.[17] At the same time, the Chinese military has taken an active stance in the Indian Ocean region, installing a military base in Djibouti and threatening to place another in Gwadar, Pakistan.[18]

Whereas distance might have been a worthwhile goal for dealing with Moscow and Washington – because it allowed New Delhi to focus on domestic development without interference from the Cold War parties – China problematizes such a stance by more aggressively spreading influence in India's own neighbourhood.

Aside from altering national aspirations and strategic objectives, economic globalization has changed the tools available for India to use in the pursuit of its foreign policy. By blossoming into a 2.3 trillion-dollar economy, the country has gained a wide range of new foreign policy options.[19] The budget of the Ministry of External Affairs alone has grown from just over Rs 5000 crore to Rs 17,884 crore.[20]

We already see the implications of rising Indian wealth for achieving foreign policy objectives. Indian development aid is heavily concentrated in its South Asian neighbourhood, with Bhutan, Nepal and Afghanistan being primary recipients.[21] The ability to take a more active stance in foreign affairs illustrates that the material constraints which made non-alignment so particularly appealing during India's early years have ceased to be serious impediments to international engagement.

Rapid economic and political changes in South Asia have rendered the old non-alignment formula anachronistic. The Indian people have different ideas of legitimate foreign policy aspirations, and the government has different tools at its disposal to fulfil those goals. Simultaneously, the rise of China poses different challenges than the Cold War rivalry of the US and the USSR. The very strengths of non-alignment – its careful proportioning between the objectives it espoused and the means at India's disposal – may not be as useful today as they were during the Cold War.

One of the chief strengths of non-alignment was that it conveyed India's foreign policy goals in an easily recognizable, straightforward manner. But modern inadequacies in the operations of the Indian government make this task difficult today; and before committing to any new doctrine, these failings must first be addressed.

New Delhi has also been reluctant to invest in long-term planning that characterizes successful approaches at grand strategy. According to the *Economist*, 'India and its leaders show little interest in military or strategic issues. Strategic defence reviews like those that take place in America, Britain and France, informed by serving officers and civil servants but led by politicians, are unknown.'[22]

This sobering assessment is confirmed by think-tanks and pundits alike, who point out that 'Indian strategic policy appears, at least from the outside, to be largely responding in piecemeal fashion to immediate events rather than following any deliberate plan.'[23] It seems intuitive that a concerted investment at developing a strategic doctrine is a prerequisite to real progress. Indeed, the success stories of rapid modernization and strategic planning all involve disciplined and powerful state institutions.

The Four Asian Tigers (the economies of Hong Kong, Singapore, South Korea and Taiwan), Japan and post-war Germany all saw tremendous economic and political expansions over the course of the twentieth century, largely because of concerted planning efforts undertaken by reformed bureaucracies. New Delhi's dearth in strategic planning infrastructure is evident in the systemic underfunding of foreign policy institutions. India's Ministry of External Affairs is the same size as tiny Singapore's, and less than one-eighth the size of China's.[24] The communication between the armed services and the civilian bureaucracy is dysfunctional, with a rampant lack of coordination over basic tasks, such as weapons procurement.[25] In a new book titled *The Absent Dialogue*, a former military officer and analyst Anit Mukherjee argues that the existing system, whereby the civilians kept the military out and the military over time became isolated into its own silos, has hurt the military's effectiveness.[26]

These problems are widely known within Indian policy circles. In 2005, an internal government audit suggested a major overhaul and expansion of the diplomatic corps. It noted that the Ministry of External Affairs's supervision of embassies 'has been weak in management and needs strengthening', training in foreign languages was 'inadequate', the work undertaken was 'not very useful', embassies should work for all ministries 'with equal interest and dispatch', career planning and selectivity in promotion was essential'. The report was simply filed away and never acted upon.[27]

Mirroring India's stymied bureaucracy is its haphazardly designed military apparatus. The army, navy and air force are only vaguely connected, making goal-sharing difficult and coordination over new priorities slow. When the Brookings Institution conducted a review of India's military organization, they found that 'despite the creation of an Integrated Headquarters of the Ministry of Defence, the three Services continue to be merely attached offices with inadequate say in policy formation.'[28]

Institutional weakness in the military bureaucracy makes coordination difficult, thereby undermining the clear articulation of uniform goals. On 24 December 2019, India appointed its first Chief of Defence Staff (CDS) who will simultaneously be permanent chairman of the Chiefs of Staff Committee (PC-COSC) as well as secretary of the newly created Department of Military Affairs (DMA).

He is supposed to ensure 'jointness' and 'reduce wasteful expenditure.' However, unless the CDS is able to set new rules for inter-service matters, he will face pushback from the civilian Ministry of Defence bureaucracy and his own service colleagues.[29] For example, the CDS, as secretary of the newly created Department of Military Affairs, is supposed to be responsible for procurement of equipment and material for all services. Yet, capital acquisition – large-scale modern equipment like planes and ships – will not fall under his purview and will remain with the secretary, Ministry of Defence.[30] Unless such anomalies are resolved, jurisdictional conflicts could further slow down India's military modernization.

Some retired generals referred to the decision as a game changer, with the CDS being able to become the 'prime mover' in the Indian military apparatus.[31] Other generals and analysts argued that since the CDS will be a four-star general, like his service chief peers, he will remain primus inter pares. Further, unlike them, he will not be head of any military command.[32]

The underdevelopment of the military compared to civil institutions, such an important facet of non-alignment, has created barriers to pivoting strategic doctrines today. This dysfunction fosters an ad hoc atmosphere towards planning, and one that is reactive, responding to threats as they arise. Such limited cooperative infrastructure is not conducive to the type of large-scale strategic shift that India needs.

The Modi administration seems to recognize the need to modernize India's planning architecture. In 2018, the administration formed a Defence Planning Committee and increased funding towards the National Security Council Secretariat (NSCS), which helps the Prime Minister's Office make decisions on strategic doctrine.[33] As part of these reforms, the NSCS added three deputy national security advisers and one military adviser to advise the NSA.[34] Such reforms are the product of the current administration's understanding that India lacks a 'comprehensive view on national security'.[35]

In a crucial step for developing new grand strategy, the NSCS is now able to issue policy recommendations, and oversees planning on intelligence, science and technology, in addition to their historic oversight over internal and external defence.[36] This comes in tandem with the formation of the external affairs ministry's Centre for Contemporary China Studies, a research group dedicated for studying the challenges and opportunities posed to India by China. Importantly, this institution reflects the growing understanding that the rise of China will play a crucial role in the development of any future Indian foreign policy doctrine.[37]

Bureaucratic reform is a crucial prerequisite for strategic modernization. Institution building is less glamorous than flashy new schemes and projects, but without strong foundations, it is impossible to create a lasting direction for grand strategy. Foreign aid, military logistics, diplomacy and negotiations, not to mention all of the domestic economic programmes which might service a potential new strategic doctrine, all require a massive coordinated effort. When the US began its post-Second World War strategic doctrine of global engagement, it spawned a massive expansion in the Washington bureaucracy. Today, China has poured billions into its state apparatus in order to facilitate its global ambitions. India needs to match these efforts if it intends on generating a clear, actionable strategic doctrine for itself.

India's rising middle class expects continued economic growth, as well as an expanded role for Indian responsibility in the Indo-Pacific as its civilizational neighbourhood. To be legitimate, a new strategic doctrine must expand the country's interests to include regional partnerships, leadership and robust economic development. Fortunately, a strategy which emphasizes integration could achieve all of these aims.

Partnerships with Japan have brought millions of dollars of investment into India, and have given New Delhi a partner to augment its influence in the region.[38] Indo-Japanese joint ventures have been met with success in Bangladesh and Sri Lanka.[39] India stands to gain considerably from these projects – South Asia's volume of intra-regional trade, less than US $28 billion, is the lowest of anywhere in the world, one-fifth that of neighbouring Southeast Asia.

India ought to prioritize building regional infrastructure and promoting integration with fellow South Asian nations and nearby heavyweights, such as Japan and Australia. Such a move would satisfy the need for economic growth and leadership which undergirds the legitimacy of Indian grand strategy.

A strategic doctrine that promotes regional engagement would address a number of India's growing security concerns. The geopolitical climate which made non-alignment workable has been replaced by a rising China and more interconnected world.

Regional engagement will curb Chinese influence and aggression in two ways. First, India-led economic schemes would give an alternative to predatory Chinese investment. Such a programme would prevent Beijing from coercing its clients by leveraging their economic relationships for strategic concession. Second, by establishing a more integrated South Asia and expanding its regional leadership, India will be better positioned to diplomatically oppose China's rise.

Beijing currently attempts to accentuate differences between India and its neighbours, using economic and political incentives to support anti-Indian interests. By creating a unified front of institutions and linking its interests to those of its neighbours through trade and security cooperation, India will be in a better position to interdict Chinese efforts at dividing South Asia. The country would benefit from supporting regional development and initiatives such as the Japanese 'Free and Open Indo-Pacific' strategy, which emphasizes maritime security cooperation between Indo-Pacific interests.

Indians must also remember that domestic stability is a prerequisite for a coherent foreign policy. A country whose internal affairs are not in order will be unable to chart a straight course for their strategic doctrine. Domestic policy affects foreign relations, whether one likes it or not, and it is not enough to say that the currently contentious issues are India's internal matters. Illiberal majoritarianism, vigilante attacks, campus protests and news stories about repression of minorities hardly paint a picture of a rising global power. A social agenda that projects the majority's religious and cultural identity as the basis of Indian nationalism seems incompatible with its global economic and strategic aspirations.

As historian Ramachandra Guha noted correctly, 'Because of its size and diversity, because of the continuing poverty of many of its citizens, because it is (in historical terms) still a relatively young nation state, and because it remains the most recklessly ambitious experiment in history, the Republic of India was never going to have anything but a rocky ride. National unity and democratic consolidation were always going to be more difficult to achieve than in smaller, richer, more homogeneous and older countries.'[40]

It is important to remember that aspirations must always be matched with capabilities. Wishful thinking about development and influence must be tempered with an understanding of India's ability to achieve its aims. Unilateralism and deep global commitments are simply not possible while the country has a long list of domestic concerns to deal with, and while GDP remains under one-eighth of China's.

British scholar Martin Wight defined a dominant power as one 'that can confidently contemplate war against any likely combination of other powers, so a great power is a power that can confidently contemplate war against any other existing single power.'[41] American international relations professor Robert Gilpin noted, 'Both individually and in interaction with one another, those states that historically have been called the great powers and are known today as the superpowers establish and enforce the basic rules and rights that influence their own behavior and that of the lesser states in the system.'[42] By those standards, India may have the potential, but has yet to make it to the ranks of greatness as a world power.

On the one hand, India's pride and its view of self come from its traditions and history. On the other, it being tradition-bound holds it back from achieving global power status in the twenty-first century. Ancient India was isolationist, which modern India cannot afford to be. Ancient India was other-worldly, but modern India needs to succeed and exercise power in this world. Only that would make India great in the eyes of the world.

Notes

INTRODUCTION: POTENTIAL AND PROMISE

1. Will Durant, *The Case for India*, New York: Simon and Schuster, 1930, p. 3.
2. Office of the Registrar General & Census Commissioner. *Census of India*, 2011; Directorate of Census Operations, Ministry of Home Affairs, Government of India, Delhi, *Census of India, 2011*. http://censusindia.gov.in/Census_And_You/age_structure_and_marital_status.aspx (accessed on 26 January 2017).
3. Alex Gray, 'These Countries Have the Most Doctoral Graduates', World Economic Forum, 27 February 2017, www.weforum.org/agenda/2017/02/countries-with-most-doctoral-graduates (accessed on 26 January 2018).
4. Rajat Gupta, Shirish Sankhe, Richard Dobbs, Jonathan Woetzel, Anu Madgavkar and Ashwin Hasyagar, 'India's Path from Poverty to Empowerment', *McKinsey Global Institute*, McKinsey & Company, February 2014, www.mckinsey.com/featured-insights/asia-pacific/indias-path-from-poverty-to-empowerment (accessed on 26 January 2017).
5. 'China's economy and the WTO: All Change', *The Economist*, 10 December 2011, www.economist.com/asia/2011/12/10/all-change (accessed on 26 January 2017).
6. 'US Interest in self-government for India,' Press Release, 25 February 1947, *The Department of State Bulletin*, Vol. XVI, No. 392, Office of Public Communication, Bureau of Public Affairs, Washington, 1947, p. 450.
7. 'Appraisal of US National Interests in South Asia,' Report by the SANACC Subcommittee for the Near and Middle East, 19 April 1949, *Foreign Relations of the United States, 1949, The Near*

159

East, South Asia and Africa, Volume VI, https://history.state.gov/historicaldocuments/frus1949v06/d3 (accessed on 26 January 2016).

8. Chester Bowles, 'New India', *Foreign Affairs*, October 1952, www.foreignaffairs.com/articles/india/1952-10-01/new-india (accessed on 26 January 2015).

9. John F. Kennedy, 'A Democrat Looks at Foreign Policy', *Foreign Affairs*, October 1957, www.foreignaffairs.com/articles/united-states/1957-10-01/democrat-looks-foreign-policy (accessed on 26 January 2015).

10. Strobe Talbott, *Engaging India: Diplomacy, Democracy, and the Bomb*, Washington, DC: Brookings Institution Press, 2004, p. 24.

11. V.S. Naipaul, *India: A Wounded Civilization*, New York: Vintage Books, 1976, p. 8.

12. Salman Rushdie, *Midnight's Children: A Novel*, New York: Random House, 1980, p. 118.

13. Shashi Tharoor, 'Globalization and the Human Imagination', *World Policy Journal*, Vol. 21, No. 2, Summer 2004, p. 88.

14. Kaunain Sheriff, 'Traffic Hazard: Tribunal concerned over animal-driven carts on roads', *The Indian Express*, 9 May 2015, https://indianexpress.com/article/cities/delhi/traffic-hazard-tribunal-concerned-over-animal-driven-carts-on-roads (accessed on 1 July 2018).

15. Alison Kroulek, 'Which Countries Have the Most English Speakers?', *K International*, 11 June 2018, www.k-international.com/blog/countries-with-the-most-english-speakers/(accessed on 1 July 2018).

16. 'BJP chief claims English bad for India, triggers outrage,' *The Times of India*, 19 July 2013, https://timesofindia.indiatimes.com/india/BJP-chief-claims-English-bad-for-India-triggers-outrage/articleshow/21178996.cms (accessed on 1 July 2018).

17. Daniel Maina Wambugu, 'The World's Largest Exporters of Beef', *World Atlas*, 10 December 2018, www.worldatlas.com/articles/the-world-s-largest-exporters-of-beef.html (accessed on 21 December 2018).

18. Reuters, 'A Ban on the Slaughter of Sacred Cows Is Hurting India's Leather Industry', *Fortune*, 15 June 2017, fortune.com/2017/06/14/india-cattle-leather-industry (accessed on 1 July 2018).

19. Ibid.

20. Tommy Wilkes and Mayank Bhardwaj, 'Cattle Slaughter Crackdown Ripples through India's Leather Industry', Reuters,

15 June 2017, www.reuters.com/article/us-india-politics-religion-insight/cattle-slaughter-crackdown-ripples-through-indias-leather-industry-idUSKBN1951OE (accessed on 1 July 2018).

21. Michael Safi, 'Indian Film *Padmaavat* Sparks Protests over "Hindu-Muslim Romance"', *The Guardian*, 16 November 2017, www.theguardian.com/world/2017/nov/16/indian-film-padmavati-sparks-protests-over-hindu-muslim-romance (accessed on 1 July 2018).

22. Romila Thapar, 'They Peddle Myths and Call it History,' *The New York Times*, 17 May 2019, https://www.nytimes.com/2019/05/17/opinion/india-elections-modi-history.html (accessed on 1 June 2019).

23. Meena Kandasamy, 'To Be an Indian Patriot,' *Al Jazeera*, 8 August 2017, www.aljazeera.com/indepth/opinion/2017/08/indian-nationalism-jnu-tank-170808075908997.html (accessed on 1 July 2018).

24. The Times Higher Education World University Rankings 2018, https://www.timeshighereducation.com/world-university-rankings/2018/world-ranking#!/page/0/length/-1/locations/IN/sort_by/rank/sort_order/asc/cols/stats (accessed on 1 July 2019).

25. 'Age Structure and Marital Status,' 2011 Census Data, http://censusindia.gov.in/Census_And_You/age_structure_and_marital_status.aspx (accessed on 22 February 2020).

26. Girija Shivakumar, 'India Is Set to Become the Youngest Country by 2020', *The Hindu*, 17 April, 2013, www.thehindu.com/news/national/india-is-set-to-become-the-youngest-country-by-2020/article4624347.ece (accessed on 1 January 2017).

27. 'India's Demographic Dividend', *The Answer Company*, Thomson Reuters, 7 July 2016, blogs.thomsonreuters.com/answerson/indias-demographic-dividend (accessed on 1 January 2017).

28. *Government Expenditure on Education, Total (% of GDP)*. The World Bank, 2015, data.worldbank.org/indicator/SE.XPD.TOTL.GD.ZS?locations=IN-1W (accessed on 1 January 2017).

29. Deon Filmer and Halsey Rogers, *World Development Report 2018: Learning to Realize Educations Promise*, The World Bank, 2018.

30. 'Most of Engineering Students Lack Employability Skills, Say Experts', *The Hindu*, 6 March 2016, www.thehindu.com/news/national/andhra-pradesh/most-of-engineering-students-lack-employability-skills-say-experts/article8319173.ece (accessed on 1 January 2017).

31. *Research and development expenditure (% of GDP)*, The World Bank, 2016, data.worldbank.org/indicator/GB.XPD.RSDV. GD.ZS?locations=IN-JP-US-CN (accessed on 1 January 2017).

32. Vivek Kaul, 'India job data spells trouble for Narendra Modi', BBC News, 31 January 2019, https://www.bbc.com/news/world-asia-india-47068223 (accessed on 1 March 2019).

33. Kinjal Pandya-Wagh, 'Training India's Millions of Unskilled Workers', BBC, 30 October 2015, www.bbc.com/news/business-3467196 (accessed on 1 January 2017).

34. *Labor force, female (% of total labor force)*. The World Bank, 2018, data.worldbank.org/indicator/SL.TLF.TOTL.FE.ZS?locations=IN-CN-1W (accessed on 1 January 2019).

35. 'World's Cities in 2018', World Urbanization Prospects, United Nations Department of Economic and Social Affairs, Population Division, https://population.un.org/wup/Publications/, pp. 6, 20 (accessed on 22 February 2020).

36. United Nations, Department of Economic and Social Affairs, Population Division (2018). *World Urbanization Prospects: The 2018 Revision*.

37. 'India Needs $1.5 trillion for Infrastructure, Arun Jaitley says', *The Times of India*, 26 June 2016, timesofindia.indiatimes.com/business/india-business/India-needs-1-5-trillion-for-infrastructure-Arun-Jaitley-says/articleshow/52928773.cms (accessed on 1 January 2017).

38. Sudeshna Ghosh Banerjee, Douglas Barnes, Bipul Singh, Kristy Mayer and Hussain Samad, *Power for All: Electricity Access Challenge in India*, Washington DC: The World Bank, 2015.

39. Asit K. Biswas, Cecilia Tortajada and Udisha Saklan, 'India Is Facing Its Worst Water Crisis in Generations', *Quartz India*, 15 March 2017, qz.com/india/931878/india-is-facing-its-worst-water-crisis-in-generations (accessed on 1 January 2018).

40. Annie Gowen, 'India's Huge Need for Electricity Is a Problem for the Planet', *The Washington Post*, 6 November 2015, www.washingtonpost.com/world/asia_pacific/indias-huge-need-for-electricity-is-a-problem-for-the-planet (accessed on 1 January 2017).

41. Maria Thomas, 'Pollution Kills More People in India than Anywhere Else in the World' *Quartz India*, 20 October 2017, qz.com/india/1107416/2-5-million-indians-died-in-2015-due-to-pollution-more-than-anywhere-else-in-the-world/ (accessed on 1 January 2018).

42. Neha Dasgupta, 'India's $230 Million Plan to Stop Crop Burning That Pollutes Delhi...' Reuters, 14 February 2018, www.reuters.com/article/us-india-pollution/indias-230-million-plan-to-stop-crop-burning-that-pollutes-delhi-falls-short-of-estimates-idUSKCN1FY0IA (accessed on 1 January 2019).

43. 'Words like Om and cow not a taboo: PM Modi hits out at critics of government's cow policies,' *India Today*, 11 September 2019, https://www.indiatoday.in/india/story/modi-cow-policy-reaction-comment-mathura-1597925-2019-09-11; 'RSS chief Mohan Bhagwat calls for nationwide ban on slaughter of cows,' *The Indian Express*, 12 April 2017, https://indianexpress.com/article/india/rss-chief-mohan-bhagwat-calls-for-nationwide-ban-on-slaughter-of-cows-4606910/; Rama Lakshmi, 'Hindu cattle patrols in India seek to protect cows from beef eaters,' *The Washington Post*, 28 October 2015, https://www.washingtonpost.com/world/asia_pacific/hindu-cattle-patrols-in-india-seek-to-protect-cows-from-beef-eaters/2015/10/28/89da1cc8-7c08-11e5-bfb6-65300a5ff562_story.html?itid=lk_inline_manual_5; Anshuman Kumar, 'Cow Welfare: Rs 500 crore Allotted for Rashtriya Kamdhenu Aayog in Budget 2019,' *The Economic Times*, 2 February 2019, https://economictimes.indiatimes.com/news/economy/policy/cow-welfare-rs-500-crore-allotted-for-rashtriya-kamdhenu-aayog-in-budget-2019/articleshow/67802769.cms?from=mdr (accessed on 22 March 2020).

44. 'BJP manifesto 2019: Top 10 promises for next 5 years,' *India Today*, 8 April 2019, https://www.indiatoday.in/elections/lok-sabha-2019/story/bjp-top-promises-1496617-2019-04-08; 'Subramanian Swamy asks Centre to acquire land for Kashi, Mathura,' *India Today*, 2 December 2019, https://www.indiatoday.in/india/story/subramanian-swamy-bjp-kashi-mathura-1624361-2019-12-02 (accessed on 22 March 2020).

45. 'What Are Anti-Romeo Squads? How Do They Operate? Points to know,' News 18, 22 March 2017, https://www.news18.com/news/india/what-are-anti-romeo-squads-how-do-they-operate-points-to-know-1362855.html; 'UP's "Anti-Romeo Squads" Are Doing the Opposite of What They're Supposed To,' The Wire, 4 April 2018, https://thewire.in/women/ups-anti-romeo-squads-are-doing-the-opposite-of-what-theyre-supposed-to (accessed on 22 March 2020).

46. Christophe Jaffrelot and Pradyumna Jairam, 'BJP Has Been Effective in Transmitting Its Version of Indian History to Next Generation of Learners,' Carnegie Endowment, 16 November 2019 https://carnegieendowment.org/2019/11/16/bjp-has-been-effective-in-transmitting-its-version-of-indian-history-to-next-generation-of-learners-pub-80373 (accessed on 22 March 2020).

47. Desk, India Today Web, 'India Jumps 23 Spots to No. 77 on World Bank Ease of Doing Business Index', *India Today*, 1 November 2018, www.indiatoday.in/business/story/india-ease-of-doing-business-index-77-position-1379663-2018-10-31 (accessed on 1 January 2019).

48. Asit Ranjan Mishra, 'India's rank jumps 14 places in World Bank's ease of doing business ranking,' Livemint, 24 October 2019, https://www.livemint.com/news/india/india-jumps-14-notches-in-world-bank-s-ease-of-doing-business-rankings-11571882591868.html (accessed on 27 October 2019).

49. Saheli Roy Choudhury, 'Ratings agency Moody's downgrades India's outlook from "stable" to "negative"', CNBC, 7 November 2019, https://www.cnbc.com/2019/11/08/moodys-lowers-indias-outlook-to-negative-from-stable.html (accessed on 10 November 2019).

50. Ibid.

51. 'GDP Growth of India', *Statistics Times*, statisticstimes.com/economy/gdp-growth-of-india.php (accessed on 31 October 2019).

52. 'GDP growth slips to 4.5% in September quarter, slowest expansion in 26 quarters,' *The Economic Times*, 30 November 2019, https://economictimes.indiatimes.com/news/economy/indicators/gdp-growth-slips-to-4-5-in-september-quarter-slowest-expansion-in-26-quarters/articleshow/72293669.cms?from=mdr (accessed on 22 February 2020).

53. *Military expenditure (% of GDP).* The World Bank, 2017, https://data.worldbank.org/indicator/MS.MIL.XPND.GD.ZS?locations=IN (accessed on 1 January 2019).

54. Rahul Bedi, 'India's low defence budget for FY 2020/21 to hit military modernization,' *Janes Defence Weekly*, 3 February 2020, https://www.janes.com/article/94060/india-s-low-defence-budget-for-fy-2020-21-to-hit-military-modernisation (accessed on 22 February 2020).

55. S. Jaishankar, Speech at India–US 2015: Partnering for Peace and Prosperity, New Delhi, India, 16 March 2015.

56. Preety Bhogal, 'India's Foreign Aid to South Asia', Observer Research Foundation, 11 November 2016, www.orfonline.org/research/indias-foreign-aid-to-south-asia (accessed on 1 January 2018).

57 Husain Haqqani, *Reimagining Pakistan: Transforming a Dysfunctional Nuclear State*, Noida: HarperCollins India, 2018.

58 Anna Pujol-Mazzini, 'India tops global pollution deaths of 9 million a year: study,' Reuters, 19 October 2017 https://www.reuters.com/article/us-global-pollution-health/india-tops-global-pollution-deaths-of-9-million-a-year-study-idUSKBN1CO39P (accessed on 1 January 2018).

1: ANCIENT CULTURE, MODERN TIMES

1. Tim McGirk, 'Hindu world divided by a 24 hour wonder,' *Independent* (UK), 23 September 1995, https://www.independent.co.uk/news/uk/hindu-world-divided-by-a-24-hour-wonder-1602382.html https://www.bbc.com/news/av/magazine-38301718/the-milk-miracle-that-brought-india-to-a-standstill (accessed on 5 January 2019).

2. Ibid.

3. Maseeh Rahman, 'Indian prime minister claims genetic science existed in ancient times,' *Guardian* (UK), 28 October 2014, https://www.theguardian.com/world/2014/oct/28/indian-prime-minister-genetic-science-existed-ancient-times (accessed on 5 January 2019). According to Hindu mythology, Ganesha's elephant head is the result of a battle between him and his father, Lord Shiva, in which Ganesha's human head that was lopped off was replaced by Shiva with the head of an elephant.

4. Yashwant Sinha and Aditya Sinha, *India Unmade: How the Modi Government Broke the Economy*, New Delhi: Juggernaut, 2018, p. 21.

5. Belinda Goldsmith and Meka Beresford, 'India most dangerous country for women with sexual violence rife - global poll,' Reuters, 25 June 2018, https://www.reuters.com/article/us-women-dangerous-poll-exclusive/exclusive-india-most-dangerous-country-for-women-with-sexual-violence-rife-global-poll-idUSKBN1JM01X (accessed on 10 January 2019).

6. 'Haryana khap blames consumption of chowmein for rapes,' Times of India News Network, 16 October 2012 https://timesofindia.

indiatimes.com/india/Haryana-khap-blames-consumption-of-chowmein-for-rapes/articleshowprint/16829882.cms (accessed on 20 January 2019); Chander Suta Dogra, 'Jeans, mobiles and khap panchayats,' *The Hindu*, 19 October 2013 (accessed on 20 January 2019).

7. Aldous Huxley, *Jesting Pilate: An Intellectual Holiday*, New York: George Doran Company, 1926, pp. 142–43.

8. 'A Vision of India's History: Dr Tagore's Lecture,' *The Times of India*, Karachi, 23 March 1923.

9. Jawaharlal Nehru, *The Discovery of India*, Calcutta: The Signet Press, 1946, p. 560.

10. Ibid., p. 59.

11. Sudipta Kaviraj, 'Modernity and Politics in India', *Daedalus*, Vol. 129, No. 1, Multiple Modernities, Winter, 2000, pp. 141–47.

12. Harihara Das and Sasmita Mahapatra, *The Indian Renaissance and Raja Rammohan Roy*, Jaipur: Pointer Publishers, 1996, p. 61.

13. Manu S. Pillai. 'Raja Rammohun Roy: India's Gentleman Reformer', Livemint, 2 June 2017, www.livemint.com/Leisure/lw9CbPNHHsosZ7oxIYq15O/Raja-Rammohun-Roy-Indias-gentleman-reformer.html (accessed on 10 January 2019).

14. Harihara Das and Sasmita Mahapatra, *The Indian Renaissance and Raja Ram Mohan Roy*, Jaipur: Pointer Publishers, 1996, p. 61.

15. Atulchandra Gupta and Jagannath Chakavorty (eds), *Studies in the Bengal Renaissance*, Calcutta: National Council of Education, Bengal, 1958, p. 394.

16. Arvind Sharma, *Hinduism as a Missionary Religion*, New York: State University of New York Press, 2011, p. 33.

17. Jawaharlal Nehru, *The Discovery of India*, Calcutta: The Signet Press, 1946, p. 314.

18. 'Raja Rammohun Roy,' Article of Unitarian Universalist History & Heritage Society Retrieved from: http://uudb.org/articles/rajarammohunroy.html (accessed on 1 January 2017).

19. Milton Kumar Dev, 'Rammohun Roy: A Study of His Religious Views,' *Journal of Philosophy and Progress*, Vols. LIX-LX, 2016, DOI: http://dx.doi.org/10.3329/pp.v59i1-2.36682, p. 101 (accessed on 1 January 2017).

20. Rabindranath Tagore, *The Message of Japan to India: A Lecture*, New York: The Macmillan Company, 1916, p. 20.

21. Mahatma Gandhi, 'In Defense of Nationalism,' *Young India*, 16 March 1921; Also, Mahatma Gandhi, *India of My Dreams*, Ahmedabad: Navjeevan Publishing House, 1947, p. 21.

22. V.D. Savarkar, *Hindutva: Who is a Hindu?*, Bombay: S.S. Savarkar, 1925.

23. Ibid., p. 41.

24. Ibid., p. 83.

25. Mahatma Gandhi's prayer discourse, 25 July 1947, *Collected Works of Mahatma Gandhi*, Vol. 88. https://indianculturalforum.in/2015/10/16/from-gandhis-prayer-july-1947/ (accessed on 1 January 2017).

26. Nehru's letter to Syed Mahmud, 12 September 1926 from Geneva. Taken from S. Gopal (ed.), *Selected Works of Jawaharlal Nehru*, Volume 2, Delhi: BR Publishing Corporation, 1974, p. 242.

27. Gurcharan Das, *India Unbound: The Social and Economic Revolution from Independence to the Global Information Age*, New York: Anchor Books, 2002, p. 34.

28. P.S. Deshmukh, *Constituent Assembly of India Debates (Proceedings)*, Vol. IX, 11 August 1949, http://cadindia.clpr.org.in/constitution_assembly_debates/volume/9/1949-08-11 (accessed on 10 January 2019).

29. Jawaharlal Nehru on discussion on citizenship, *Constituent Assembly of India Debates (Proceedings)*, Vol. IX, 12 August 1949, http://cadindia.clpr.org.in/constitution_assembly_debates/volume/9/1949-08-12 (accessed on 10 January 2019).

30. Sunil Khilnani, *The Idea of India*, New York: Farrar, Straus, Giroux, 1997, pp. 5–9.

31. Edward Luce, *In Spite of the Gods: The Strange Rise of Modern India*, London: Abacus, 2011, pp. 194–95.

32. Inaugural speech by First Temporary Chairman Sachchidananda Sinha, *Constituent Assembly of India Debates (Proceedings)*, Vol. I, 9 December 1946, http://cadindia.clpr.org.in/constitution_assembly_debates/volume/1/1946-12-09 (accessed on 10 January 2019).

33. Rajendra Prasad, Speech on taking over as Chairman of Constituent Assembly, *Constituent Assembly of India Debates (Proceedings)*, Vol. 11 December 1946, http://cadindia.clpr.org.in/constitution_assembly_debates/volume/1/1946-12-11 (accessed on 10 January 2019).

34. B.R. Ambedkar on Nehru's resolution, *Constituent Assembly of India Debates (Proceedings)*, Vol. I, 17 December 1946, http://cadindia.clpr.org.in/constitution_assembly_debates/volume/1/1946-12-17 (accessed on 10 January 2019).

35. Jawaharlal Nehru, *Discovery of India*, Calcutta: The Signet Press, 1946, p. 53.

36. Nehru's letter to Syed Mahmud, 12 September 1926 from Geneva. Taken from S. Gopal (ed.) *Selected Works of Jawaharlal Nehru*, Volume 2, Delhi: BR Publishing Corporation, 1974, p. 242.

37. According to *Encyclopedia Britannica*, Intelligent design is an '… argument intended to demonstrate that living organisms were created in more or less their present forms by an "intelligent designer."' https://www.britannica.com/topic/intelligent-design (accessed on 1 January 2017).

38. Meera Nanda, 'How Modern Are We? Cultural Contradictions of India's Modernity', *Economic and Political Weekly*, Vol. 41, No. 6 (11–17 February 2006), p. 491.

39. Ibid.

40. Ibid.

41. Rahul Bedi, 'India Had Planes and Test Tube Babies Thousands of Years Ago, Science Conference Told', *The Telegraph*, 7 January 2019, https://www.telegraph.co.uk/news/2019/01/07/indian-scientists-condemn-irrational-claims-hindu-epics-contain (accessed on 12 January 2019).

42. Shah Alam Khan, 'Remembering Nehru as a "Friend of Science"', The Wire, 22 June 2018, https://thewire.in/society/remembering-nehru-as-a-friend-of-science (accessed on 15 January 2019).

43. Swami Shraddhananda, 'Hindu Sangathan: Saviour of the Dying Race', 1924 https://archive.org/details/in.ernet.dli.2015.66063/page/n1 (accessed on 1 January 2017).

44. Rupam Jain and Tom Lasseter, 'By rewriting history, Hindu nationalists aim to assert their dominance over India,' Reuters, 6 March 2018, https://www.reuters.com/article/us-india-modi-culture-specialreport/special-report-by-rewriting-history-hindu-nationalists-aim-to-assert-their-dominance-over-india-idUSKCN1GI170 (accessed on 15 January 2019).

45. 'Rewriting history: Akbar lost to Maharana Pratap; Mahatma, Nehru missing from texts,' *Hindustan Times*, 25 July 2017, https://www.hindustantimes.com/india-news/rewriting-history-akbar-lost-to-maharana-pratap-no-mahatma-or-nehru-in-texts/

story-N0xOT7Pqq6XGEvAgFXnBvI.html; see also, Rupam Jain and Tom Lasseter, 'Special Report: By rewriting history, Hindu nationalists aim to assert their dominance over India', Reuters, 6 March 2018, https://www.reuters.com/article/us-india-modi-culture-specialreport/special-report-by-rewriting-history-hindu-nationalists-aim-to-assert-their-dominance-over-india-idUSKCN1GI170 (both accessed on 10 January 2019).

46. Priya Ranjan Sahu, 'Gandhi Died Due to "Accidental Sequence of Events", Says Odisha Government Booklet', The Wire, 14 November 2019, https://thewire.in/education/odisha-gandhi-nathuram-godse (accessed on 15 November 2019).

47. Ayeshea Perera, 'Cows to planes: Indian ministers who rewrote scientific history,' BBC News, 22 September 2017 https://www.bbc.com/news/world-asia-india-41344136 (accessed on 20 January 2019).

48. 'India had internet and satellites during Mahabharata, claims Tripura CM Biplab Deb,' *The Indian Express*, 18 April 2018, https://indianexpress.com/article/north-east-india/tripura/india-had-internet-and-satellites-during-mahabharata-claims-tripura-cm-biplab-deb-5141521 (accessed on 20 January 2019).

49. 'India: Vigilante "Cow Protection" Groups Attack Minorities', *Human Rights Watch*, 19 February 2019, https://www.hrw.org/news/2019/02/18/india-vigilante-cow-protection-groups-attack-minorities (accessed on 20 February 2019).

50. Anshuman Kumar, 'Cow Welfare: Rs 500 Crore Allotted for Rashtriya Kamdhenu Aayog in Budget 2019, *The Economic Times*, 2 February 2019, https://economictimes.indiatimes.com/news/economy/policy/cow-welfare-rs-500-crore-allotted-for-rashtriya-kamdhenu-aayog-in-budget-2019/articleshow/67802769.cms (accessed on 3 February 2019).

51. Jawaharlal Nehru on secularism, *Constituent Assembly of India Debates (Proceedings)*, Vol. IX, 12 August 1949, http://cadindia.clpr.org.in/constitution_assembly_debates/volume/9/1949-08-12 (accessed on 20 January 2019).

52. Christophe Jaffrelot, *The Hindu National Movement and Indian Politics 1925-1990s*, New Delhi: Penguin Books, 1996, pp. 102–04.

53. Ibid.

54. Taken from Sarvepalli Gopal, *Jawaharlal Nehru: An Anthology*, Delhi: Oxford University Press, 1980, p. 330.

55. Ian Copland (2017), 'Cows, Congress and the Constitution: Jawaharlal Nehru and the Making of Article 48', *South Asia: Journal of South Asian Studies*, Vol. 40, No.4, p. 724.

56. Edward Luce, *In Spite of the Gods: The Strange Rise of Modern India*, London: Abacus, 2011, pp. 194–95.

57. For more, please read Tagore's works: *Sampatti* (1891–92), *Nastanirh* (1901) and *A Wife's Letter* (1914).

58. 'Haryana khap blames consumption of chowmein for rapes,' The Times of India News Network, 16 October 2012, https://timesofindia.indiatimes.com/india/Haryana-khap-blames-consumption-of-chowmein-for-rapes/articleshowprint/16829882.cms (accessed on 20 January 2019).

59. Chander Suta Dogra, 'Jeans, mobiles and khap panchayats,' *The Hindu*, 19 October 2013 (accessed on 20 January 2019).

60. Richa Taneja (ed.), 'Khap Panchayats Stopping Marriages Is Illegal, Top Court Issues Rules', NDTV, 27 March 2018, https://www.ndtv.com/india-news/khap-panchayats-stopping-marriages-is-illegal-top-court-issues-rules-1829069 (accessed on 20 January 2019).

61. Anuj Pant (ed.), 'Don't Wear Jeans, T-Shirts To Work: Rajasthan Labour Department's Diktat', NDTV, 27 June 2018 https://www.ndtv.com/india-news/rajasthan-labour-departments-diktat-dont-wear-jeans-t-shirts-to-work-1874044 (accessed on 20 January 2019).

62. Christophe Jaffrelot, *The Hindu National Movement and Indian Politics 1925-1990s*, New Delhi: Penguin Books, 1996, pp. 102–104.

63. Chitra Sinha, 'Rhetoric, Reason and Representation: Four Narratives in the Hindu Code Bill Discourse,' p. 4, https://uu.diva-portal.org/smash/get/diva2:874167/FULLTEXT02.pdf (accessed on 1 January 2017).

64. Akshaya Mukul, *Gita Press and the Making of Hindu India*, Noida: HarperCollins India, 2015, p. 259.

65. Chitra Sinha, 'Rhetoric, Reason and Representation: Four Narratives in the Hindu Code Bill Discourse,' p. 8, https://www.ndtv.com/india-news/rajasthan-labour-departments-diktat-dont-wear-jeans-t-shirts-to-work-1874044 (accessed on 1 January 2017).

66. Ibid.

67. Kartik Kwatra, 'What a narrowing Hindu-Muslim fertility gap tells us,' Livemint, 21 February 2019, https://www.livemint.com/news/india/what-a-narrowing-hindu-muslim-fertility-gap-tells-us-1550686404387.html (accessed on 1 March 2019).

68. Chitra Sinha, 'Rhetoric, Reason and Representation: Four Narratives in the Hindu Code Bill Discourse,' p. 8, https://uu.diva-portal.org/smash/get/diva2:874167/FULLTEXT02.pdf (accessed on 1 January 2017).

69. Ibid.

70. Ibid.

71. Reba Som, 'Jawaharlal Nehru and the Hindu Code: A Victory of Symbol over Substance?', *Modern Asian Studies*, Vol. 28, No. 1 (February 1994), pp. 180–81.

72. Speech at Mahila Vidyapith, Allahabad, 31 March 1928, S. Gopal (ed.), *Selected Works of Jawaharlal Nehru*, Vol. 3, New Delhi: Nehru Memorial Trust and Oxford University Press, 1972, p 361.

73. Please read the Gita Press's forty-six-page monograph *Stri Dharma Prashnottar* (Questions and Answers on Women's Dharma) written by Hanuman Prasad Poddar in 1926 and other such pamphlets published by the Press over the decades. For more read Akshaya Mukul, *Gita Press and the Making of Hindu India*, Noida: HarperCollins India, 2015, p. 349.

74. 'Indian President's Son Apologizes over Rape Comments', BBC News, 27 December 2012 https://www.bbc.com/news/world-asia-india-20852513 (accessed on 20 January 2019).

75. Mohd Faisal Fareed, 'Mulayam's shocker: Boys will be boys, they make mistakes... Will you hang them for rape?,' *The Indian Express*, 11 April 2014, https://indianexpress.com/article/india/politics/mulayam-singh-yadav-questions-death-penalty-for-rape-says-boys-make-mistakes (accessed on 20 January 2019).

76. Ian Copland (2017), 'Cows, Congress and the Constitution: Jawaharlal Nehru and the Making of Article 48', South Asia: *Journal of South Asian Studies*, Vol. 40, No. 4, pp. 735–36.

77. Article 48, Directive Principles of State Policy, *Constitution of India*.

78. Ian Copland (2017), 'Cows, Congress and the Constitution: Jawaharlal Nehru and the Making of Article 48', South Asia: *Journal of South Asian Studies*, Vol. 40, No. 4, p. 725.

79. Balmurli Natarajan and Suraj Jacob, 'What India Really Eats', The Wire, 5 March 2018, https://thewire.in/food/india-food-eating-vegetarianism and https://www.epw.in/journal/2018/9/special-articles/provincialising-vegetarianism.html (accessed on 20 January 2019).

80. 'India Is World's Third-Biggest Beef Exporter: FAO Report', *The Indian Express*, 29 July 2017 https://indianexpress.com/article/world/india-third-biggest-beef-exporter-fao-report-4772389 (accessed on 20 January 2019).

81. Jeffrey Gettleman, and Suhasini Raj, '"Tell Everyone We Scalped You!" How Caste Still Rules in India' *The New York Times*, 17 November 2018, https://www.nytimes.com/2018/11/17/world/asia/tell-everyone-we-scalped-you-how-caste-still-rules-in-india.html (accessed on 20 January 2019).

82. Mahatma Gandhi's speech at Round Table Conference, London, 1931. Citation from *Constituent Assembly of India Debates*, Vol. IX, 10 September 1949, https://www.constitutionofindia.net/historical_constitutions/constituent_assembly_of_india_debates__proceedings____volume_ix_10th%20September%201949 (accessed on 1 January 2017).

83. Ibid.

84. Stanley Wolpert, *Gandhi's Passion: The Life and Legacy of Mahatma Gandhi*, New York: Oxford University Press, 2002, p. 91.

85. Jawaharlal Nehru, *The Discovery of India*, Calcutta: The Signet Press, 1946, p. 84

86. S. Senthalir. 'In Tamil Nadu, Beheading of a 14-Year-Old Is Suspected to Be a Caste Crime', Scroll.in, 28 October 2018, https://scroll.in/article/899899/in-tamil-nadu-beheading-of-a-14-year-old-is-suspected-to-be-a-caste-crime (accessed on 20 January 2019).

87. 'Dalit Ragpicker Mukesh Vaniya Beaten to Death in Rajkot; Five People Arrested', *The Indian Express*, 22 May 2018, https://indianexpress.com/article/india/dalit-ragpicker-beaten-to-death-in-rajkot-5184794 (accessed on 20 January 2019).

88. 'Indian Lowest-Caste Dalit Man Killed "for Owning Horse"', BBC News, 31 March 2018, https://www.bbc.com/news/world-asia-india-43605550 (accessed on 20 January 2019).

2: HUMAN CAPITAL

1. The Kumbh Mela is 'a mass Hindu pilgrimage of faith in which Hindus gather to bathe in a sacred or holy river. Traditionally, four fairs are widely recognized as the Kumbh Melas: the Prayagraj Kumbh Mela, Haridwar Kumbh Mela, the Nashik–Trimbakeshwar Simhastha, and Ujjain Simhastha.' These four fairs are held periodically at one of the following places by rotation: Allahabad

(Prayagraj), Haridwar, Nashik district (Nashik and Trimbak), and Ujjain. ('Kumbh Mela,' Encyclopedia Brittanica, https://www. britannica.com/topic/Kumbh-Mela (accessed on 22 February 2020). First two sentences are quoted verbatim.

2. Facts have been taken from Kumbh mela, https://kumbh.gov.in/en/ making-of-kumbh

3. Jeffrey Gettleman and Hari Kumar, 'Millions of Indians Trek to the Ganges, and Modi Chases Their Votes,' *The New York Times*, 10 February 2019, https://www.nytimes.com/2019/02/10/world/asia/ modi-india-kumbh-mela-ganges.html (accessed on 12 February 2019).

4. Gurcharan Das, *India Unbound: The Social and Economic revolution from Independence to the Global Information Age*, New York. Anchor Books, 2002, p xviii.

5. Dale Weldeau Jorgenson, J. Steven Landefeld, and Paul Schreyer, *Measuring Economic Sustainability and Progress*, Chicago: University of Chicago Press, 2014.

6. The Human Capital Project. World Bank Group, https://openknowledge.worldbank.org/bitstream/ handle/10986/30498/33252.pdf?sequence=5&isAllowed=y (accessed on 31 January 2019).

7. Ibid.

8. Ibid.

9. Ibid.

10. Ibid.

11. Vijay Joshi, *India's Long Road: The Search for Prosperity*, Gurgaon: Penguin, 2016, p. 51.

12. 'Literacy rate, adult (percentage of people ages fifteen and above), World Bank, https://data.worldbank.org/indicator/SE.ADT.LITR. ZS (accessed on 22 February 2020).

13. Vijay Joshi, *India's Long Road: The Search for Prosperity*, Gurgaon: Penguin, 2016, p. 51.

14. James Heitzman and Robert L. Worden (eds), *India: A Country Study*, Washington: GPO for the Library of Congress, 1995, http:// countrystudies.us/india/37.htm (accessed on 1 January 2018).

15. Office of the Registrar General & Census Commissioner. *Census of India*, 2011; Directorate of Census Operations, Jammu & Kashmir, *Census of India, 2011*. http://censusindia.gov.in/Census_And_You/ age_structure_and_marital_status.aspx (accessed on 1 January 2018).

16. Arvind Subramanian, *Of Counsel: The Challenges of the Modi–Jaitley Economy*, Gurgaon: Penguin Random House, 2018, p. 230.

17. Ibid., p. 232.

18. 'Economic Survey warns of India's ageing population, says retirement age should rise,' Livemint, 4 July 2019, https://www.livemint.com/budget/economic-survey/eco-survey-warns-of-india-s-ageing-population-says-retirement-age-should-rise-1562248716749.html (accessed on 22 February 2020).

19. Arvind Subramanian, *Of Counsel: The Challenges of the Modi–Jaitley Economy*, Gurgaon: Penguin Random House, 2018, p. 233.

20. 'School Education System in India before and after Independence', http://shodhganga.inflibnet.ac.in/bitstream/10603/69112/5/chapter%203.pdf (accessed on 1 January 2018).

21. Ibid.

22. Roshni Chakrabarty, 'Jawaharlal Nehru and His Views on Education', Newsgram, November 2015, https://www.newsgram.com/jawaharlal-nehru-and-his-views-on-education (accessed on 1 January 2018).

23. 'Remembering Maulana Abul Kalam Azad, India's first education minister,' *The Indian Express*, 11 November 2017, https://indianexpress.com/article/india/remembering-maulana-abul-kalam-azad-indias-first-education-minister-4932256 (accessed on 1 January 2018).

24. 'National Education Day: Celebrating the legacy of Maulana Abul Kalam Azad and his contribution to Indian education system,' *The Economic Times*, 11 November 2017, https://economictimes.indiatimes.com/news/politics-and-nation/national-education-day-celebrating-the-legacy-of-maulana-abul-kalam-azad-and-his-contribution-to-indian-education-system/the-man-behind-iits-ugc-and-other-universities/slideshow/61605224.cms (accessed on 1 January 2018).

25. 'University and Higher Education', Department of Higher Education, Ministry of Human Resource Development, 19 April 2016, https://mhrd.gov.in/university-and-higher-education (accessed on 1 January 2018).

26. Rachel Williams, 'Why girls in India are still missing out on the education they need,' *The Guardian*, 11 March 2013, https://www.theguardian.com/education/2013/mar/11/indian-children-education-opportunities (accessed on 1 January 2018).

27. Ibid.

28. Vijay Joshi, *India's Long Road: The Search for Prosperity*, Gurgaon: Penguin, 2016, p. 173.
29. PTI, 'India's R&D spend stagnant for 20 years at 0.7% of GDP'. *The Economic Times*, 29 January 2018, https://economictimes. indiatimes.com/news/economy/finance/indias-rd-spend-stagnant-for-20-years-at-0-7-of-gdp/articleshow/62697271.cms (accessed on 1 January 2019).
30. Neetu Chandra Sharma, 'Need more funds, contribution from private sector, varsities for research: Survey', Livemint, January 2018. https://www.livemint.com/Politics/xaD1dr8Ucgwcg4oPHRqyPL/ Need-more-funds-contribution-from-private-sector-varsities.html (accessed on 1 January 2019).
31. Ananya Bhattacharya, 'As Asia drives ahead on innovation highway, India sputters', Quartz, October 2017, https://qz.com/india/1090423/ as-asia-drives-ahead-on-innovation-highway-india-sputters/ (accessed on 1 January 2018).
32. Suparna Dutt D'Cunha, '90% of Indian Startups Will Fail Because of Lack of Innovation, Study Says', *Forbes*, May 2017 (accessed on 1 January 2018).
33. Ibid.
34. National Academies of Sciences, Engineering and Medicine, 'Building America's skilled technical workforce', National Academies Press, 2017, https://www.nap.edu/read/23472/chapter/3, pp. 6–7 (accessed on 1 January 2019).
35. Laurence Chandy (ed.), 'The Future of Work in the Developing World: Brookings Blum Roundtable 2016 Post-conference Report', Global Economy and Development at Brookings, 2016. https://www.brookings.edu/wp-content/uploads/2017/01/ global_20170131_future-of-work.pdf., pp. 17–18 (accessed on 1 January 2019).
36. Sarosh Kuruvilla and Rodney Chua, 'How Do Nations Develop Skills? Lessons from the Skill Development Experiences of Singapore' (2000), https://digitalcommons.ilr.cornell.edu/cgi/viewcontent.cgi? article=1007&context=cbpubs, pp. 13–15 (accessed on 1 January 2019).
37. Ibid.
38. Prashant Nanda, 'Economic Survey 2018: Jobs set to be a pressing challenge in the medium term,' Livemint, 30 January 2018, https:// www.livemint.com/Politics/jtUrXJSVD9V7U6oroWU6aK/

Economic-Survey-2018-Jobs-set-to-be-a-pressing-challenge-in.html (accessed on 1 January 2019).

39. K. Sujatha Rao, *Do We Care? India's Health System*, New Delhi: Oxford University Press, 2017, p. xii.

40. Vijay Joshi, *India's Long Road: The Search for Prosperity*, Gurgaon: Penguin, 2016, p. 179.

41. Ibid., p. 181.

42. Ibid., p. 180.

43. Srinivasan, K., and Raka Sharan, 'Organization of Indian Health Bureaucracy and its Delivery System', *Productivity, A Quarterly Journal of the National Productivity Council, India*, Vol. 46, No. 4 (2006), pp. 477–86, https://www.researchgate.net/profile/Srinivasan_Kannan2/publication/24115331_Organization_of_Indian_Health_Bureaucracy_and_its_Delivery_System/links/00b4952b15e7021311000000/Organization-of-Indian-Health-Bureaucracy-and-its-Delivery-System.pdf (accessed on 1 January 2019).

44. Vijay Joshi, *India's Long Road: The Search for Prosperity*, Gurgaon: Penguin, 2016, p. 189.

45. Mohan Rao, Krishna Rao, Shiva Kumar and Mirai Chatterjee, 'Human resources for health in India', *The Lancet*, Vol. 377, Issue 9765, pp. 587–98, https://www.thelancet.com/journals/lancet/article/PIIS0140-6736(10)61888-0/fulltext) (accessed on 1 January 2019).

46. K. Sujatha Rao, *Do We Care? India's Health System*, New Delhi: Oxford University Press, 2017, p. 31.

47. Gilles Duranton, 'Cities: Engines of Growth and Prosperity for Developing Countries,' World Bank Commission on Growth and Development, Working Paper No. 12, 2008, http://siteresources.worldbank.org/EXTPREMNET/Resources/489960-1338997241035/Growth_Commission_Working_Paper_12_Cities_Engines_Growth_Prosperity_Developing_Countries.pdf (accessed on 1 January 2019).

48. Brad Cunningham, 'Why Growth Economics Needs to Understand Cities', Brookings, 28 November 2016, https://www.brookings.edu/blog/the-avenue/2016/11/28/why-growth-economics-needs-to-understand-cities (accessed on 1 January 2019).

49. Richard Florida, 'Why Big Cities Matter in the Developing World', *CityLab: The Atlantic Monthly Group*, 14 January 2014, www.citylab.com/life/2014/01/why-big-cities-matter-developing-world/6025 (accessed on 1 January 2019).

50. Vijay Joshi, *India's Long Road: The Search for Prosperity*, Gurgaon: Penguin, 2016, p. 123.

51. Shirish Sankhe and Ireena Vittal, 'India's urban awakening: Building inclusive cities, sustaining economic growth', McKinsey & Company, April 2010, https://www.mckinsey.com/featured-insights/urbanization/urban-awakening-in-india (accessed on 1 January 2019).

52. Ibid.

53. Edward Luce, *In Spite of the Gods: The Strange Rise of Modern India*, London: Abacus, 2011, p. 10.

54. Vijay Joshi, *India's Long Road: The Search for Prosperity*, Gurgaon: Penguin, 2016, p. 123.

55. V. Anantha Nageswaran and Gulzar Natarajan, *Can India Grow?: Challenges, Opportunities, and the Way Forward*, Washington DC: Carnegie Endowment for International Peace, 2016., p. 92.

56. Pretika Khanna, 'These two Indian cities are in Global Liveability Index 2019,' Livemint, 4 September 2019, https://www.livemint.com/news/india/these-two-indian-cities-are-in-global-liveability-index-2019-1567582279267.html (accessed on 22 February 2020).

57. Richard Dobbs and Shirish Sankhe, 'Comparing urbanization in China and India', McKinsey & Company, July 2010, https://www.mckinsey.com/featured-insights/urbanization/comparing-urbanization-in-china-and-india (accessed on 1 January 2019).

58. Ibid.

59. Shirish Sankhe and Ireena Vittal, 'India's urban awakening: Building inclusive cities, sustaining economic growth', McKinsey & Company, April 2010, https://www.mckinsey.com/featured-insights/urbanization/urban-awakening-in-india (accessed on 1 January 2019).

3: ECONOMIC POTENTIAL

1. T.N. Ninan, *The Turn of the Tortoise: The Challenge and Promise of India's Future*, New Delhi: Penguin Books, 2015, p. 307.

2. Ibid.

3. TNN, 'India No Longer Home to the Largest Number of Poor: Study', *The Times of India*, 27 June 2018, timesofindia.indiatimes.com/india/india-no-longer-home-to-the-largest-no-of-poor-study/articleshow/64754988.cms (accessed on 1 January 2019).

4. 'Yogi Adityanath cites Lohia's "prediction", suggests Narendra Modi will run nation for 25 years,' PTI, 15 May 2019, https://economictimes.indiatimes.com/news/elections/lok-sabha/uttar-pradesh/yogi-adityanath-cites-lohias-prediction-suggests-narendra-modi-will-run-nation-for-25-years/articleshow/69342314.cms?from=mdr (accessed on 1 June 2019).

5. Lynn Parramore, 'How India's Traumatic Capitalism is Reshaping the World', Institute for New Economic Thinking, 2 March 2015, https://www.ineteconomics.org/perspectives/blog/how-indias-traumatic-capitalism-is-reshaping-the-world (accessed on 1 January 2019).

6. Poonam Gupta, 'This Is the Story of India's GDP Growth' World Economic Forum, 13 April 2018, www.weforum.org/agenda/2018/04/india-s-remarkably-robust-and-resilient-growth-story (accessed on 1 January 2019).

7. Preetika Rana and Joanna Sugden, 'India's Record Since Independence', *The Wall Street Journal*, Dow Jones & Company, 15 August 2013, blogs.wsj.com/indiarealtime/2013/08/15/indias-record-since-independence/ (accessed on 1 January 2019).

8. B.B. Bhattacharya and Arup Mitra, 'Excess Growth of Tertiary Sector in Indian Economy: Issues and Implications', *Economic and Political Weekly*, Vol. 25, No. 44, 1990, pp. 2445–2450, JSTOR, www.jstor.org/stable/4396935 (accessed on 1 January 2019).

9. Poonam Gupta, 'This Is the Story of India's GDP Growth' World Economic Forum, 13 April 2018, www.weforum.org/agenda/2018/04/india-s-remarkably-robust-and-resilient-growth-story (accessed on 1 January 2019).

10. Ibid.

11. Vijay Joshi, *India's Long Road: The Search for Prosperity*, Gurgaon: Penguin, 2016, p. 6.

12. Ibid., p. 4.

13. Ibid., p. 6.

14. Ibid., p. 7.

15. Yashwant Sinha and Aditya Sinha, *India Unmade: How the Modi Government Broke the Economy*, New Delhi; Juggernaut, 2018, pp. 61–62.

16. Ibid., p. 22.

17. T.N. Ninan, *The Turn of the Tortoise: The Challenge and Promise of India's Future*, New Delhi: Penguin Books, 2015, p. 3.

18. 'Rana Safvi, 'No, Mughals didn't loot India. They made us rich', 16 September 2017. https://www.dailyo.in/politics/mughals-contribution-indian-economy-rich-culture-tourism-british/ story/1/19549.html (accessed on 1 January 2019).

19. 'World history by per capita GDP', Livemint, 25 August 2010, https://www.livemint.com/Opinion/Nb7KkZ3yOVSNW3vHf9K1oM/ World-history-by-per-capita-GDP.html (accessed on 1 January 2019).

20. Gurcharan Das, *India Unbound: The Social and Economic Revolution from Independence to the Global Information Age*, New York: Anchor Books, 2002, p. 19.

21. Ibid., p. 25.

22. Rama P. Kanungo, Chris Rowley and Anurag N. Banerjee (eds), *Changing the Indian Economy. Renewal, Reform and Revival*, Oxford and New York: Elsevier, 2018., p. 92.

23. Swaminathan S. Anklesaria Aiyar, '25 Years of Indian Economic Reform', Cato Institute, October 2016, https://www.cato.org/ publications/policy-analysis/twenty-five-years-indian-economic-reform (accessed on 1 January 2019).

24. Kaushik Basu, *An Economist in the Real World: The Art of Policymaking in India*, Gurgaon: Penguin Viking, 2016, p. 11.

25. Ibid., pp. 14–16.

26. Ibid.

27. Ibid.

28. Edward Luce, *In Spite of the Gods: The Strange Rise of Modern India*, London: Abacus, 2011, p. 11.

29. Ibid.

30. Kaushik Basu, *An Economist in the Real World: The Art of Policymaking in India*, Gurgaon: Penguin Viking, 2016, pp. 14–16.

31. Gurcharan Das, *India Unbound: The Social and Economic Revolution from Independence to the Global Information Age*, New York: Anchor Books, 2002, p. 10.

32. The signatories of the Plan were Jehangir Ratanji Dadabhoy (JRD) Tata, Ghanshyam Das Birla, Ardeshir Dalal, Lala Shri Ram, Kasturbhai Lalbhai, Ardeshir Darabshaw Shroff, Sir Purshottamdas Thakurdas and John Mathai.

33. P.S. Lokanathan. 'The Bombay Plan', *Foreign Affairs*, July 1945, https://www.foreignaffairs.com/articles/india/1945-07-01/bombay-plan (accessed on 1 January 2019).

34. Gurcharan Das, *India Unbound: The Social and Economic Revolution from Independence to the Global Information Age*, New York: Anchor Books, 2002, pp. 63–64.

35. Jagdish Bhagwati and Arvind Panagariya, *Why Growth Matters: How Economic Growth in India Reduced Poverty and the Lessons for Other Developing Countries*, New York: Public Affairs, 2013, p. vii.

36. Ibid., p. xii.

37. Ibid., pp. xii–xiii.

38. Vijay Joshi, *India's Long Road: The Search for Prosperity*, Gurgaon: Penguin, 2016, p. 18.

39. Ibid.

40. Ibid.

41. Ibid.

42. Ibid., p. 19.

43. Gurcharan Das, *India Unbound: The Social and Economic Revolution from Independence to the Global Information Age*, New York: Anchor Books, 2002, p. 75.

44. Ibid.

45. Ibid., p. 158.

46. Sudeep Chakravarti, 'In an India known for thinking small, Rajiv Gandhi generated high-stakes optimism', *India Today*, 15 June 1991, https://www.indiatoday.in/magazine/cover-story/story/19910615-in-an-india-known-for-thinking-small-rajiv-gandhi-generated-high-stakes-optimism-814461-1991-06-15 (accessed on 1 January 2019).

47. Ibid.

48. Gurcharan Das, *India Unbound: The Social and Economic Revolution from Independence to the Global Information Age*, New York: Anchor Books, 2002, p. 161.

49. Kaushik Basu, *An Economist in the Real World: The Art of Policymaking in India*, Gurgaon: Penguin Viking, 2016, p. 26.

50. Ibid.

51. Ibid.

52. Swaminathan S. Anklesaria Aiyar '25 Years of Indian Economic Reform', Cato Institute, October 2016, https://www.cato.org/publications/policy-analysis/twenty-five-years-indian-economic-reform (accessed on 1 January 2019).

53. Vijay Joshi, *India's Long Road: The Search for Prosperity*, Gurgaon: Penguin, 2016, p. 26.

54. T.N. Ninan, *The Turn of the Tortoise: The Challenge and Promise of India's Future*, New Delhi: Penguin Books, 2015, p. 23.

55. Ibid.

56. Ibid.

57. Kaushik Basu, *An Economist in the Real World: The Art of Policymaking in India,* Gurgaon: Penguin Viking, 2016, pp. 27–28.

58. 'India's Forex Reserves Soar Past $400 Billion-Mark Again' Livemint, 8 March 2019, www.livemint.com/industry/banking/india-s-forex-reserves-soar-past-400-billion-mark-again-1552049140380.html (accessed on 1 April 2019).

59. 'One more push', *The Economist*, July 2011. https://www.economist.com/leaders/2011/07/21/one-more-push (accessed on 1 January 2019).

60. Shankar Acharya, 'India: Crisis, Reforms and Growth in the Nineties', Working Paper, Stanford Center for International Development, July 2002, https://siepr.stanford.edu/sites/default/files/publications/139wp.pdf (accessed on 1 January 2019).

61. Swaminathan S. Anklesaria Aiyar, '25 Years of Indian Economic Reform, Cato Institute, October 2016, https://www.cato.org/publications/policy-analysis/twenty-five-years-indian-economic-reform (accessed on 1 January 2019).

62. Yashwant Sinha and Aditya Sinha, *India Unmade: How the Modi Government Broke the Economy*, New Delhi: Juggernaut, 2018, p. 34.

63. Ibid., p. 37.

64. Ibid., p. 38.

65. T.N. Ninan, *The Turn of the Tortoise: The Challenge and Promise of India's Future*, New Delhi: Penguin Books, 2015, p. 23.

66. Manoj Kumar, 'Exclusive: India Needs Land, Labor Reform to Aid Manufacturing - chief economic advisor', Reuters, 4 March 2019, www.reuters.com/article/us-india-economy-adviser-exclusive/exclusive-india-needs-land-labor-reform-to-aid-manufacturing-chief-economic-adviser-idUSKCN1QL17K (accessed on 1 January 2019).

67. Ibid.

68. Vijay Joshi, *India's Long Road: The Search for Prosperity*, Gurgaon: Penguin, 2016, p. 65.

69. Vibhudatta Pradhan and Vrishti Beniwal, 'Modi's Labour Reform Push May Remove Key Hurdle For Investors,' Bloomberg,

25 November 2019 https://www.bloomberg.com/news/articles/2019-11-25/modi-s-labor-reform-push-may-remove-key-hurdle-for-investors (accessed on 1 December 2019).

70. Anirban Nag and Vrishti Beniwal, 'Modi Pivots to India Reforms to Shift Focus From Hindu Base,' Bloomberg, 21 November 2019, https://www.bloomberg.com/news/articles/2019-11-21/modi-brings-india-s-economy-into-focus-amid-privatization-push (accessed on 1 December 2019).

71. Asit Ranjan Mitra, 'Govt to invite bids for Air India privatization,' Bloomberg, 8 October 2019, https://www.livemint.com/companies/news/govt-to-invite-bids-for-air-india-privatization-11570557355060.html (accessed on 1 November 2019).

72. Prashant K. Nanda, 'Job creation still a challenge after four years of Modi govt', Livemint. May 2018, https://www.livemint.com/Industry/dlzi6Osi2iB7UC18znYe1I/Job-creation-still-a-challenge-after-four-years-of-Modi-govt.html (accessed on 1 January 2019).

73. Manoj Kumar, 'As "foreign" economic advisers leave, a protectionist India returns', Reuters, July 2018, https://www.reuters.com/article/us-india-politics-economists-insight/as-foreign-economic-advisers-leave-a-protectionist-india-returns-idUSKBN1K20UB (accessed on 1 January 2019).

74. Vijay Joshi, *India's Long Road: The Search for Prosperity*, Gurgaon: Penguin, 2016, p. 98.

75. Ibid.

76. Ibid., p. 99.

77. Ibid., p. 98.

78. Arvind Subramanian, *Of Counsel: The Challenges of the Modi–Jaitley Economy*, Gurgaon: Penguin Random House, 2018, p. 206.

79. Yashwant Sinha and Aditya Sinha, *India Unmade: How the Modi Government Broke the Economy*, New Delhi: Juggernaut, 2018, p. 89.

80. Vijay Joshi, *India's Long Road: The Search for Prosperity*, Gurgaon: Penguin, 2016, p. 105.

81. Ibid., p 106.

82. T.N. Ninan. *The Turn of the Tortoise: The Challenge and Promise of India's Future*, New Delhi: Penguin Books, 2015, pp. 6–7.

83. Ibid.

84. Ibid., p. 88.

85. Ibid., pp. 100–01.

86. Ibid., pp. 6–7.

87. Ibid.
88. Ibid., p, 7.

4: GEOPOLITICS AND FOREIGN POLICY

1. Jawaharlal Nehru, *India's Foreign Policy*, New Delhi, Publications Division, Government of India, 1961, p. 22.
2. Stephen Cohen, *India: Emerging Power*, Washington DC: Brookings Press, 2001, p. 62.
3. 'FS's Keynote address to the 1st Disarmament and International Security Affairs Fellowship,' Ministry of External Affairs Media Center, Speeches and Statements, 14 January 2019, https://www.mea.gov.in/Speeches-Statements.htm?dtl/30910/FSs_Keynote_address_to_the_1st_Disarmament_and_International_Security_Affairs_Fellowship (accessed on 23 February 2020).
4. Ibid.
5. Jawaharlal Nehru's speech on 22 January 1947 during the Constituent Assembly Debates. Taken from *Constituent Assembly Debates of India, Official Report,* Vol. II (20th January to 25th January 1947) https://www.constitutionofindia.net/constitution_assembly_debates/volume/2/1947-01-22 (accessed on 22 March 2020).
6. Sisir K. Bose and Sugata Bose (eds), *The Essential Writings of Netaji Subhas Chandra Bose*, New Delhi: Oxford University Press, 2004, pp. 105, 205, 216–18.
7. Venkaiah Naidu, 'Make India Vishwaguru again', *The Indian Express*, 5 September 2018, 'India should once again become Vishwa Guru and hub of innovation and knowledge: Vice President,' Press Information Bureau, 22 October 2019, https://pib.gov.in/newsite/PrintRelease.aspx?relid=193941; 'Next 5 years will make India Vishwaguru: PM Modi in Gujarat,' *The Times of India*, 27 May 2019, https://timesofindia.indiatimes.com/india/next-5-yrs-will-make-india-vishwa-guru-modi-in-gujarat/articleshow/69510732.cms (accessed on 22 March 2020).
8. Jawaharlal Nehru, 'Changing India', *Foreign Affairs*, April 1963, Volume 41, No 3, p. 457, https://www.foreignaffairs.com/articles/asia/1963-04-01/changing-india (accessed on 23 February 2020).
9. Jawaharlal Nehru's speech at closed door session at the Afro-Asian Conference, Bandung, 22 April 1955. Taken from Sarvepalli Gopal, *Jawaharlal Nehru: A Biography*, Volume II (1947-56), Delhi: Oxford University Press, 1979, p. 241.

10. Werner Levi, 'Indian Neutralism Reconsidered,' *Pacific Affairs*, Vol. 37, No. 2, Summer 1964, pp. 137–47.

11. George Tanham, 'Indian Strategic Thought: An Interpretive Essay', RAND Corporation, 1 January 1992, www.rand.org/pubs/reports/ R4207.html (accessed on 1 January 2017).

12. Alex Wooley, 'Report: China, India Winning Friends in the Developing World, but Lag Far behind US', AidData, a Research Lab at William and Mary College, 30 October 2018, www.aiddata. org/blog/china-india-winning-friends-in-the-developing-world-but-lag-far-behind-u-s (accessed on 1 January 2019).

13. 'India and United Nations: Peacekeeping and Peacebuilding,' Permanent Mission of India to the UN, New York, https://www. pminewyork.gov.in/pdf/menu/submenu__668040979.pdf (accessed on 21 February 2020).

14. 'Country Summary: India,' World Bank Group Finances, Washington DC: World Bank, https://finances.worldbank.org/ countries/India (accessed on 1 January 2019).

15. 'World Bank Group to Focus on India Growth, Jobs, Human Capital', World Bank, 20 September 2018, www.worldbank.org/en/ news/press-release/2018/09/20/world-bank-group-focus-on-india-growth-jobs-human-capital (accessed on 1 January 2019).

16. 'At a Glance: India and the IMF,' International Monetary Fund, Washington DC: International Monetary Fund, https://www.imf. org/external/country/IND/rr/glance.htm (accessed on 1 January 2019).

17. Raphael Minder, Jamil Anderlini and James Lamont, 'China blocks ADB India loan plan,' *Financial Times*, 10 April 2019, https://www. ft.com/content/033935c2-25e4-11de-be57-00144feabdc0 (accessed on 22 March 2020).

18. Anjli Raval, 'India eyes oil demand growth top spot,' *Financial Times*, 22 July 2016, https://www.ft.com/content/bacac870-4f46-11e6-8172-e39ecd3b86fc (accessed on 1 January 2019).

19. Sudarshan Varadhan, 'Canada, US Gain as India Cuts Dependence on Australian Coking Coal', Reuters, 25 June 2019, https://www. reuters.com/article/us-india-coal-imports/canada-u-s-gain-as-india-cuts-dependence-on-australian-coking-coal-idUSKCN1TQ234 (accessed on 22 March 2020).

20. Figures have been taken from Y.D. Gundevia, *Outside the Archives*, Hyderabad: Sangam Books, 1984, pp. 48–49.

21. 'The worldwide web: India should make more of a valuable asset abroad,' *The Economist*, 23 May 2015, https://www.economist. com/special-report/2015/05/21/the-worldwide-web (accessed on 1 January 2019).

22. 'India highest recipient of remittances at $79 bn in 2018: World Bank', *The Times of India*, 9 April 2019, https://economictimes. indiatimes.com/nri/forex-and-remittance/india-highest-recipient-of-remittances-at-79-bn-in-2018-world-bank/articleshow/68788815. cms?from=mdr (accessed on 1 July 2019).

23. For details please look at various Presidential speeches. Here are a few: Giani Zail Singh, Address to the Parliament, New Delhi, 20 February 1986. Taken from, *Speeches of President Giani Zail Singh, Vol II*, New Delhi: Publications Division, Ministry of Information and Broadcasting, Government of India, 1992, pp. 14–23; Giani Zail Singh, Address to the Parliament, New Delhi, 23 February 1987. Taken from *Speeches of President Giani Zail Singh, Vol II*, New Delhi: Publications Division, Ministry of Information and Broadcasting, Government of India, 1992, pp. 139–51; A.P.J. Abdul Kalam address to joint session of Parliament 2003, 24 March 2003. Taken from http://www.indianembassy.ru/index. php/en/component/content/article/113-media/statements-speeches-interviews-archives/258-24032003-the-president-of-india-dr-apj-abdul-kalam (accessed on 1 January 2017), A.P.J. Abdul Kalam's address to joint session of Parliament 2004, 7 June 2004. Taken from http://architexturez.net/doc/az-cf-21867#off-canvas (accessed on 1 January 2017).

24. Interview with Ambassador Husain Haqqani, Washington DC, 1 February 2017.

25. S.D. Muni, 'India and Regionalism in South Asia: A Political Perspective,' in Bimal Prasad (ed.), *India's Foreign Policy: Studies in Continuity and Change*, New Delhi: Vikas Publishing House, 1979, pp. 107–08.

26. 'Nehru vows to Bar invasion of Nepal,' *The New York Times*, 17 March 1950, https://urldefense.proofpoint.com/v2/ url?u=https-3A__www.nytimes.com_1950_03_18_archives_ nehru-2Dvows-2Dto-2Dbar-2Dinvasion-2Dof-2Dnepal-2Dstates-2Dhe-2Ddoes-2Dnot-2Dbelieve-2Dit.html&d=DwMF-g&c=hh7v4vz1gCZ__1Ci-hUEVZfsSwlOcPhT2q8Zs1ka6Ao&r=TefW0vqYwtPtyVSBLgYs7T4AAeU8rYPASXnsBCv1XkC8yJfHw

ncAA2GKMhI_TcuJ&m=bE--6SKTL5AuUWNrTy7s-6XhdFwnw
8Hy9zYwDlWqPxg&s=g6AUqCWgTIi_Ar245t8Jjnxpz3EoNJlX-
L97ag4W73A&e=" https://www.nytimes.com/1950/03/18/
archives/nehru-vows-to-bar-invasion-of-nepal-states-he-does-
not-believe-it.html; Robert Trumbull, 'India, Bhutan sign
perpetual Pact, Himalayan Kingdom gets Subsidy,' *The New
York Times*, 8 August 1949 https://urldefense.proofpoint.com/v2/
url?u=https-3A__www.nytimes.com_1949_08_09_archives_india-
2Dbhutan-2Dsign-2Dperpetual-2Dpact-2Dhimalayan-2Dkingdom-
2Dgets-2Dsubsidy.html-3FsearchResultPosition-3D1&d=DwMF-
g&c=hh7v4vz1gCZ__1Ci-hUEVZfsSwlOcPhT2q8Zs1ka6Ao&r=T
efW0vqYwtPtyVSBLgYs7T4AAeU8rYPASXnsBCv1XkC8yJfHwn
cAA2GKMhI_TcuJ&m=bE--6SKTL5AuUWNrTy7s-6XhdFwnw8
Hy9zYwDlWqPxg&s=MZ4BRmarJ4eLZSJnqRMMFMq13I5Rk1h
XRj-dl085z8k&e=" https://www.nytimes.com/1949/08/09/archives/
india-bhutan-sign-perpetual-pact-himalayan-kingdom-gets-subsidy.
html?searchResultPosition=1; Robert Trumbull, 'India assumes
Defense of Sikkim, Strategic Principality in Himalayas', *The New
York Times*, 5 December 1950 https://urldefense.proofpoint.com/v2/
url?u=https-3A__www.nytimes.com_1950_12_06_archives_india-
2Dassumes-2Ddefense-2Dof-2Dsikkim-2Dstrategic-2Dprincipality-
2Din-2Dhimalayas.html-3FsearchResultPosition-3D1&d=DwMF-
g&c=hh7v4vz1gCZ__1Ci-hUEVZfsSwlOcPhT2q8Zs1ka6Ao&r=T
efW0vqYwtPtyVSBLgYs7T4AAeU8rYPASXnsBCv1XkC8yJfHwn
cAA2GKMhI_TcuJ&m=bE--6SKTL5AuUWNrTy7s-6XhdFwnw8
Hy9zYwDlWqPxg&s=1mQYCK2JH9Y4fkWt8FmjrKZM3FkDTU
YowHU0YwKCvws&e=" https://www.nytimes.com/1950/12/06/
archives/india-assumes-defense-of-sikkim-strategic-principality-
in-himalayas.html?searchResultPosition=1 (all three accessed on 1
January 2018).

27. Ashok Kapur, 'Strategic choices in Indian foreign policy,'
International Journal, Vol. 27, No. 3, Summer 1972, pp. 448–50.

28. For details, please read the author's *Explaining Pakistan's Foreign
Policy: Escaping India*, London: Routledge, 2011.

29. Press Trust of India, 'India Announces Rs 4,500 Crore Assistance
to Bhutan', *The Times of India*, 28 December 2018, timesofindia.
indiatimes.com/india/india-announces-rs-4500-crore-assistance-to-
bhutan/articleshow/67285038.cms (accessed on 1 January 2019).

30. Sanjeev Miglani, 'India's Modi Gives $1.4 Billion Aid to Maldives
amid Worry over Its...' Reuters, 17 December 2018, www.reuters.

com/article/us-india-maldives/indias-modi-gives-1-4-billion-aid-to-maldives-amid-worry-over-its-china-debt-idUSKBN1OG0RO (accessed on 1 January 2019).

31. 'India Lends a Helping Hand to Sri Lanka', Indian Navy, www.indiannavy.nic.in/content/india-lends-helping-hand-sri-lanka (accessed on 1 January 2019).

32. Steve Coll, *Ghost Wars: The Secret History of the CIA, Afghanistan, and Bin Laden, from the Soviet Invasion to September 10, 2001*, New York: Penguin Press, 2004, p. 175.

33. 'Statement by External Affairs Minister at the Second Session of the India-Central Asia Dialogue', Ministry of External Affairs, Government of India, 13 January 2019, mea.gov.in/Speeches-Statements.htm?dtl%2F30906%2FStatement_by_External_Affairs_Minister_at_the_Second_Session_of_the IndiaCentral_Asia_Dialogue (accessed on 19 January 2019).

34. For further details please read John Garver, *Protracted Contest: Sino-Indian Rivalry in the Twentieth Century* Seattle: University of Washington Press, 2001.

35. For further details please see the following: Bharat Karnad, 'Habit of Free Riding,' *Seminar India*, Vol. 599, July 2009, http://www.india-seminar.com/2009/599/599_bharat_karnad.htm; Gurmeet Kanwal, 'Countering China's encirclement plan,' *The Deccan Herald*, 2 November 2011, https://www.deccanherald.com/content/202077/countering-chinas-encirclement-plan.html (both accessed on 1 January 2019).

36. 'What does China really spend on its military?,' China Power Project, Center for Strategic and International Studies, https://chinapower.csis.org/military-spending/ (accessed on 23 February 2020); L.K. Behera, 'India's Defence Budget 2020-21,' Institute for Defence and Strategic Analyses, 4 February 2020, https://idsa.in/issuebrief/india-def-budget-2020-21-lkbehera-040220 (accessed on 23 February 2020).

37. Letter from Sardar Patel to Nehru, 27 April 1948 on the issue of the recruitment of services. Taken from Durga Das (ed.) *Sardar Patel's Correspondence, 1945–50, Vol. IV*, Ahmedabad: Navjivan Publishing House, 1972, pp. 324–25.

38. Ibid.

39. Jayantanuja Bandyopadhyaya, *The Making of India's Foreign Policy: Determinants, Institutions, Processes and Personalities*, Bombay: Allied Publishers, 1970, pp. 211–12.

40. Elizabeth Roche, 'Ministry of External Affairs to hire from private sector', Livemint, 18 June 2015, https://www.livemint.com/Politics/viacY3ov7WTeGmcLdle8yK/MEA-to-hire-from-private-sector.html (accessed on 1 January 2017).

41. Indrani Bagchi, 'Crisis point: Not enough diplomats in India,' *The Times of India*, 30 April 2007 http://articles.timesofindia.indiatimes.com/2007-04-30/india/27878506_1_indian-diplomat-mea-foreign-policy (accessed on 1 January 2019).

42. Elizabeth Roche, 'Ministry of External Affairs to hire from private sector,' Livemint, 18 June 2015. https://www.livemint.com/Politics/viacY3ov7WTeGmcLdle8yK/MEA-to-hire-from-private-sector.html (accessed on 1 January 2017).

43. Ibid.

44. 'Modi government to restructure Ministry of External Affairs,' *The New Indian Express*, 1 February 2020 https://www.newindianexpress.com/nation/2020/feb/01/modi-government-to-restructure-ministry-of-external-affairs-2097285.html (accessed on 22 February 2020).

45. Pranab Dal Samanta, 'NSA gets teeth, Secretariat put in government business rules,' *The Economic Times*, 3 October 2019, https://economictimes.indiatimes.com/news/politics-and-nation/nsa-gets-teeth-secretariat-put-in-government-business-rules/articleshow/71416098.cms?from=mdr (accessed on 1 December 2019).

5: MILITARY AND GRAND STRATEGY

1. Hedley Bull, *The Anarchical Society: A Study of Order in World Politics'*, New York: Columbia University Pres, 1977, pp. 200–03.

2. Lewis Carroll, *Alice's Adventures in Wonderland,* commonly known as *Alice in Wonderland*, London: Macmillan, 1865.

3. John Lewis Gaddis, *On Grand Strategy*, New Haven, Connecticut: Yale University Press, 2018.

4. Aparna Pande, *From Chanakya to Modi: Evolution of India's Foreign Policy*, Noida: HarperCollins India, 2017.

5. S.D. Muni, *India's Foreign Policy: The Democracy Dimension, With Special Reference to Neighbours*, New Delhi: Foundation Books/Cambridge University Press, 2009, p. 29.

6. '2018 India Military Strength', Global Firepower Index, https://www.globalfirepower.com/country-military-strength-detail.asp?country_id=india (accessed on 1 January 2019).

7. Ibid.
8. Iain Marlow, 'India Joins World's Top Five Defense Spenders, Surpassing France', Bloomberg.com, 1 May 2018, www.bloomberg. com/news/articles/2018-05-01/china-tensions-push-india-into-world-s-top-five-defense-spenders (accessed on 1 January 2019).
9. Rahul Bedi, 'India's low defence budget for FY 2020/21 to hit military modernization,' *Janes Defence Weekly*, 3 February 2020 https://www.janes.com/article/94060/india-s-low-defence-budget-for-fy-2020-21-to-hit-military-modernisation (accessed on 22 February 2020).
10. 'SIPRI Military Expenditure Database', Stockholm International Peace Research Institute, https://www.sipri.org/databases/milex (accessed on 1 January 2019).
11. Sanjib Baruah, '68 per cent of weapons outdated: Army Vice-chief', *Deccan Chronicle*, 14 March 2018, https://www.deccanchronicle. com/nation/current-affairs/140318/68-per-cent-of-weapons-outdated-army-vice-chief-lt-gen-sarath chand.html (accessed on 1 January 2019).
12. Winston Churchill's speech 'The Landslide,' House of Commons, 26 January 1931. Taken from Winston Churchill, *India: Defending the Jewel in the Crown*, London: Dragonwyck Publications Co, 1931, Chapter IV.
13. From a discussion between Winston Churchill and General Claude Auchinleck, Commander of British forces in Western desert, Spring 1942. Taken from Arthur Herman, *Gandhi & Churchill: The Epic Rivalry That Destroyed an Empire and Forged Our Age*, New York: Bantam Books, 2008, p. 482.
14. Elisabeth Mariko Leake, 'British India versus the British Empire: The Indian Army and an Impasse in Imperial Defense, circa 1919–39', *Modern Asian Studies*, Vol. 48, No. 1, January 2014, pp. 319–20.
15. 'Indian Army in World War II - Military History - Oxford Bibliographies – Obo', Oxford Bibliographies, Oxford University Press, 18 May 2018, www.oxfordbibliographies.com/view/document/obo-9780199791279/obo-9780199791279-0159.xml (accessed on 1 January 2019).
16. Ibid.
17. Ibid.
18. Alan Jeffreys, *The Indian Army 1939-47*, Farnham, UK: Ashgate Publishing 2012.

19. Stephen Peter Rosen, *Societies and Military Power: India and Its Armies*, Ithaca: Cornell University Press, 1996, p. 162.

20. Ibid., p. 169.

21. 'Data on the Division of Armed Forces in India at Partition', CIA, 19 March 1959, https://www.eisenhower.archives.gov/research/online_documents/Declassified/fy_2012/1959_03_19.pdf (accessed on 1 January 2019).

22. Srinath Raghavan, 'Liberal thought and colonial military institutions,' in Kanti Bajpai, Saira Basit, V. Krishnappa (eds), *India's Grand Strategy: History, Theory, Cases*, New Delhi: Routledge, 2014, p. 91.

23. Ibid., p. 99.

24. Iqbal Singh, *India's Foreign Policy*, Bombay: Hind Kitab Limited, 1946, pp. 15–16.

25. Taraknath Das, 'The War comes to India,' *The Antioch Review*, Vol. 2, No. 3, Autumn 1942, p. 480.

26. Iqbal Singh, *India's Foreign Policy*, Bombay: Hind Kitab Limited, 1946, pp. 20–21.

27. Ibid.

28. Muchkund Dubey, 'Nehru's Vision of the International Order,' in Nehru Centre (ed.), Bombay, *Witness to History: Transition and Transformation of India, 1947-64*, New Delhi: Oxford University Press, 2011, p. 60.

29. Srinath Raghavan, 'Liberal thought and colonial military institutions,' in Kanti Bajpai, Saira Basit, V. Krishnappa (eds), *India's Grand Strategy: History, Theory, Cases*, New Delhi: Routledge, 2014, p. 108.

30. Steven Wilkinson, *Army and Nation: The Military and Indian Democracy Since Independence*, Cambridge, Massachusetts: Harvard University Press, 2015, front flap.

31. 'Resolution re recruitment of all classes to the Indian army, 13 March 1935, moved by P.N. Sapru, Council of State Debates, 13 March 1935, Simla: Government of India Press, 1935, pp. 541–68. See also 'Council of State: Plea to throw open army ranks to all classes,' *The Times of India*, 14 March 1935; Steven Wilkinson, *Army and Nation: The Military and Indian Democracy Since Independence*, Cambridge, Massachusetts: Harvard University Press, 2015, pp. 2–3.

32. Steven Wilkinson, *Army and Nation: The Military and Indian Democracy Since Independence*, Cambridge, Massachusetts: Harvard University Press, 2015, pp. 1–2.

33. Ibid.
34. Field Marshal Claude Auchinleck, draft response to Nehru's letter of 12 September 1946, 'Auchinleck Papers', Manchester University, Rylands Library, cited in Steven Wilkinson, *Army and Nation: The Military and Indian Democracy Since Independence, Cambridge, Massachusetts: Harvard University Press, 2015*, p. 4.
35. 'Young soldiers warned against politics, Army must be worth of people's trust,' *The Times of India*, 19 March 1949. See also 'Encroachment on Few Privileges,' *The Times of India*, 4 September 1950, and 'Maintenance of Internal Peace: Gen Cariappa against Use of army,' *The Times of India*, 5 December 1950, all cited in Steven Wilkinson, *Army and Nation: The Military and Indian Democracy Since Independence*, Cambridge, Massachusetts: Harvard University Press, 2015, p. 5.
36. Steven Wilkinson, *Army and Nation: The Military and Indian Democracy Since Independence*, Cambridge, Massachusetts: Harvard University Press, p. 92.
37. Ibid., pp. 22–23.
38. General J.N. Chaudhuri, 'Nehru and the Indian Armed Forces', Fifth Nehru Memorial Lecture, Cambridge Trust, 5 May 1973, https://www.cambridgetrust.org/assets/documents/Lecture_5.pdf (accessed on 1 January 2019).
39. Stephen P. Cohen and Sunil Dasgupta, *Arming without Aiming: India's Military Modernization*, Washington DC: The Brooking Institutions, 2016, https://www.brookings.edu/wp-content/uploads/2016/07/armingwithoutaimingrevised_chapter.pdf (accessed on 1 January 2019).
40. Speech given by Nehru at Lucknow, 13 May 1963. Taken from K. Satchidananda Murty, *Indian Foreign Policy*, Calcutta: Scientific Book Agency, 1964, n. 20, pp. 7–8.
41. Lawrence James, *Raj: The Making and Unmaking of British India*, New York: St Martin's Press, 1997, p. 640.
42. Olaf Caroe, *Wells of Power: The Oilfields of Southwestern Asia, A Regional and Global Study*, New York: Da Capo Press, 1976, p. 33.
43. 'India–Oman Bilateral Relations', Ministry of External Affairs. Government of Indian, 2018, https://mea.gov.in/Portal/ForeignRelation/India-Oman_Bilateral_Realtions_for_MEA_Website.pdf (accessed on 1 January 2019).

44. Devirupa Mitra, 'How India nearly gave in to US pressure to enter the Iraq Killing zone', The Wire, 8 July 2016, http://thewire. in/50028/india-nearly-gave-us-pressure-join-iraq-war (accessed on 8 July 2016).

45. Author's interview of former senior government official, Delhi, October 2012.

46. K. Subrahmanyam, 'Nehru and Defense Policy'. Taken from *Nehru Revisited,* Mumbai: Nehru Centre, 2003, pp.89–90.

47. Emily Crawford, 'Made in China 2025: The Industrial Plan that China Doesn't Want Anyone Talking About', 7 May 2019, https:// www.pbs.org/wgbh/frontline/article/made-in-china-2025-the-industrial-plan-that-china-doesnt-want-anyone-talking-about (accessed on 23 February 2020).

48. Neha Kohli, 'Defence Reform: A National Imperative', Brookings Institution, https://www.brookings.edu/wp-content/ uploads/2018/04/book-defence-reform-3.pdf (accessed on 1 January 2019).

49. Ibid.

50. Ibid.

51. Ibid.

52. Henderson Brooks–Bhagat report, Government of India. https:// smedia2.intoday.in/indiatoday/HENDERSON_BROOKS1.pdf (accessed on 1 January 2019).

53. Neha Kohli, 'Defence Reform: A National Imperative', Brookings Institution, https://www.brookings.edu/wp-content/ uploads/2018/04/book-defence-reform-3.pdf (accessed on 1 January 2019).

54. Ibid.

55. K. Subrahmanyam, 'Nehru and Defense Policy,' taken from *Nehru Revisited,* Mumbai: Nehru Centre, 2003, pp. 93–95.

56. K. Subrahmanyam in the Foreword to Jaswant Singh, *Defending India,* Bangalore: Macmillan Press, 1999, pp. x–xiv.

57. Jaswant Singh, *Defending India,* Bangalore: Macmillan Press, 1999, pp. 34–35

58. Pratibha Patil's speech before the joint session of parliament, 2009. Taken from http://pib.nic.in/newsite/erelease.aspx?relid=49043 (accessed on 1 January 2017).

59. Mohannan B. Pillai and L. Premashekhara (eds), *Foreign Policy of India: Continuity & Change,* New Delhi: New Century Publications, 2010, pp. 20–23.

60. Author's interview with a former senior government official, New Delhi, October 2012.

61. Author's interview with a retired diplomat and former ambassador, New Delhi, October 2012.

62. Kanti Bajpai, Saira Basit, V. Krishnappa (eds), *India's Grand Strategy: History, Theory, Cases*, New Delhi: Routledge, 2014, Foreword by Arvind Gupta, pp. ix–x.

63. Kanti Bajpai, 'Indian Grand Strategy: Six schools of thought', in Kanti Bajpai, Saira Basit, V. Krishnappa (eds), *India's Grand Strategy: History, Theory, Cases*, p. 108.

64. Ibid., p. 134.

65. Ibid., p. 135.

66. Ibid., p. 138.

67. Ibid., p. 145.

68. Ibid., p. 131.

69. Ibid., p. 145.

70. 'Know Your Own Strength', *The Economist*, 30 March 2013, www.economist.com/briefing/2013/03/30/know-your-own-strength (accessed on 1 January 2018).

CONCLUSION

1. Robert Burns, 'To a Louse,' (1786) http://www.gutenberg.org/ebooks/1279?msg=welcome_stranger#2H_4_0107 (accessed on 1 January 2018).

2. Minister Anurag Thakur to ANI, 5 July 2019, https://www.aninews.in/videos/national/angrez-chale-gaye-angrezon-ki-paramaparayein-bhi-chali-jani-chahiye-anurag-thakur-fms-bahi-khata/ (accessed on 1 August 2019).

3. Gurcharan Das, *India Unbound: The Social and Economic Revolution from Independence to the Global Information Age*, New York: Anchor Books, 2002, p. 348.

4. Ibid., p. 349.

5. 'Japanese economic takeoff after 1945', Indiana University Northwest, http://www.iun.edu/~hisdcl/h207_2002/jecontakeoff.htm (accessed on 1 January 2019).

6. Nake M. Kamrany and Frank Jiang, 'China's Rise to Global Economic Superpower', Huffington Post, February 2015. https://www.huffpost.com/entry/chinas-rise-to-global-eco_b_6544924 (accessed on 1 January 2019).

7. Doris Goodwin, 'The Way We Won: America's Economic Breakthrough During World War II, *The American Prospect*, Fall 1992. http://prospect.org/article/way-we-won-americas-economic-breakthrough-during-world-war-ii (accessed on 1 January 2019).

8. Editorial Board' 'The world has made great progress in eradicating extreme poverty', *The Economist*, March 2017, https://www.economist.com/international/2017/03/30/the-world-has-made-great-progress-in-eradicating-extreme-poverty (accessed on 1 January 2019).

9. 'India No Longer Home to the Largest Number of Poor: Study', *The Times of India,* 27 June 2018, https://timesofindia.indiatimes.com/india/india-no-longer-home-to-the-largest-no-of-poor-study/articleshow/64754988.cms (accessed on 20 October 2018).

10. N.R. Bhanumurthy and Arup Mitra, 'Declining Poverty in India: A Decomposition Analysis', Institute of Economic Growth, Delhi University Enclave.

11. 'India's Middle-Class Population to Touch 267 Million in 5 Yrs', *The Economic Times*, 6 February 2011, economictimes.indiatimes.com/news/economy/indicators/indias-middle-class-population-to-touch-267-million-in-5-yrs/articleshow/7435793.cms (accessed on 1 January 2019).

12. Vir Sanghvi, 'How Will India's Modi-Loving Middle Class Shape the Future?', *South China Morning Post*, 18 September 2018, www.scmp.com/week-asia/politics/article/2164551/old-values-die-how-will-indias-new-modi-loving-middle-class-shape (accessed on 1 January 2019).

13. John Mearsheimer, 'Why the Ukraine Crisis Is the West's Fault', *Foreign Affairs*, September/October 2014, https://www.foreignaffairs.com/articles/russia-fsu/2014-08-18/why-ukraine-crisis-west-s-fault (accessed on 1 January 2019).

14. Krishnappa Venkatshamy and Princy George, *Grand Strategy for India 2020 and Beyond*, New Delhi: Institute for Defence Studies & Analyses, 2012, https://idsa.in/system/files/book/book_GrandStrategyIndia.pdf (accessed on 1 January 2019).

15. Ibid.

16. Ibid.

17. Manoj Kumar Mishra, 'India and China Vying for Influence in South Asia', *South Asia Journal*, 7 August 2018, http://southasiajournal.net/india-and-china-vying-for-influence-in-south-asia (accessed on 20 October 2018).

18. Minnie Chan, 'First Djibouti ... Now Pakistan Tipped to Have Chinese Naval Base', *South China Morning Post*, 5 January 2018, https://www.scmp.com/news/china/diplomacy-defence/article/2127040/first-djibouti-now-pakistan-port-earmarked-chinese (accessed on 1 January 2019).

19. Data has been taken from World Bank documents.

20. 'A Visual Guide to the External Affairs Ministry's Share of the Budget 2020 Pie,' The Wire, 3 February 2020, https://thewire.in/external-affairs/ministry-external-affairs-union-budget Ministry of External Affairs (accessed on 1 January 2019); *Annual Reports*, https://www.mea.gov.in/annual-reports.htm?57/Annual_Reports (accessed on 1 January 2019).

21. Ibid.

22. 'Know Your Own Strength', *The Economist*, 30 March 2013, www.economist.com/briefing/2013/03/30/know-your-own-strength (accessed on 1 January 2019).

23. Rajesh Rajagopalan, 'India's Strategic Choices: China and the Balance of Power in Asia', Carnegie India 2017, https://carnegieendowment.org/files/CP_312_Rajesh_Strategic_Choices_FNL.pdf (accessed on 1 January 2019).

24. Rudra Chaudhuri, 'Does India Have a Grand Strategy?', Centre for the Advanced Study of India (CASI), 2 June 2014, casi.sas.upenn.edu/iit/chaudhuri (accessed on 1 January 2019).

25. Stephen P. Cohen and Sunil Dasgupta, 'The Drag on India's Military Growth', Brookings, 28 July 2016, www.brookings.edu/research/the-drag-on-indias-military-growth (accessed on 1 January 2019).

26. Anit Mukherjee, *The Absent Dialogue: Politicians, Bureaucrats and the Military in India*, New Delhi: Oxford University Press, 2020.

27. Kishan S. Rana, *Asian Diplomacy*, Washington, DC: John Hopkins University, Woodrow Wilson Press, 2007.

28. Neha Kohli, 'Defence Reform: A National Imperative', Brookings Institution, https://www.brookings.edu/wp-content/uploads/2018/04/book-defence-reform-3.pdf (accessed on 1 January 2019).

29. Manoj Joshi, 'CDS Rawat to Face Hurdles, Sabotage Lest Rules Are Rewritten,' The Quint, 1 January 2020, https://www.thequint.com/voices/opinion/the-minefield-general-bipin-rawat-must-cross-as-first-cds (accessed on 24 February 2020).

30. Manvendra Singh, 'Stop celebrating CDS. Gen Rawat will barely be able to command forces thanks to bureaucracy,' The Print, 10

January 2020, https://theprint.in/opinion/stop-celebrating-cds-gen-rawat-will-barely-be-able-to-command-forces-thanks-to-bureaucracy/347138 (accessed on 24 February 2020).

31. Lt. Gen (Retd) Prakash Menon, 'CDS was needed. But Modi govt also creating Department of Military Affairs is a big bonus,' The Print, 25 December 2019, https://theprint.in/opinion/modi-govt-creating-department-of-military-affairs-with-cds-a-big-bonus/340495 (accessed on 24 February 2020).

32. 'Modi govt's CDS-Dept of Military Affairs: Cosmetic change or increasing defence efficiency?,' The Print, 25 December 2019, https://theprint.in/talk-point/modi-govts-cds-dept-of-military-affairs-cosmetic-change-or-increasing-defence-efficiency/340625 (accessed on 24 February 2020).

33. Nitin Gokhale, 'Major Revamp of India's National Security Architecture', Bharat Shakti, 9 October 2018, bharatshakti.in/major-revamp-of-indias-national-security-architecture (accessed on 1 January 2019).

34. Ibid.

35. Ibid.

36. Nitin Gokhale, 'How Revamped NSCS Is Helping Shape Coherent National Security Policy', Bharat Shakti, 1 November 2018, bharatshakti.in/how-revamped-nscs-is-helping-shape-coherent-national-security-policy (accessed on 1 January 2019).

37. 'India's MEA to set up first in-house China-centric center', Politics, CGTN News, November 2017, https://news.cgtn.com/news/7855544e33597a6333566d54/share_p.html (accessed on 1 January 2019).

38. Tridivesh Singh Maini, 'Improving Japan-India Infrastructure Cooperation in South Asia', The Diplomat, June 2018, https://thediplomat.com/2018/06/improving-japan-india-infrastructure-cooperation-in-south-asia (accessed on 1 January 2019).

39. Ibid.

40. Ramachandra Guha, 'Democratic to a fault?,' The Prospect Magazine, January 25, 2012, https://www.prospectmagazine.co.uk/magazine/democratic-to-a-fault-ramachandra-guha-indias-future (accessed on 23 February 2020).

41. Martin Wight, Power Politics, London: Holmes and Meier, 1978, p. 52.

42. Robert Gilpin, War and Change in World Politics, Cambridge: Cambridge University Press, 1981, p. 30.

Index

Acknowledgements

THIS BOOK WOULD not have been possible without the guidance and support of my colleagues at Hudson Institute, especially Mr Eric Brown, Dr Hillel Fradkin, Mr John Walters, Dr Kenneth Weinstein, Mr Lewis Libby and Chairman Sarah Stern.

I would like to thank friends with whom I have discussed and who helped me think through many of the ideas of the book. They include Dr Christophe Jaffrelot, Mr Lalit Jha, Mr Nirmal Ghosh, Mr Prakhar Sharma, Prof. C. Christine Fair, Mr Sadanand Dhume and Ms Seema Sirohi. A special thanks also to Ms Farahnaz Ispahani for her friendship and support.

A number of research interns helped with my book, including Akaash Palaparthy, Ben Silvian, Bernardo Soares de Affonseca Ribenboim, Molly McCammon, Nicholas Newton-Cheh, Rohil Sabherwal, Siddhidatri Mishra and Spencer Wong. A special note of thanks to my former research intern, Jacob Urda, for his research assistance and support for this book project.

I would also like to thank HarperCollins India for publishing this book. They have done so in a remarkably short period of time. My particular thanks to Ananth Padmanabhan, Antony Thomas and Udayan Mitra.

My older brother, Chaitanya, and sister-in-law, Mona Pande, have always been a source of support over the years. Finally, none of this would have been possible without the love and affection of my parents, Vinita and Kamal Pande, who have made me who I am today.

About the Author

DR APARNA PANDE is director of the Initiative on the Future of India and South Asia at the Hudson Institute, Washington DC

Born in India, Pande received her bachelor's and master's degrees in History from St Stephen's College, University of Delhi, before receiving an M. Phil in International Relations from Jawaharlal Nehru University. She completed her Ph.D. in Political Science at Boston University in the United States.

She is the author of *From Chanakya to Modi: Evolution of India's Foreign Policy* (HarperCollins, 2017), *Explaining Pakistan's Foreign Policy: Escaping India* (Routledge, 2010) and is the editor of *Contemporary Handbook on Pakistan* (Routledge, 2017).

**ALSO BY
APARNA PANDE**

'An Insightful Account Of India's World view'
SHIVSHANKAR MENON

FROM
CHANAKYA
TO
MODI

WITH
A NEW
FOREWORD

THE
EVOLUTION
OF INDIA'S
FOREIGN
POLICY

APARNA PANDE

As India pursues modernity and seeks to exercise influence in the contemporary world, an examination of India in the context of its history and tradition is crucial. Aparna Pande's *From Chanakya to Modi* explores the deeper civilizational roots of Indian foreign policy in a manner reminiscent of Walter Russel Mead's seminal *Special Providence* (2001). It identifies the neural roots of India's engagement with the world outside. An essential addition to every thinking person's library.

'*From Chanakya to Modi* is a magnificently readable survey of Indian foreign policy. Aparna Pande has interrogated the ideational, material and institutional underpinnings of India's efforts to cope with its external environment.'

– Ashley J. Tellis, *Tata chair for strategic affairs, Carnegie Endowment for International Peace*